J. MASSYNGBAERDE FORD

My Enemy Is My Guest

Jesus and Violence in Luke

ORBIS BOOKS
Maryknoll, New York 10545

The Catholic Foreign Mission Society of America (Maryknoll) recruits and trains people for overseas missionary service. Through Orbis Books Maryknoll aims to foster the international dialogue that is essential to mission. The books published, however, reflect the opinions of their authors and are not meant to represent the official position of the society.

Manuscript Editor: William E. Jerman

Indexes prepared by William H. Schlau

The statue depicted on the front cover is part of the Tetrarch Group, third century AD, in the facade of St. Mark's, Venice.

Library of Congress Cataloging in Publication Data
Ford, J. Massyngbaerde (Josephine Massyngbaerde)
   My enemy is my guest.

   Bibliography: p.
   Includes index.
   1. Bible. N.T. Luke—Criticism, interpretation, etc.
2. Jesus Christ—History of doctrines—Early church,
ca. 30–600.   3. Nonviolence—Biblical teaching.
I. Title.
BS2595.2.F67   1984   226′.406   84-5812
ISBN 0-88344-348-1 (pbk.)

To

Professor David Daube,

*formerly Regis Professor of Law, Oxford, England,
presently Professor of Law, University of California,
to whom I owe so much in my academic career,*

and to

Ms. Sharon A. Wildey,

*attorney at law,
who has devoted so much talent and professional skill
in winning equal opportunities for women.*

CONTENTS

PREFACE

Nonviolence is the most crucial issue in the Western world today. It is a subject about which every Christian should be informed. This book is intended for that purpose; it offers some reflections based on critical examination of sacred scripture.[1]

Nonviolence has often been treated thematically but this book takes a different approach, that of redaction criticism—the way that Luke has used his sources. It is not my claim that the entire New Testament—even the four gospels—teaches a nonviolence ethic. On the contrary, parts of the Christian scriptures are definitely belligerent—for example, the Book of Revelation, 2 Thessalonians, and Romans 13.

Paul's writings are dated prior to the gospels: approximately 52-67 C.E., the Gospels 65-100 C.E. Paul may never have seen even one of our canonical Gospels. Hence we cannot always expect the gentleness and openness of the Christ whom we meet in the Gospel of Luke.

It is my claim that Christian thought in the scriptures matures in the later works. We have a prime example in the Gospel of Luke. Luke portrays a dramatically new picture of Jesus. He does so because, more than Matthew and Mark, he is aware of the political conditions of Palestine, Syria, and the Diaspora after the great Jewish war against the Romans (66-74 C.E.). He is probably cognizant, too, of certain political allegations against Jesus and the early Christians during and after that war.

The unrest in Palestine in the first century C.E. will be treated in the pages that follow. I give special attention to the Lukan infancy narratives, understanding them as nonpacifist material. They represent a Judaism that looked forward to a military leader. John the Baptist was not apolitical and he too expected a warrior Messiah.

With the coming of Jesus and his ministry, according to Luke, we have a provocatively novel approach to nonviolence, nonresistance and, more importantly, forgiveness and practical love of erstwhile enemies among both one's own people and foreigners. The latter two points show how Jesus' message differs from the peace-seeking, nonviolent resistance of the Jews of the first century.

For, it must be noted, even if many in Palestine breathed a warlike spirit, nonviolence and nonresistance were live options in the first century. It is remarkable that, although Josephus records the deeds of the Maccabees and the heroic stand at Masada, the Talmud, a later Jewish work, has no reference to Masada and only six very indirect references to the Maccabees.

This might be illustrative of the mind of the Pharisees who followed the tradition of the "peace-seeking" Hillelites, the disciples of the Babylonian Pharisee Hillel. Rhoads has pointed out that the Pharisees as a whole worked for reconciliation with Rome and avoidance of war.[2] N. N. Glatzer remarks that, although Hillel could not accept the Herodian state, he did not engage in futile struggles with it but rather formed a community of peace-loving persons, the early *hasidim*, pious ones.[3] This community reached a climax in the establishment of Jamnia, the Pharisaic academic center, by Yohanan ben Zakkai, who followed the philosophy of Hillel. Hillel exhorted:

> Be of the disciples of Aaron [the priest],
> loving peace, pursuing peace.
> Be one who loves his fellow creatures
> and draws them near to the Torah [*Aboth* 1:12].

This contrasts with the Hasmonean priest leaders, who had been men of war. Hillel sought to establish peace within families, neighbors, cities, nations, and governments (*Mekl.* on Exod. 20:25). He taught: "The more charity, the more peace."[4] Glatzer alludes to another peace-loving *hasid*, Onias.[5] When there was domestic fighting he refused to pray for either side and was stoned to prevent a further demonstration of such impartiality. The patriarch Judah, Hillel's descendant, deleted from the Mishnah the political background to the Hanukkah story and centered it on the miracle of the oil that lasted eight days. Glatzer notes:

> The Maccabean heroes gave rise to the Hasmonean kings, who usurped the throne of David, and finally gave way to the Hellenist kingdom of Herod. Herod's contemporaries, Hillel and Shammai, heirs of the traditions of Hasidism and of ancient priesthood, used the symbol of the humble jar of oil as the expression of their nonpolitical stand, their choice of a nonviolent resistance to the sword and their determination to go the way of gentleness.[6]

Messianic ideas were prominent from the time of the writing of Daniel (ca. 167 B.C.E.) until the Bar Kochba revolt (132–135 C.E.), but Hillel was silent about messianism and placed emphasis on the pursuit of the Torah and a disciplined life.

One may also observe that the peace seeking of Hillel was in harmony with the teaching on nonresistance to foreign powers found in the classical prophetic tradition—that is, First Isaiah (Isa. 1–39) with reference to the Assyrians; Jeremiah vis-à-vis the Babylonians; and Second Isaiah (Isa. 40–55), especially in the servant songs.

Further, seemingly independent of the Hillelites, Josephus records specific instances of nonviolent resistance on the part of the Jewish people. First, Pontius Pilate's bringing Roman banners into Jerusalem by night (26 C.E.) was offensive to the Jews because the standards were used in pagan ceremonies. Crowds of Jews went to Caesarea, the residence of the Roman governor, to protest (*B.J.* 6:316). Josephus describes how they remained there for several days and bared their necks to the Roman sword. They preferred death to disobeying the Torah. Pilate, fearing a revolt and moved by their devotion, removed the standards.

Secondly, when Pilate took funds from the sacred treasury to build an aqueduct, the Jews were scandalized: a gentile was using sacred monies (*B.J.* 2:175–77; *Ant.* 18:60–62). They protested when Pilate came to Jerusalem. However, when Pilate's troops made a surprise attack on them, they were found to be unarmed.

In fact there seems to have been little armed conflict between the Jews and the Romans between 6 and 26 C.E. except for the rebellion of Judas the Galilean (see below).

Thirdly, another outstanding example of Jewish nonviolent resistance is found when Petronius was bidden by Emperor Gaius to place his statue in the Temple. The Jews replied:

> . . . that they offered sacrifice twice daily for Caesar and the Roman people, but that if he wished to set up these statues, he must first sacrifice the entire Jewish nation; and that they presented themselves, their wives and their children, ready for slaughter [*B.J.* 2:197; cf. *Ant.* 18:271].

Under this threat the people refused to till the fields as a nonviolent economic protest against Gaius (Josephus, *Life* 71; Philo, *Leg.* 248–53, 257).

Thus on three occasions the Jews were unarmed and expressed a willingness to die for their laws (see Philo, *Leg.* 115, 209, 229–33). There seems to have been no indication of revolt (*Leg.* 190).

Rhoads remarks:

> In each of the disturbances which Josephus relates in the period from 26 to 44 C.E. the Jewish protest was a spontaneous response to offensive Roman activity in Palestine. Jewish outrage was expressed non-violently, and when it appeared that there may have been potential for violence (*B.J.* 2:175–77), it was a matter of the tumult of an angry crowd rather than any kind of armed uprising. The people as a whole, including elements from all major groups in Israel, reacted to these disturbances, and there is no evidence of a small group or sect urging the nation to revolt.[7]

Rhoads also observes that the prewar prophets (see below), except the Egyptian prophet, were nonviolent.[8] Josephus does not mention conspiracies from 6 to 44 C.E. Tacitus (*Hist.* 5:9) says that under Tiberius "all was quiet." The aristocracy prevented one crisis by petitions to Rome (Philo, *Leg.*

38:209–306). A nonbiblical Jewish work, the *Assumption of Moses* (9:7), encourages the Jews to undergo martyrdom by the Romans and trust that God will vindicate the people.

However, only one record of passive resistance is recorded between 44 and 66 C.E., when the Jews protested against the burning of a Torah scroll by a Roman soldier (*B.J.* 2:229–30; *Ant.* 20:114–17).

Added to this stance of nonviolence, suicide, and martyrdom, the cult emanating from Maccabean days was an important aspect of pacifist resistance, which could have affected both Jesus and Luke, although Christians did not advocate suicide.

In his conclusion Rhoads observes:

> During the prewar period, resistance took many forms: nonviolent protest, popular clamors, riots, petitions, appeals, delegations, acts of defiance, strikes, plundering, assassinations, kidnaping, extortions, threats, bribery.[9]

This means that Jesus lived in a period when there was some, but not overwhelming, violence vis-à-vis Rome. Hence the earlier gospels do not concentrate on nonresistance. Some time after Jesus' death, organized militant opposition to Rome increased (after 44 C.E.). Some Christians must have been involved in this. They, and some Jews, may have conceived of Jesus as a political leader who would return with the glory and power of the war god of the exodus (see 2 Thess. and Rev.).

Under these circumstances the Lukan communities were faced with a situation different from that at the time of Jesus. Therefore Luke writes with a new purpose. He shows Jesus had no political or belligerent aspirations.

However, more interestingly, the Lukan Jesus is more progressive than the peace-seeking Pharisees. We see this from three aspects: (1) Jesus forgives enemies; (2) he does them good deeds; (3) he admits them to intimate relationship with him, a relationship that is covenantal.

It is this last point that would cause profound astonishment on the part of Jews and pagans alike. It is particularly shocking when Jesus dines with those who were normally ostracized by religious persons. Among the synoptic writers it is Luke who portrays so poignantly this characteristic of Jesus and his teaching.

I should like to coin a word from Greek and aver that Jesus plants the seed of a new theology, that of "philo-echthrology" (love of the enemy). This is the science I seek to develop.

In the chapters below I will consider Luke's depiction of the nonviolent Jesus in the order he presents the material in his Gospel. Discussion questions for each chapter have been provided at the end of the book and focus on the understanding and application of Luke's principles in our own contemporary circumstances. While these are intended primarily for study groups, they may also be an aid to the reflection of the individual reader.

ACKNOWLEDGMENTS

None of my other books underwent such a protracted and vicissitudinous period of gestation. I owe the inspiration of this thesis to an invitation from the Pittsburgh Theological Seminary to deliver the Schaff Lectures in 1974. I was honored by the privilege, and spent a fruitful and happy week with friends, scholars, and students. Further opportunities for research were available to me when I accepted the Bernard Hanley Chair at Santa Clara University during the academic year 1976–77. I spent a most rewarding nine months there and enjoyed great hospitality from California scholars. My hypothesis on revolutionaries in the first century C.E. was stimulated further by the honor of delivering the E. T. Earl Lectures at the Pacific School of Religion, Berkeley, California, in 1979. On this occasion I experienced the joy of witnessing my interpretation of the Book of Revelation set to musical drama, creatively and exquisitely composed by Dr. Wayne Rood. My gratitude is also due to the College of Arts and Letters of Notre Dame University, which gave me a summer grant in 1980.

The writing of this manuscript was prolonged because of illness and a series of surgical operations. I wish to express my appreciation to Dr. John A. McQuade for his unfailing devotion over the years and his almost uncanny gift for diagnosis; to Dr. John M. Stenger, my prosontologist, without whose professional skill I should be unable to speak audibly and painlessly; and to Dr. Paul Howard and Dr. Nermin Tutunji, who gave me a new lease of life through three thoracotomies and the implantation of an atrial pacemaker.

I wish to thank Dr. Willard Swartley and Dr. John Howard Yoder for their helpful comments and encouragement; Ms. Sharon Pace and Sr. Mary T. Treanor for their generous help in proofreading; and Rev. Charles Hohenstein for his proofreading and remarks. My sincere appreciation goes also to Betty Hillerman, M.A., editor, teacher, and writer, for editing my manuscript, which she helped me to shorten and simplify. I wish to thank Mrs. Cheryl Reed, Ms. Janet Wright, and Ms. Sandy DeWulf for their patience and forbearance in typing my manuscript.

Last but not least, I must not forget my four-footed friends whose companionship and daily needs have enabled me to persevere in the face of peculiar difficulties. Lady Martina Marie, my Appoloosa mare, named after Dr. Martin Luther King, Jr., and the Queen of Peace, enabled me to enjoy relaxation, physical exercise, and the countryside—all of which are generally inaccessible to a handicapped person. Sir Winston, my retriever, was usually my sole companion on the innumerable occasions when I was semi- or wholly unconscious; his joie de vivre, sense of humor, and unfailing fidelity remain a source of wonder to me. Finally, my Arabian colt, Lord Christian Alcuin Winrare, was attacked by a jealous gelding as I was mounting to ride astride. His opponent's hooves, aimed at him, landed over my cardiac area and, if Winrare had not embraced the philosophy of nonretaliation, by not kicking back, I should have precipitously shuffled off "this mortal coil."

Thus this book has been possible through the agape of humans and animals. I can only hope that, to some degree, it may help to contribute peace and happiness to a troubled world by persuading women and men to embrace the love of enemies presented so brilliantly in the Lukan portrayal of Jesus of Nazareth.

ABBREVIATIONS

Ann.	*Annals,* Tacitus
Ant.	*Antiquities of the Jews,* Josephus
BA	*Biblical Archaeologist*
b. Yoma	Babylonian Talmud *Yoma*
B.B.	*Baba Bathra*
Bek.	*Bekhoroth*
B.J.	*Jewish War,* Josephus
B.K.	*Baba Kamma*
b. Kidd.	Babylonian Talmud *Kiddushin*
B.M.	*Baba Metzia*
b. Sanh.	Babylonian Talmud *Sanhedrin*
BZ	*Biblische Zeitschrift*
CBQ	*Catholic Biblical Quarterly*
CD	Damascus Document (Qumran)
Coll. Brug.	*Collationes* (Bruges)
EphT	*Ephemerides Theologicae Lovanienses*
ET	*Expository Times*
EvT	*Evangelische Theologie*
Hag.	*Hagigah*
HE	*Ecclesiastical History,* Eusebius
HJ	*Heythrop Journal*
HTR	*Harvard Theological Review*
IEJ	*Israeli Exploration Journal*
J. Ber.	Jerusalem Talmud *Berakoth*
JBL	*Journal of Biblical Literature*
JJS	*Journal of Jewish Studies*
JQR	*Jewish Quarterly Review*
JRS	*Journal of Roman Studies*
JTS	*Journal of Theological Studies*
Ket.	*Ketuboth*
Kidd.	Mishnah *Kiddushin*
Leg.	*Embassy to Gaius,* Philo
LXX	Septuagint
Mart. Isa.	*Martyrdom of Isaiah*
Mekl.	*Mekhilta*
Mid.	Midrash

MT	Massoretic text
Nov. Test.	*Novum Testamentum*
ns	new series
NTS	*New Testament Studies*
P. Sheb.	Palestinian (Jerusalem) *Shebiith*
Ps. Sol.	*Psalms of Solomon*
QH	Hymn Scroll (Qumran)
QM	War Scroll of the Sons of Light against the Sons of Darkness (Qumran)
QS	Rule of the Community (Qumran)
RB	*Revue Biblique*
Ref. Haer.	*Refutation of Heresies,* Hippolytus
Rev. Hist.	*Revue de l'Histoire des Religions*
RHPR	*Revue d'Histoire et de Philosophie Religieuses*
RSR	*Revue des Sciences Religieuses*
Sanh.	*Sanhedrin*
S-B	H. L. Strack and P. Billerbeck, *Kommentar zum Neuen Testament aus Talmud und Midrasch,* Munich, 1956
Shek.	*Shekalim*
Sifre Dt.	Sifre on Deuteronomy
SLA	*Studies in Luke-Acts,* L. E. Keck and J. L. Martyr, eds., Nashville, 1966
Targ.	Targum
TDNT	*Theological Dictionary of the New Testament,* G. Kittel and G. Friedrich, eds., Grand Rapids, 1964–76
Test.	*Testament of the Twelve Patriarchs (Test. Levi = Testament of Levi,* etc.)
TU	*Texte und Untersuchungen*
TZ	*Theologische Zeitschrift*
ZNW	*Zeitschrift für die neutestamentliche Wissenschaft*
ZTK	*Zeitschrift für Theologie und Kirche*

Chapter 1

THE SEETHING CAULDRON
OF FIRST-CENTURY PALESTINE

One of the most turbulent and belligerent centuries of Jewish history was the one into which Jesus of Nazareth was born and in which the early church expanded. It has been called the "seething cauldron" of first-century Judaism. The climax of numerous and diverse revolts came with the outbreak of the memorable war with the Romans in 66 C.E. and ceased for some sixty years after the mass suicide at Masada in 74 C.E.—that is, until the second rebellion against the Romans, instigated by the Jewish leader Bar Kochba (132–35 C.E.). It is important to realize that the Gospels—indeed, the whole of the New Testament—were written against this background of unrest, an unrest that had repercussions in some countries beyond the Palestine where Jews resided.

I shall sketch some of the causes of these revolts, to assist the reader in understanding what is called "redaction" in the Gospel of Luke. Redaction in the Gospels is the editorial work that authors perform on their source or sources for the purpose of conveying a certain theological point of view. In the present case we are examining Luke to discover whether he has used his sources in such a way as to portray Jesus as a model for nonviolence.

For the purposes of this study I shall hold that Luke's sources were the following: the Gospel of Mark; a source that appears to be common to Luke and Matthew, which scholars call "Q" (from the German word *Quelle*, "source"); and material that is found only in Luke, designated "L."

It will be especially important for our investigation that we note the following points with regard to redaction:

(1) Where Luke has altered his source—for example, he has only four beatitudes compared with Matthew, who has eight or nine (depending on how we divide the last one).

(2) Where Luke has different material or has changed material—for example, we find:

1

Matt. 10:34–36	Luke 12:51–53
"Do not think that I have come to bring peace on earth; I have not come to bring peace, but a *sword.* . . ."	"Do you think that I have come to give peace on earth? No, I tell you, but rather *division.* . . ."

Luke did not use the more pugnacious word "sword."

(3) Where he has omitted material—for example, he does not include the narrative of James and John's ambitious request for places of honor in Jesus' kingdom.

(4) Where he has changed the position of certain material in the structure of the Gospel—for example, he has placed the dispute about greatness in the setting of the Last Supper, whereas it is in the prepassion material in Mark and Matthew.

(5) Where he has added to his source or used a source of his own. For example, he leaves his Markan source at Luke 9:51 and does not return to it until 18:15. This part of his Gospel (9:51–18:14) is called the "central section" of Luke. It contains much material from his special source.

Luke's Gospel and Acts, which he also wrote, are tailored to the needs of the Christian communities for which his works were written. Whether those communities were in Syria, where his Gospel was probably compiled, or whether they were diaspora communities, they could not have been unaffected by the revolutions preceding the war, or by the war itself and its aftermath. Josephus called it the greatest war of his period.

It is very possible that Luke wrote to persuade his readers that violence was not the way in which the kingdom of God could be established and that the destruction of Jerusalem (70 C.E.) did not hinder the people from enjoying the fruits of Christ's redemption. However, we must first sketch the condition of Palestine in the time of Jesus and the early church.

Palestine, An Occupied Country

Alexander the Great conquered Palestine in the fourth century B.C.E. He and his successors introduced Greek culture into the holy land. When he died, in 323 B.C.E., Palestine was first under the rule of the Egyptians (323–142 B.C.E.) and then of the Syrians (200–142 B.C.E.) until Jewish nationalists arose and secured an independent Jewish state for some seventy years (142–63 B.C.E.). This ended when Pompey conquered Palestine for the Roman Empire in 63 B.C.E. In 37 B.C.E. Herod the Great was permitted to be king of the Jewish people under the auspices of Rome. However, he was not acceptable to many Jews, partly because of his Idumean (non-Jewish) ancestry and partly because of his cruelty and his oppressive taxation, which accompanied his introduction of Greek and Roman culture into Palestine and the Diaspora. When he died, in 4 B.C.E., various revolts occurred and they continued sporadically until the fierce outbreak of the war in 66 C.E. We are concerned here with the Roman period. Although the Romans did bring some benefits with them, they were also guilty of violence, sacrilege, robbery, devastation, rape, and selling persons into slavery, especially families that could not pay their taxes and debts.

Although there was no open rebellion in the time of Herod the Great, his reign was one of terror. He exhibited extreme hatred toward his opponents and tried to obliterate the successors of the Jewish nationalists, the followers of the Hasmoneans. Josephus reports that Herod was continually trying to control the tactics of "bandits." This, however, is probably a misnomer, for the so-called bandits appear to have been revolutionaries who favored the Hasmonean house. They displayed remarkable discipline, often dwelt in the caves that honeycombed the Judean desert, and were noted for their military prowess and their religious devotion. Thus from the time of Herod the Great, there were anti-Roman rebels who waged continual guerrilla warfare, and sometimes pitched battles, against the Romans or their protégés, such as Herod. This sowed the seed for the great war from 66 to 74 C.E.

When Herod died (about the time that Jesus was born, according to Matthew), much of the land went into Roman hands or was auctioned off. The indigenous farmers fared badly. Even if they retained their land, they were obliged to give a considerable amount of produce to their landlords in addition to paying taxes and tithes. Drought intensified these difficulties. The preponderance of large estates also threatened the small farmers. They became a source of recruitment for the revolutionaries. Guerrilla war was conducted against the rich, both Jew and gentile.

The Romans punished the turbulence and revolts that followed Herod's death (4 B.C.E.) by the slaughter of three thousand Jews in the courts of the Temple and the looting of four hundred talents from the sacred treasury. Two thousand insurgents were crucified.

The chief centers of unrest were the royal agricultural estates, where tension existed between tenants and landlords (recall the parable of the wicked tenants).

Causes of Unrest in First-Century Palestine

In addition to trouble during and after the reign of Herod the Great, there were other causes of unrest. The main ones were: (1) occupation by foreign troops; (2) class conflicts, which included anticlericalism; (3) social banditry; (4) religious fanaticism and the concept of God as divine warrior; (5) revolutionary prophets and messianic pretenders; (6) misconduct on the part of Roman officials; (7) strife between the various factions of Jewish revolutionaries; (8) taxation, both by the Romans and by Herod and his successors; and (9) the bitter hostility between the Jews and the Samaritans. In this chapter we shall touch on the first seven points; the other two—taxation and the Samaritans—are dealt with in chapters 5 and 6, respectively.

1. Occupation by Foreign Troops

With and after the conquest of the East by Alexander the Great, the Greek armies had a direct effect upon the economies of the countries they conquered. The moving army itself was a source of commerce. Thousands of civilians traveled with the army: wives, concubines, children, servants, slaves, merchants, moneylenders, traffickers in booty, veterinarians, doctors, and others. The Hellenistic army was "an enormous moving city, comparable to the moving cities of the Oriental nomads in eastern Europe and in Asia."[1] Alexander shared his wealth with his soldiers and left many of them as colonists in the cities that he founded. This led to the formation of a new social class composed of foreigners; practicing Jews did not serve in pagan armies. This military factor is important because, after the death of Alexander, Palestine was invaded or occupied by seven or eight armies in approximately 370 years. What has been said about the Greek army may be applied just as well to the Roman army.

The presence of foreign troops caused havoc. For example, as well as providing for the soldiers, their families, and servants—"billeting" them—the Jews would witness the destruction of their forests and the loss of other materials used for Roman earthworks, battering rams, quick-fire devices, and so forth. The feeding and watering of an army's horses, camels, and elephants, and herds of animals for human consumption, would vastly diminish resources for local populations. Persons and animals were pressed into the service of the Roman soldiers; think of Simon of Cyrene, who carried the horizontal shaft of Jesus' cross.

Added to all this, personal tragedy and psychological trauma prevailed. To mention only one problem area, women and children were captured and often raped. Even if a woman had only been in danger of rape, a pious Jew could not sleep with her, because she had been "defiled."

2. Class Conflicts

Marked class conflict was found in Palestine in the first century because of the effects of foreign occupation, of taxation (Roman and Herodian), and of confiscation of land by the Romans and the Herodians for various reasons, but especially for unpaid taxes. The loss of small holdings increased unemployment; only seasonal employment was possible for many (recall the parable of the workers in the vineyard). Famine and drought also caused the peasants to lose their holdings and fall into the hands of moneylenders (the parable of the two debtors and the parable of the unmerciful servant). This was one of the reasons why revolutionaries burned the public archives in 66 C.E.: to destroy evidence of debts. There was a great rift between rich and poor, a subject to which Luke frequently returns.

Class conflict was also aggravated by anticlericalism. The priesthood fell into two classes, upper (Jerusalem priests) and lower (rural priests). The Jewish aristocracy, including especially the Sadducean high priests, collaborated with Rome and enriched themselves. The high priestly families were especially corrupt, and the office was often obtained by bribery. The immense luxury of the high priests was a cause of great indignation on the part of the masses. A priest once received a thousand ships as *part* of his inheritance! The aristocratic priests were "big business" people.

There was open class warfare when the high priests sent their slaves to rob the poorer country priests of their tithes. There were quarrels between the high priests and the lay nobility. So great was the conflict that the high priests could not prevent the other priests from declaring war on the Romans and refusing sacrifices brought by foreigners, including representatives of the Roman emperor. Class hatred induced revolutionaries to choose, by lot, an uneducated peasant to be high priest. The lay aristocracy lost prestige because of its violence and oppression (*Ant.* 20:214), together with its submission to Rome.

Luke often deals with class conflicts, especially in his parables and in the passion narrative, where the priestly aristocracy is shown to be pitted against Jesus and against those who would defend him.

3. Social Banditry

One important result of social and economic unrest was banditry, often accompanied by violence. Richard A. Horsley writes that banditry was "a recurrent and widespread phenomenon in Jewish Palestine and increased dramatically during the decades prior to the Revolt."[2] He says that it had become epidemic under the last Roman governors before the war and was "a significant, perhaps the most significant, identifiable social form" taken by the nascent Jewish rebels against the Romans as well as against the sacerdotal aristocracy.[3]

Social bandits were the Robin Hoods of the ancient world. The phenomenon of social banditry arises as a protest in conditions existing prior to the development of genuine political consciousness. Bandits appear when the state or local rulers are seen to be upholding an unjust system. Bandits are usually guilty of crimes in the eyes of the state, but innocent in the eyes of the general populace. In fact, they are often seen as heroes and, at times, are endowed with magical characteristics—for instance, invisibility or invulnerability. Social bandits usually appear in rural areas. Hobsbawm writes:

> Social banditry is universally found wherever societies are based on agriculture and consist largely of peasants and landless laborers ruled, oppressed, and exploited by someone else—landlords, towns, governments, lawyers, and even banks.[4]

Social bandits are a symbol of hope for the people. They correct wrongs, avenge offenses, and help the poor. Often they are anticlerical, although they are not against religion itself. Just at the outbreak of the war, we find a dramatic increase in rural bandits, and some well-organized urban bandits in the Zealots, who appear between 66 and 68 C.E., and in the *sicarii* (rebels carrying daggers). When the war broke out the bandits sided with the revolutionaries.

The Lukan beatitudes—"Blessed are you poor"—would be understandable in the context of an audience that supported social banditry.

Together with banditry we find the phenomena of apocalypticism and messianic pretenders. The oppressed peasants dreamed of a world without woes, a new society of freedom and equality. Jewish apocalypticism permeated society except for the upper classes, the high priests, and the Sadducees. At times social banditry embraced the concept of millenarianism, a temporary reign of the Messiah on earth.

Bandits are usually armed and there is often only a thin line between them and revolutionaries. Josephus very frequently calls revolutionaries "bandits" (*lestai*). Social banditry is pertinent to the subject of nonviolence.

4. Religious Fanaticism and God as Divine Warrior

Religious zeal, sometimes developing into fanaticism and terrorism, was a common phenomenon from the time of the Maccabees and their successors, the Hasmoneans, and even throughout the first century C.E. Many of these religious zealots believed in "holy war" or acts of violence perpetrated to ensure the observance of the Torah and religious purity. They directed their ardor not only against gentiles but also against any fellow Jews whom they deemed "unorthodox."

These zealots, and many revolutionaries, took as their model the high priest Phinehas, who thrust his spear through an Israelite and a pagan woman who were cohabiting. Mixed marriages were taboo. He also led a holy war against the Midianites (Num. 25 and 31). Zealots believed that zeal like Phinehas's would turn away God's wrath, atone for sin, and remove hindrances to the breaking in of salvation. For them the murder of the godless was a religious, expiatory act and directly associated with the offering of sacrifice. Martyrdom was also seen as an aspect of sacrifice. This unconditional readiness for sacrifice was linked with the idea of the eternal priesthood of Phinehas, which was important to the revolutionaries. Martyrdom among the revolutionaries was linked with belief in resurrection and eternal life.

The prophet Elijah was also seen as following in the footsteps of those who were zealous for God. He was zealous and righteous when he killed the prophets of Baal. Queen Jezebel persecuted him for his zeal. In later tradition Elijah is identified with Phinehas and even endowed with the priesthood. Many believed Elijah would be the leader of the eschatological war.

There was a strong tradition that when someone was disobedient a pious zealot would come with a weapon in hand. Hence it is understandable that the first-century revolutionaries did not hesitate to deal harshly with, or kill, even their own friends and relatives. It is this mentality that Luke rejects. He mentions Simon the zealot both in his Gospel and in Acts. Simon did not belong to the Zealot political party because that did not begin until about 67 C.E. He must have been a religious zealot.

Beliefs Commonly Found among Zealots and Revolutionaries. The religious zealots, whom we may identify to some extent with the various groups of revolutionaries, maintained some or all of the following beliefs:

(1) They emphasized the sovereignty of God and saw submission to foreign powers as a transgression of the first commandment.

(2) They had a passionate belief in freedom and political independence.

(3) They embraced the concept of the kingship of God, which could be understood in three ways: (a) God as universal king; (b) God as king of Israel; (c) God as king in an eschatological sense. The eschatological sense was often fused with political ideas, for many thought that the Messiah would bring about the liberation of Israel and reestablishment of a theocratic state. This emphasis on the kingship of God can be accounted for if it is seen against the background of the cult of the Hellenistic rulers and, subsequently, the Roman emperors whom gentiles believed to be divine.

(4) They believed that they could cooperate with God in obtaining the redemption of Israel and national independence. Armed combat would be an integral part of this cooperation.

(5) They believed they were justified in seizing the property of landowners.

(6) They believed that a census and taxation of the people was sacrilegious.

(7) Many revolutionaries were opposed to all images, both of human beings and animals. Archeological discoveries have certified that images were destroyed from the time of the Maccabees to the start of the Jewish war in 66 C.E. Many refused to handle or even look upon foreign moneys because of the pagan symbols and inscriptions on them. Roth says that the "anti-iconic tendency in Judaism reached its climax in the second half of the Christian century, at the time of the great revolt."[5] Recall the passage about the tribute money in all three synoptic Gospels.

(8) Certain revolutionaries also believed in circumcision, even involuntary, in order to prevent the desecration of the land and Torah through the presence of unclean persons. Male circumcision was a source of keen debate in the early church.

(9) The pious also believed in separation from the heathen—in sharp contrast with Jesus' association with them.

In the first century eighteen laws were passed to prevent defilement from association with the heathen. There was an intensified desire for pure food, dietary laws, and table fellowship, all designed to keep Jews separate. The pious Jew would not accept anything from heathens—their food, their gifts, their first fruits, or their sons and daughters in marriage. This was to be a source of great controversy in the early church.

The climax of segregation was the refusal to accept heathen sacrifices in the Temple. This refusal was initiated by one Eleazar, who was a priest himself although probably from the lower order. It started in 66 C.E. and was an immediate cause of the war.

Trial and suffering were no deterrents to the revolutionaries; they saw them as purification before the final redemption. They felt that as long as they submitted to Rome, God's wrath would perdure, but if they began a holy war, the end of affliction and the time of redemption would begin.

It is obvious that the ideology of the revolutionaries in Luke's time clashed with many Christian beliefs.

Martyrdom. The cult of martyrdom is found in the Maccabean era; it gave birth to popular legends about martyrs. Many of those killed by the Romans were regarded as martyrs by the Jews. The revolutionaries were willing to undergo not only death, but even death by torture, for the sake of the Torah.

Crucifixion was often the preferred mode of execution by the Romans. Florus crucified many Jews before the outbreak of the war (*B.J.* 2:308). Titus crucified more than five hundred each day during the seige of Jerusalem. He allowed his soldiers to torture their victims by crucifying them in different positions. His purpose was to persuade the Jews to capitulate.

In view of the widespread practice of crucifixion, especially for political causes, Luke was obliged to show his readers—and perhaps the Romans—that, although Jesus was crucified, he was innocent of political intrigue and conducted himself in a nonviolent manner. We shall see this clearly in chapter 8, on the passion and death of Jesus.

Holy War. The concept of holy war is found throughout the Hebrew scriptures, at least after the age of the patriarchs (Abraham, Isaac, and Jacob). Both charismatic leaders and priests were involved in belligerent undertakings. New vigor was given to the holy war by the Maccabees, who were inspired by the accounts of the exodus and the conquest of Canaan.

The concept of holy war is dramatically portrayed in the *War Scroll of the Sons of Light against the Sons of Darkness*, a document found at Qumran and dated probably from the time of Herod. Here holy war is a direct inauguration of judgment and involves human and supernatural forces. In the war the priests recite the necessary prayers, blow the trumpets, and generally oversee the proceedings. God is the principal warrior. In the Qumran *Rule of the Community* (1 *QSb* 5:24–27) the leader from Judah must break the power of the enemy. The Messiah as warrior also appears frequently in nonbiblical Jewish literature. The Lukan Jesus repudiates the very notion of a holy war.

5. Revolutionary Prophets and Messianic Pretenders

Although the revolutionaries counted prophets among their numbers, they were not necessarily war leaders; in fact, only one Egyptian prophet (mentioned below) appears to have taken up arms. Nevertheless, the revolutionary prophets exhorted the masses and encouraged them to expect "salvation," often sought by recourse to arms.

There were seven such prophets of whom we have some historical verification:

(1) In 36 C.E. there arose a Samaritan whose name is unknown to us. He promised his followers that he would reveal to them the sacred vessels that Moses had hidden on Mt. Gerizim (*Ant.* 18:85–87).

(2) Between 44 and 48 C.E., Theudas, mentioned in Acts 5, arose and persuaded his followers "to take up their possessions and follow him to the Jordan." He thought that the Jordan would be divided when he entered it (*Ant.* 20:97–99; cf. Acts 5:36).

(3) Between 52 and 60 C.E. another prophet summoned the masses to the desert (*Ant.* 20:167–68). He promised "unmistakable marvels" and "signs of freedom."

(4) During the same period an Egyptian prophet appeared (*Ant.* 20:168–72; *B.J.* 2:261–63; cf. Acts 21:38). He led his adherents from the desert to the Mount of Olives and expected the walls of Jerusalem to fall down at his command, as the walls of Jericho had done at the command of Joshua. His aim was to defeat the Roman garrison and establish himself as ruler.

(5) From 60 to 62 C.E. another prophet, whom Josephus calls a "god," urged his adherents to follow him to the desert, where they would receive "salvation and rest from troubles" (*Ant.* 20:188).

(6) Before the war the prophet Jesus ben Ananias bewailed the destruction of the city for seven years and five months. After severe punishment, he was stoned to death (*B.J.* 6:300ff.).

(7) At the end of the Roman siege, when the Temple was already burning (70 C.E.), a prophet announced to the six thousand refugees that they would receive "tokens of their deliverance" and "help from God" (*B.J.* 6:285–86).

Barnett notes that all these prophets came after the time of Jesus and he is of the opinion that they sought to imitate him.[6] Luke does present Jesus as "the prophet" but one unlike the revolutionary prophets who predicted marvels. In his passion account Luke emphasizes that Jesus was not a false prophet.

Messianic pretenders were not anarchists; they looked for a leader raised up by God to overthrow a foreign power and reestablish a theocracy. Two examples will suffice. One was Menahem, the son or grandson of Judas the Galilean; the latter had rebelled against Rome in 6 C.E. Menahem seems to have claimed messianic honors, when the war reached a critical point in Jerusalem. He appeared in royal attire with his followers but was soon struck down by his opponents from other Jewish factions in the holy city.

Another messianic pretender was Simon bar Giora (see below, under "Jewish Revolutionary Factions").

In the Lukan passion narrative Jesus is devoid of all political messianic features.

6. Misconduct of Roman Officials

There was very little conflict between Jews and Romans from 6 to 26 C.E., except for the rebellion of Judas the Galilean. Josephus does not mention any conspiracies on the part of the Jews from 6 to 44 C.E., although there was some nonviolent resistance of the Jews against some of the Roman governors' actions. The first major troubles began under the Roman governor Cumanus (48–52 C.E.), when some Roman soldiers behaved offensively at a Jewish feast (B.J. 2:223–27; Ant. 20:105–12). Some Jews attacked the caravan of a slave official of Caesar near Bethhoron in Judaea (B.J. 2:228; Ant. 20:113–14). Cumanus' troops plundered the neighboring villages and arrested local Jewish officials (B.J. 2:229–30; Ant. 20:114–17). Roman soldiers also tore and burned a copy of the Torah (B.J. 2:229–30). Many Jews rushed to Caesarea and offered passive resistance. This appears to be the last act of passive resistance recorded by Josephus.

Then began a year-long, bitter, and bloody conflict (to be discussed in chap. 6) between the Jews and the Samaritans. After this clash with the Samaritans, Josephus reports:

Many of them [the Jews], however, emboldened by impunity, had recourse to robbery; raids and insurrections, fostered by the more reckless, broke out all over the country [B.J. 2:239].

Attempts to gain independence from the Romans during the Judeo-Samaritan conflict were not an organized effort, but the result of frustration at the failure of Roman responsibility in the province.

From 52 to 60 C.E., Felix was the Roman governor. The conduct of his life was offensive to the Jews (Tacitus, Hist. 5:9). At the end of his term the country was infested with brigands. During his time, too, the sicarii (dagger-carrying revolutionaries) appeared, and apocalyptic prophets increased.

Festus (60–62 C.E.) and Albinus (62–64 C.E.) could do little against the "brigands." Albinus's corruption aggravated the situation. He plundered both private and public funds, accepted bribes to release brigands and, at the end of his procuratorship, released the worst criminals from prison.

Florus (64–66 C.E.) was the worst procurator of all. He made unjust extractions of money from the people (Ant. 20:252; B.J. 2:227–83) and indulged in other cruelties. Many prophets and messianic pretenders appeared in his time. Josephus reports that imposters and brigands united and stimulated many to revolt (*B.J.* 2:264–65). Josephus says of Florus that he was the one who "constrained us to go to war with the Romans, for we preferred to perish en masse rather than one by one" (*Ant.* 20:257–58).

Thus, after several attempts at nonviolent resistance, the whole country was aroused to war, although the philo-Roman aristocracy, which had a great deal to lose by such a war, continued to urge the people to come to terms. The various factions were stronger than they, and war resulted. It was facilitated at several points by Roman domestic conflicts, chiefly the political anarchy that reigned in the year of the four emperors (68–69 C.E.) and Rome's constant fear of the Parthians, for Israel was a buffer state between Parthia and Rome.

7. Jewish Revolutionary Factions

At the beginning and during the war the Jews did not offer a united front against the Romans, and this was one of the reasons for their defeat by the enemy. Five different parties can be distinguished among the Jews.

The Sicarii. In the summer of 66 C.E. a revolutionary group named the *sicarii* (dagger-bearers) took possession of Masada. They went to Jerusalem and during the wood festival joined the worshipers and attacked the high priests and royalists with daggers. A messianic figure appeared among them—Menahem (mentioned above).

The *sicarii* attacked the upper class, and this suggests a social uprising. They may have been associated with a struggle for a new order in the land, the order prescribed in Leviticus 25 and Deuteronomy 15. They defended Masada until 74 C.E. They also went into the Diaspora (Egypt and Cyrene). They seem to have been the first among the organized revolutionary groups. They committed suicide at Masada rather than submit to Rome.

The Zealot Party. The Zealot party was probably a democratic body comprised of lower-class priests, lay persons from Jerusalem, and small farmers, including "bandits," from the countryside. They appeared as a recognizable faction in 67–68 C.E. They formed a group who were in conflict with the established social order and they were nationalistic. The Temple was their central focus. They do not seem to have produced a messianic figure. Their terrorism cost them popular support.

The Party of John of Gischala. Initially John opposed Rome, then he became a moderate and, afterward, a revolutionary. He does not appear to have been a social revolutionary but rather a nationalist. Although he could not provide strong leadership, he was important because he helped the Zealots to overthrow the government.

The Idumeans. The Idumeans were a citizen force from Idumea and not part of a social reform. They were important because they helped other factions.

The Party of Simon bar Giora. The name "bar Giora" means "son of a proselyte." Simon was victorious over the Romans led by Cestius in 66 C.E.

He headed many "bandit" groups in the countryside. The high priest Ananus sent out forces to disarm him and he fled to the *sicarii* at Masada. After the death of Ananus he launched his social program in earnest. He opposed the rich in order to help the poor and he freed many slaves, who became his followers. His religious rationale may have been Isaiah's prophecy on bringing good tidings to the poor (see chap. 4, below). He appears to have seen himself as a messianic liberator and a warrior fighting the eschatological war. In 69 C.E. the high priests and Idumeans supported Simon. He was hailed as savior and protector (*B.J.* 4:575). He attacked John of Gischala and the Zealots. During the siege he was in main control of the troops. He was a strict disciplinarian to the point of executing people without trial if they showed signs of desertion. After the siege of Jerusalem, Simon, dressed in white garments (as a martyr), asked the Romans for safe passage. This was denied him. He was taken to Rome for the celebration of the military triumph of Vespasian and Titus and was executed in the Roman forum (*B.J.* 7:153–54).

The revolutionary parties could have suggested models for the Lukan churches. However, the revolutionary parties used violence, and it was important for Luke to portray Jesus as the pioneer and proclaimer of a non-violent program for reform and salvation.

Luke's task was all the more formidable in that many of his readers lived in a war-torn country; violence, robbery, rape, and devastation had been their meat and drink for many a year.

Chapter 2

REVOLUTIONARY MESSIANISM AND THE FIRST CHRISTMAS

Most Christians have been accustomed to view the infancy narratives recorded by Matthew and Luke as idyllic, romantic stories of the gentle, infant Messiah. This has been encouraged by the Christmas liturgy, music, hymns, homilies, and, above all, Christmas cards. On the other hand, many scholars have been deeply skeptical about the historicity of the narratives and have seen them, and still see them, as nothing but pious legends.

It is not the purpose of this chapter to give a critique of this complex question, but rather, in examining the narratives of Luke, to pay special attention to the concept of the Messiah and the hope for a Jewish theocratic state contained in them. It would appear that the Lukan material, anything but irenic, comes from a source (or sources) bearing a political, militant, and even belligerent motif natural enough in the revolutionary era in which Christ was born and in which Luke wrote his Gospel. Later we shall see that this militant trait stands in sharp contrast to the policy of Jesus.

Gabriel and Zechariah (Luke 1:5–25)

First of all we must place this portion of the infancy narratives against the revolutionary background sketched in chapter 1. Luke records that Gabriel appeared to Zechariah during the reign of Herod the Great, king of Judea from 40 to 4 B.C.E. As we have seen, this was a period of oppressive taxation, social banditry, political discontent, and rebelliousness. It was a time that would nurture eschatological hope among the masses: the oppressed mitigate their abject condition by dreaming of a "golden age."

Luke indicates that Zechariah, the father of John the Baptist, was a rural priest. He would have fulfilled his duties in Jerusalem about twice a year (Luke 1:9). Be it recalled that the conflict between the lower-class priests and the sacerdotal aristocracy was a vital issue in the first century. The revolutionaries, for their part, did not oppose the Temple in Jerusalem, as did the members of Qumran; indeed, most of them regarded it as central to their worship. They sought to purify it—for instance, by reverting to the ancient practice of electing the high priest by lot instead of his being chosen by political leaders such as Herod or the Roman governors (*B.J.* 4:153–57). The revolutionaries vehemently defended the Temple in the great war from 66 to 74 C.E., and many perished in its final conflagration. Zechariah, like them, is represented as a devotee of Temple worship, and he and his wife righteous and blameless with regard to the Torah (Luke 1:6), as were the religious rebels. Zechariah, as a lower-class priest, may have been opposed to the pro-Roman priestly aristocracy and may have entertained eschatological hope.

As Zechariah was performing his priestly duties there appeared to him Gabriel, the angel of the Lord. We are accustomed to see Gabriel portrayed as a winged, white-robed figure. This is an anachronism, in terms of Jewish sources. For the Jewish people Gabriel, as his name denotes, is the warrior of God: *geber* (warrior), *el* (God)—a war angel.

In the Bible it is Gabriel who appears to Daniel to explain his visions (Dan. 8:16–26; 9:21–27). The Book of Daniel was written during the persecution of the Hellenistic ruler Antiochus Epiphanes, in the second century B.C.E. It encourages active resistance to oppressors and kindles apocalyptic hope in Israel to win victory over its enemies. Gabriel also appears as an important figure in nonbiblical Jewish writings. He is associated with metals and is clothed like a metal worker. He is the angel who executes God's will on earth. He slays bastards (*1 Enoch* 10:9) and will make war on the leviathan, the mythological monster (*B.B.* 74b). He killed Sennacherib, the king of Assyria (*Sanh.* 95b). He is reported to have taken fire from the hand of a cherub and thrown it upon the city of Jerusalem and the Temple when the Jews were disobedient. According to these and other sources, therefore, Gabriel is an aggressive, warlike figure.

Gabriel appears as a warrior most clearly in the Qumran scrolls. Together with the angels Michael, Uriel, and Raphael, he plays a significant role in the eschatological holy war. He is described as being in the "battalions of the mighty angels . . . girding themselves for battle" (1 *QM* 15:14).

Clearly, it is one of the principal war angels who appears to Zechariah.

It is important to note that John is to go before the Lord in the spirit and power of Elijah (Luke 1:17). The concept of Elijah's preceding the Lord is found in Malachi 4:5–6 (cf. 3:1). These passages are well known. Less known and less frequently quoted or cited in popular works is Sirach 48:1–12. The whole passage reads:

> Till like a fire there appeared the prophet
> whose words were as a flaming furnace.
> Their staff of bread he shattered,
> in his zeal he reduced them to straits;
> by God's word he shut up the heavens
> and three times brought down fire. . . .

You [Elijah] brought a dead man back to life
from the nether world, by the will of the Lord.
You sent kings down to destruction,
And nobles, from their beds of sickness.
You heard threats at Sinai,
at Horeb avenging judgments.
You anointed kings who should inflict vengeance,
and a prophet as your successor.
You were taken aloft in a whirlwind,
in a chariot with fiery horses.
You are destined, it is written, in time to come
to put an end to wrath before the day of the Lord,
to turn back the heart of fathers towards their sons,
and to reestablish the tribes of Jacob.
Blessed is he who shall have seen you before he dies,
O Elijah, enveloped in the whirlwind.

This text portrays Elijah as a "zealot" in the sense of one who performs righteous acts—even to the point of violence—for God's sake. Sirach praises Elijah as righteous inasmuch as he caused famine and drought, he brought down kings and nobles, and he helped to inflict vengeance. This, apparently, was the vision of Elijah that prevailed in the second century B.C.E. (when Sirach was written) and was apparently acceptable to the Maccabees.

Zechariah, the father of the Baptist, probably lived in the same tradition. John is not actually identified with Elijah, but Gabriel predicts that he will be endowed with characteristics of Elijah. Elijah is often identified with Phinehas, the zealous priest of God (see chap. 1). He was one of the "patron saints" of the Maccabees and the revolutionaries.

It seems to me that this background is necessary in order to understand the words of the war angel that the son of Zechariah would go before the Lord in the power and spirit of Elijah and, probably, follow in the footsteps of the warlike Phinehas.

Gabriel's words contain no mention of the Messiah. John's lifework is to be in the service of God. As a priest's son he could have striven to purify the priesthood for God and cooperated with other observant Jews to reestablish a theocratic state (see Luke 1:74–75, which mentions the purified worship that will follow victory).

Annunciation of the Birth of Jesus (Luke 1:26–38)

As Hengel points out, the activity of the revolutionaries was determined not only by the political orientation of their movement, but also by prophecy in the sense of an eschatological reinterpretation of scripture through the inspiration of the Spirit.[1] This is true also of the Qumran community members, who interpreted scripture in the light of contemporary events.

Josephus remarks that the revolutionaries were inspired by two oracles.[2] One predicted that the "sanctuary would be taken when the temple should become foursquare"; the source and meaning of this prediction is unknown. A second, and more important one for our purposes, he calls an "ambiguous oracle." It is likewise found in the revolutionaries' sacred scriptures. It appears to predict that a person from the Jewish nation would become ruler of the world (B.J. 6:311). The revolutionaries naturally expected a person of Jewish birth to fulfil this prophecy, whereas Josephus was confident that it referred to the Roman Vespasian, who was in Palestine in the sixties. It meant that he would rule the world. In fact Vespasian did become emperor, in 69 C.E.

Thus the expectation of a Jewish international leader was "in the air" in the first century. In the light of this expectation, the words of Gabriel, war angel, to Mary are highly significant. Luke informs us that Joseph, Mary's betrothed, was from the house of David, from which the political Messiah was expected (Luke 1:27). He announces that the name of her son will be "Jesus."

This name is vitally important. First of all it means "savior." This appellation is not only Jewish; it was frequently given to Hellenistic and Roman military leaders.[3]

More pertinently, "Jesus" is the Greek form of the Hebrew "Joshua." Indeed, Greeks reading the Hebrew scriptures translated into their own language would see the names of the Old Testament books as Genesis, Exodus, Leviticus, Numbers, Deuteronomy, Jesus, Judges. . . . Throughout the narratives concerning Joshua, the Greek reader would read "Jesus." For example:

> And Jesus the son of Nun was full of the spirit of wisdom, for Moses had laid his hands upon him; so the people of Israel obeyed him, and did as the Lord had commanded Moses [Deut. 34:9].

Thus for the Greek the successor of Moses is Jesus. It is Jesus who conquers Canaan and establishes the twelve tribes in the promised land. Jesus, the son of Nun, was the military man par excellence in Israelite history because he gained the promised land for the Hebrews, gained it through military prowess. It would be worthwhile to read again the entire Book of Jesus (Joshua) reading "Jesus" every time the name "Joshua" occurs.

If, as is very likely, the infancy source narratives were written in Hebrew or Aramaic, the text would clearly read that the child was to be called Joshua. Jesus' family, disciples, and Jewish opponents would call him "Joshua of Nazareth" if they spoke Aramaic. Syrian Christians would later speak of "Joshua of Nazareth."

The implication of these words is that Mary's son will be a military leader, in all likelihood destined to reconquer Palestine and make it an international power. Jesus was a popular name in the first century C.E.; Josephus mentions several revolutionaries who bore that name.

Gabriel also tells Mary that her son will assume the throne of David and enjoy an everlasting reign. This is primarily a political, not a spiritual, statement; there is no hint that Mary's son will die in atonement for sin or repudiate a political kingship (recall Jesus' temptations, Luke 4:5–8 and Matt. 4:8–10). A political interpretation would be natural from a Jewish point of view, but Christians would later discover a spiritual interpretation.

The reference to an everlasting kingdom is very interesting in the light of discoveries from Qumran. Among the scrolls were found what are called *testimonia:* messianic proof texts—texts selected to support theological (here, messianic) theses. These texts include the important text from 2 Samuel 7:10–14, where God promises to be a father to the descendants of David, who will occupy his throne. The original text makes two statements: (1) David's kingdom will be everlasting in that his line of successors will be preserved; (2) the Davidic kings will be the adopted sons of God. With regard to the first point, the Qumran proof text and the words of Gabriel share a new insight. The Qumran *testimonium* speaks not of a succession of rulers, but of a particular one who will reign forever. In the same way the Lukan text has changed the idea of a continuing line of kings to a single Davidic king. Brown observes:

> The "forever" for both Qumran and Luke is, then, not an endless series of reigns by different kings, but an eschatological description. And there is nothing *distinctively Christian* in Gabriel's words in vv. 32–33 of Luke, except that the expected Davidic Messiah has been identified with Jesus.[4]

The observation that Gabriel's words have a Jewish, not necessarily Christian, character encourages one to see them as historically possible. Brown thinks that the angel's words are a free rendering of 2 Samuel 7:9–16, which he cites thus:

9: I shall make for you a *great* name.
13: I shall establish *the throne of his kingdom forever.*
14: I shall be his father, and he will be *my* son. . . .
16: And your *house* and your *kingdom* will be made sure *forever.*

The italicized words show affinity with the annunciation text (Luke 1:31–36).

With regard to the second point (the Davidic kings will be the adopted sons of God) the annunciation text goes an appreciable step further. Jesus will not be only the adopted son of God but the very Son of God. However, another important discovery from Qumran has shown that there was a similar, but not identical, concept in the Qumran community. Fitzmyer translates an Aramaic fragment as follows:

[But your son] 7 shall be great upon the earth, 8 [O King! All (men) shall] make [peace], and all shall serve 9 [him. He shall be called the son of] the [G]reat [God], and by his name shall he be named. (Col. ii). 1 He shall be hailed (as) the Son of God, and they shall call him Son of the Most High. As comets (flash) 2 to the sight, so shall be their kingdom. (For some) year[s] they shall rule upon 3 the earth and shall trample everything (under foot); people shall trample upon people, city upon ci[t]y, 4 *(vacat)* until there arises the people of God, and everyone rests from the sword [4 Q 243 (4 *Qps* Dan. Aᵃ)].[5]

In this text one notes surprising affinities with Luke 1 in the following phrases:

(1) he will be great (cf. Luke 1:32);
(2) he will be called Son of the Highest (cf. Luke 1:32);
(3) he will be called Son of God (cf. Luke 1:35);
(4) he will reign . . . forever (cf. Luke 1:33);
(5) . . . will come upon you (cf. Luke 1:35).[6]

This text is of singular importance because before its discovery "sons of the Highest" (in the plural) was known to exist in Semitic texts but not "Son of the Highest" (in the singular). This is the first Aramaic text to refer to a Jewish leader as "Son of the Highest."

Fitzmyer has warned that even the occurrence of the title "Son of the Highest" together with "Son of God" in the same fragment does not necessarily mean that the members of Qumran actually expected a divine Messiah. They anticipated many different eschatological figures: two messiahs, one priestly and one political; a prophet like Moses; a teacher of righteousness. Our text does not indicate to which eschatological figure these titles are attributed or whether they belong to the whole people of God. The fragment is dated to the last third of the first century B.C.E. It appears to be apocalyptic in character. The last part describes a brief rule by the enemy and then rest from war and an everlasting rule by the king or by the people.[7] Fitzmyer thinks that the titles may refer to an enthroned king, possibly from the house of David.[8]

We can at least say that there is a very exalted view of a Jewish leader in this text. Further, another text from Qumran may be considered in the same light. Appendix 1 of the *Rule of the Community* (1 *QSa* 2:11–12) possibly reads: "When God *will have begotten* the Messiah among them" (italics added). However, one must be careful not to overemphasize this interpretation: the text is fragmentary and may read "When God *leads forth* the Messiah." The difficulty arises from the reading of one letter in the Hebrew text.

These texts from Qumran suggest that the members of the Qumran community expected a divine figure (not necessarily a messiah) among the eschatological ones who would appear. In their light it can be argued that the words of Gabriel to Mary may be based on pre-Christian—that is, Jewish—tradition. In this case Luke reports an important Jewish expectation. He does not "read back" Christian concepts into the infancy narratives. Indeed, he will underplay Jesus' Davidic descent in the main part of his Gospel.

The Visitation (Luke 1:39–56)

When Mary learned of Elizabeth's condition she went with haste to visit her kinswoman, and both of them rejoiced in the messianic expectation. Elizabeth greeted Mary as one who was "blessed among women." This phrase or beatitude is found in only two places in the Old Testament, Judges 5:24–27 and Judith 13:18. These texts would immediately spring to the minds of Luke's readers. They concern two women, Jael and Judith. The first text reads:

> Blessed among women be Jael, . . .
> blessed among tent-dwelling women.
> He [Sisera, the leader of the enemy] asked for water,
> she gave him milk;
> in a princely bowl she offered curds.
> With her left hand she reached for the peg,
> with her right, for the workman's mallet.
> She hammered Sisera, crushed his head;
> she smashed, stove in his temple.
> At her feet he sank down, fell, lay still;
> down at her feet he sank and fell;
> where he sank down, there he fell, slain [Judg. 5:24–27].

Jael is praised for a heroic, yet violent, action on behalf of Israel. She is blessed as an assassin. The story of Jael appears in the canticle of Deborah, who was a prophetess and charismatic judge, and led a war against the Canaanites. The description of Jael's action is full of religious jubilation.

The second example is Judith. The Book of Judith does not appear to be historical. However, for our purposes it does depict a heroine who, purportedly, went into the camp of the Assyrians, who were fighting Israel, and decapitated Holofernes, their general. On Judith's return to her native city, one of the chief elders, Uzziah, praised her for her violent act:

> "Blessed are you, daughter, by the Most High God, above all the women on earth; and blessed be the Lord God, the creator of heaven and earth, who guided your blow at the head of the chief of our enemies. Your deed of hope will never be forgotten by those who tell of the might of God. May God make this redound to your everlasting honor, rewarding you with blessings, because you risked your life when your people were being oppressed, and you averted our disaster, walking uprightly before our God." And all the people answered, "Amen! Amen!" [Jth. 13:18–20].

It is interesting that these two women are blessed for a heroic, nationalistic, but violent course of action. In other words they were women zealots, somewhat analogous to Phinehas and Elijah. Mary is praised by Elizabeth in words that would clearly remind Jewish readers of these two women zealots.

Like Mary, Judith sings a canticle to God (Jth. 16:1–17). Skehan finds its prototype in the exodus canticle (Exod. 15:1–9), which is associated with Miriam. He sees the Book of Judith as nurturing a postexilic piety characterized by "lowliness, . . . chastity, faith, and prayer." Yet he also finds the victory of Judith "interwoven with dreams of . . . earthbound and militaristic ushering in of God's kingdom, in which the gentiles are treated as the Jews had been treated."[9] Mary may have entertained similar dreams.

A similar idea is found in the Qumran *War Scroll:*

> For you will give over the enemies in all lands into the hand of the poor, and the hand of those groveling in the dust . . . to bring low the warriors of the peoples. . . .[10]

By recalling the memory of Jael and Judith through the words of Elizabeth to Mary, Luke allows us to see Mary as a political figure in the eyes of her kinsfolk. Brown observes that the martial tone of Luke 1:51–52, where the arrogant and proud are cast down, "is scarcely explained by Mary's conception of a child."[11] But it is understandable if Jesus were expected to be an aggressive, political messiah who would cut down the enemies of Israel, and Mary is greeted as the mother of a political figure.

Elizabeth uses the title "Lord" with reference to Mary's child. This title was used of God and of important persons, such as kings and owners of slaves. In Luke's Gospel Jesus is called "Lord" before the resurrection appearances, but in the other Gospels the title is reserved for God and for the resurrected Jesus.[12] Danker sees Elizabeth as a prophetess who is able to discern the mysteries of God in Jesus and his superiority to her son John.[13]

After Elizabeth's greeting Mary proclaims the canticle that the Christian church has called the Magnificat. We have been accustomed to hearing the Magnificat sung to exquisite Gregorian or classical music and interpreted in a very devotional manner. Yet if we look objectively at the wording of this hymn and study both its affinity to the Hebrew scriptures and nonbiblical Jewish texts, it can be seen to be very warlike.

Both the Magnificat and the Benedictus emanate from a Jewish milieu. It has been suggested that they were originally Maccabean war hymns. Indeed, there is nothing specifically Christian about them. Brown summarizes the views of most modern scholars when he remarks that the canticles have greatest affinity to Jewish hymns and psalms found in literature dating from 200 B.C.E. to 100 C.E.—for instance, the Maccabean books (1–4 Maccabees), Judith, 2 Baruch, 4 Ezra, the Qumran hymns, and the *War Scroll* from Qumran.[14] They have the same religious outlook and a confidence in the (political) victory of God.

The Magnificat has been described as a mosaic of Old Testament allusions. A Jewish person contemporaneous with Jesus or Luke would know the scriptures very well. In preliterary society memories are quite astounding. I recall attending a production of *Hamlet* at a seminary in Uganda. The actors were seminarians for whom English was a second or third language. I asked how long it took the one playing Hamlet to learn his part; this would be difficult because of the Elizabethan English. I was told that he was word-perfect in twenty-four hours! Similarly, in the ancient world an allusion to an Old Testament passage would immediately evoke the original text and context.

The contexts of Old Testament texts alluded to in the Magnificat are military (martial) in nature. Verses 47–48 show affinity to Habukkuk 3:18:

> Yet will I rejoice in the Lord
> and exult in my saving God.

This verse occurs after one of the most famous and dramatic descriptions of Yahweh as a god of war. He comes from Mount Paran with all his glory, riding in his war chariot with his weapons—his bow, arrows, and spear. He bestrides the earth in his wrath and tramples the nations in his fury. Habakkuk predicts that God will pierce with his shafts the heads of princes and will tread the sea with his steeds (war horses).

Verses 47–48 are also reminiscent of Psalm 35:9:

> But I will rejoice in the Lord,
> I will be joyful because of his salvation.

This again is in a martial context: the psalmist asks God to come to war, to take up his shield, buckler, and lance, and to scatter the enemy like chaff before the wind.

There is a less close parallel to 1 Samuel 2:1 (the Song of Hannah when she offered Samuel to God):

> My heart exults in the Lord,
> my horn is exalted in my God.

Again, this is in a martial context. Hannah's song rejoices in Israelite victory and reports reversal of fortunes, as does the Magnificat: the mighty are broken, the well-fed hire themselves out for bread, the barren woman gives birth to seven sons, and so forth (see also *Ps. Sol.* 3:7; 17:3—a messianic psalm found in early nonbiblical Jewish literature).

Thus the first two verses of the Magnificat are reminiscent of Old Testament texts that portray God as Warrior and speak of political victory. From its beginning, then, the hymn does strike a military tone.

In verse 49 Mary addresses God as "He who is Mighty." This attribution is most frequently found in the Old Testament when God is described as mighty in battle. It is a clear echo of Psalm 24:8–10:

Who is this king of glory?
The Lord, strong and mighty,
the Lord *mighty in battle* . . .
the Lord of *hosts (armies)* [italics added].

Jones, in an article investigating the Jewish background of the Lukan canticles, speaks of the "divine warrior-champion of Israel" and of Mary's conception of Jesus as a "supreme turning point in history."[15] Zephaniah 3:17 calls God a "mighty savior." Once again this phrase occurs in a context where God is conquering Israel's enemies.

It is, however, the whole clause "He who is mighty has done great things" (Latin *magnalia)* that is borrowed directly from the theology of holy war. F. M. Cross speaks of the reenactment of the *magnalia Dei* at the covenant renewal festivals either in the autumn or spring among the early Israelites.[16] God wins the first victories over enemies in the cosmic struggle and then continues them on an earthly dimension in the events of the exodus and the conquest of Canaan—that is, in the history of redemption when God's mighty armies come from Sinai (also called Horeb) to win battles for the Israelites. These are the mighty deeds of Yahweh in the Hebrew scriptures. Thus the confession of the *magnalia Dei* or the recitation of the epic concerning God's prowess in battle belongs intrinsically to the covenant-renewal ritual. Hence the reference, at the end of the Magnificat, to God's covenant with Abraham, to whom the land was promised (Gen. 15), is readily understandable. Yahweh is a guardian deity who entered into intimate relationship with the people and directed and won their battles.

The Day of Yahweh (or of the Lord) is both the day of God's enthronement and of God's victory over Israel's enemies. Even in late prophetic eschatology the Day of Yahweh is still the day of victory in the "holy war." This is abundantly clear in the Qumran *War Scroll*.

The second part of verse 49 refers to the sanctity of God's name; that holiness is demonstrated in triumph over God's enemies (cf. Ps. 99:1-3).

In verses 51-55 the hymn changes from God's personal favors to Mary to ones of more general application.[17] According to the Magnificat, God shows the same power in Mary's time as was shown at the time of the exodus (Ps. 89:13; 118; Exod. 6; Deut. 3:24). The canticle continues to use the language and concept of holy war—for example, the phrase "with his arm" is found in the exodus story (e.g., Exod. 6:6; Deut. 4:34) and is frequently associated with God's prowess in battle.

Beginning with verse 52 we find the reversal-of-fortune motif, which, again, is characteristic of God's victory. Court officials, potentates, and princes are cast down from their thrones. Marshall remarks that "the overthrow of rulers who do not obey God's will is a sign of his power at work in history" and is "here ascribed to the agency of the Messiah."[18] Jones sees in the verse "the classical vocabulary of the Day of the Lord," which also dominates the Song of Hannah, Tobit 13:2, and the Psalm of Return from the *War Scroll* (1 *QM* 14:10-11).[19]

Verse 53 moves to social situations. Schürmann notes that the coming of the kingdom of God is expected to bring, above all else, a political and social revolution.[20]

Verses 54–55 focus particularly on Israel. God will remember or, more accurately, implement the parts of the covenant with the people—again, a concept linked closely with holy war. There is no mention of the incorporation of the gentiles.

In summary, just as there is a political and militant tone in the narrative of the conception of the Baptist, there is a similar tone in the annunciation to Mary. Gabriel's words to her must be understood against the revolutionary background at the time of Jesus and of the Lukan churches when many messianic pretenders arose (after 44 C.E.). In the Lukan infancy narratives Jesus is to be the Davidic Messiah endowed with military prowess. Yet he is to be more than this. He is the Son of the Highest and the Son of God. Parallel to this pronouncement is the Qumran fragment (4 Q 243) that appears to speak of an eschatological and apocalyptic figure who will have a glorious and victorious kingdom. The description of Mary's visit to Elizabeth suggests that to her contemporaries Mary was a Jael-Judith figure, perhaps even a feminine zealot. The canticle that she sings bears all the marks of a holy-war song. This is not exactly our own image.

The Birth of John the Baptist (Luke 1:57–66)

In the ancient world, names were very important because they were meant to express the character or calling of a person. To know the name of a person was to have power over that person. To bestow a special name on someone was to give that person special characteristics or a particular role. If one gave a name from history, then one bestowed characteristics similar to that historical figure.

In Luke 1:60 the son of Elizabeth and Zechariah is given the name John instead of the name of his father or, according to the prevailing custom, of his grandfather. We must ask whether there were any important Jewish heroes who bore the name John, an alternative form of Jonathan. It is important to look into Maccabean history.

Farmer notes that an investigation of the genealogy of the Maccabean (Hasmonean) family shows that, in addition to the Greek names that they possessed—Hyrcanus, Aristobolus, and so forth—those heroes also bore Jewish names.[21] Farmer continues:

> . . . in every case where we are able to establish what Jewish name a particular Maccabean ruler bore, we find it to be one of the names borne by the early Maccabean heroes. This test holds true without a single exception over a period of six generations and brings us right down to the period with which we are dealing [first century C.E.]. We conclude that these names were family names passed on from one generation to another within the royal Maccabean house.

In examining the names recorded by Josephus, Farmer produces the following chart:

Jews Bearing Non-Maccabean Names	Jews Bearing Maccabean Names
Actively resisted Rome, 11%	Actively resisted Rome, 65%
Neutral or ambiguous records, 78%	Neutral or ambiguous records, 35%
Positive collaborators with Rome, 11%	Positive collaborators with Rome, none

He finds that of the revolutionary leaders *two out of three* have Maccabean names.

The most common Maccabean names are Mattathias and the names of his five sons: John, Simon, Judas, Jonathan, and Eleazar. Another famous Eleazar was the elderly hero whose martyrdom is described in 2 Maccabees 6 and in nonbiblical Jewish texts.

The Maccabean names that were popular during the period of resistance to Rome were Judas, Simon, Eleazer, and John (or Jonathan)—for example, Judas of Galilee; Simon of Peraea; James and Judas, sons of Judas the Galilean; Eleazer ben Dinai; Simon ben Giora; Eleazar, son of Ananias; John of Gischala; Eleazar, son of Simon; and Simon and Judas, sons of Ari.

Among prominent men called John in the Old Testament is Jonathan, son of Saul, the beloved companion of David; John, son of Kareah, who was a war leader and member of the "resistance movement" against Babylon; and Jonathan, the Maccabean, who assumed the leadership of the holy war against the Hellenistic rulers. He performed a number of violent actions—for example, he massacred a wedding procession out of vengeance for the death of his brother John (1 Macc. 9:37–42). Jonathan became a judge and performed the zealous duty of "rooting the godless out of Israel" (1 Macc. 9:65–73). He is called a "mighty warrior" (1 Macc. 10:19–20) and given regal honors (1 Macc. 10:20–21; 10:67–89; 11:57–58).

Jonathan's memory was deeply respected, especially by those who were either from the Maccabean house or lived in the Maccabean spirit. The biblical references give an excellent insight into the warrior angel's insistence that the Baptist be named John.

In Josephus' works fourteen important men are named Jonathan.[22] Luke may have known many of them. Among them were priests, resistance fighters, a *sicarius*, and a foe of Josephus.

It is possible that the Baptist's parents wanted to associate John with the freedom fighters; they expected him to serve the Messiah in a military capacity.

As many scholars have pointed out, there is a tandem relationship between John and Jesus just as there was between Elijah and Elisha.[23] In addition to the military prowess associated with the name of John, perhaps there is another motif in the infancy narratives. Jesus is descended from David. The son of Zechariah and Elizabeth is to be called John. An obvious parallel would be the relationship between David and Jonathan, son of King Saul and intimate friend of David. The friendship was secured by a covenant (1 Sam. 18:1–3). Jonathan bestowed on David part of his clothing and armor to share his personality with his friend. Later he became David's protector when he was persecuted by Saul. The infancy narratives may suggest a quasi-covenant relationship between John and Jesus. They may expect John to be the protector or aide-de-camp of Jesus.[24]

The Benedictus (Luke 1:68–79)

The Benedictus, the canticle sung by Zechariah, comes as a climax to the naming ceremony of the Baptist. It not only emphasizes the importance of this event but throws into higher relief the miraculous recovery of Zechariah's speech, which in turn confirmed the choice of the name of John.

The Benedictus falls into two parts. The first, verses 68–75, blesses God for bringing salvation to Israel; the second, verses 76–79, rejoices in the birth of a child. It has been suggested that originally this was two hymns, the first Jewish and the second Christian. The first is messianic; the second concerns John and, perhaps, a supernatural being. However, there is nothing specifically Christian in verses 76–79. The structural unity of the canticle is maintained by leading scholars. Our inquiry into this material will focus on the question of whether it is Jewish or Christian and whether, like the Magnificat, it contains warlike elements.

The hymn has a stereotyped beginning (v. 68) but, in contrast to Luke's theology in the main part of his Gospel and in Acts, it is significant that Zechariah addresses God as "God of Israel": the hymn shows no favor toward gentiles; rather, it is nationalistic in character. As Jones points out, the first line ("Blessed be the God of Israel") is a blessing formula that is rare in the Old Testament.[25] It is found in the Book of Psalms but not at the beginning of any psalm. The psalter is divided into five parts and this formula occurs at the end of four of the parts—namely, Ps. 40 (41):14; 71 (72):18; 88 (89):53; 105 (106):48 (see also Tobit 13:18).

On the other hand, important for our thesis, this formula is found in a significant place in the *War Scroll* from Qumran. It occurs at the beginning of the "Hymn of Return" from battle after the slaughter of the enemy in the eschatological war (1 *QM* 14:4). Several of the Qumran hymns also have the phrase but not at their beginning (1 *QH* 5:20; 10:14; 11:27, 32; 16:8). The phrase, therefore, is known from the Qumran scrolls and is found in a martial context.

Indeed, there is quite a striking parallel to the first verse of the Benedictus in the thanksgiving hymn in the *War Scroll*:

Blessed be the God of Israel who keeps favor unto His Covenant and testimonies of salvation to the people whom He has redeemed! He has

called them that staggered to marvelous salvation but has wiped out the
assembly of the nations unto destruction. . . . He raises in righteousness the discouraged in heart and *opens the mouth of the dumb that it
may cry out with joy* because of His lofty deeds [1 *QM* 14:4–6; italics
added].

This quotation has the following affinities to the Lukan pericope: a reference
to the dumb speaking (parallel: the restoration of Zechariah's speech), the
blessing of the God of Israel, the emphasis on redemption, the remembering
of the covenant, the rescue from enemies, the reference to righteousness.
"Salvation" has political connotations, and salvation events can be understood to have already been partially realized in the birth of John and the
conception of Jesus.

Jones also draws attention to 1 Kings 1:48, where David, learning that
Solomon is to succeed him, says, "Blessed be the Lord, the God of Israel,
who has granted one of my offspring to sit on my throne this day, my own
eyes seeing it." This may be significant because the Benedictus emphasizes
the Davidic covenant (the "horn of salvation" from the house of David in v.
69). There is no reference to the Davidic covenant in the Magnificat.

In verse 69 we find another martial note in the phrase "God has raised up a
horn of salvation." "Horn" in ancient times would immediately bring to
mind the image of a fighting animal and may refer to the horn of the ram that
often symbolizes the Messiah.

In Daniel's vision of the four beasts (Dan. 7) the last beast has ten horns,
then a little horn arises:

. . . before which three of the first horns were plucked up by the roots;
and behold, in this horn were eyes like the eye of a man, and a mouth
speaking great things [Dan. 7:8].

After this Daniel describes the appearances of one like a son of man who will
have sovereignty over all peoples (Dan. 7:9–14). The small horn in Daniel
appears to be Antiochus Epiphanes, the great persecutor of the Jews who
would eventually succumb to the saints of the Most High (and the "Son of
Man").

In 2 Samuel 22:3 the "horn of salvation" refers to God but in Psalm 132:17
it is God who will make a horn sprout for David. The horn or power of the
anointed is found in 1 Samuel 2:10. An illuminating text is the "Animal
Apocalypse" found in the nonbiblical Jewish book *1 Enoch,* where the Jews
are symbolized by kosher animals, such as sheep, rams, and bulls, and their
enemies by nonkosher animals, such as hyenas and wolves.[26]

The horned lamb is a well-known figure in the Revelation of John. The
background to the Benedictus would indicate that the offspring of David
would be expected to be a military figure. The symbolism is wholly consonant
with purely Jewish thought.

Verses 71–75 describe salvation but add no particular Christian tone.

Salvation is political deliverance from the enemy. God promises the people freedom of worship. An outstanding example of attaining freedom of worship is furnished by Judas Maccabee's victories, which led to his reconsecration of the altar and the establishment of the feast of Hannukah (2 Macc. 10:1–8). The ideal of perfect worship was of particular interest to the Qumran community and also to the revolutionaries who purified the Temple.[27]

With verse 76 the content and style of the canticle changes. The son of Zechariah and Elizabeth will be called the prophet of the most High. This appellation appears in a nonbiblical Jewish work called the *Testament of Levi* (8:15) where it is predicated of the anointed king who will establish a new pattern of priesthood, perhaps referring to the Hasmonean priest-kings. In the context of Luke 1:76 it is an obvious contrast to Jesus who is designated the Son of the Most High (Luke 1:32). John is to prepare the way of the Lord, as Elijah was expected to, according to Malachi: 3:1 and 4:5, and as the Qumran members did by study, prayer, and observance of the Torah (1 *QS* 8:13f. and 9:19f.).

At first glance verse 77 might seem to show Christian characteristics because of the reference to forgiveness of sin. However, forgiveness of sin and knowlege (of salvation) is found in the hymn of the perfect sectarian in the *Rule of the Community:*

> He [God] has justified me by His true justice and by His immense goodness. He will pardon all my iniquities. . . . Blessed be Thou, O my God, who hast opened unto knowledge the heart of Thy servant! [1 *QS* 16:14–16].

Jones remarks that the epiphany of Yahweh brings with it forgiveness of sin (see, e.g., Ps. 98:8). However, he concludes: "On the whole it may be said that forgiveness of sins is never a central feature of the messianic hope."[28] Yet here John is a prophet who will prepare for *God* to bring forgiveness: there is no question of the Messiah's being the agent of forgiveness of sin, as in Christian teaching.

Yet the Messiah appears to be mentioned in verse 78 in the phrase "day" or "dayspring" from on high. The Greek is *anatole* and can refer to a star and its rising, a shoot or branch, or the rising of the Messiah. The star (Num. 24:17) and the branch (Jer. 23:5; 33:15; 40:15, LXX; Zech. 3:8; 6:12; cf. Isa. 4:2) are symbols of the Messiah. Thus John is preparing the way not only for God but also for the Messiah.

Thus the Benedictus shows no clear Christian features; rather, it expresses a messianic and salvific hope that is consonant with the Old Testament and the Judaism of the first century B.C.E. and C.E. The deliverance expected comprises social and political freedom, which was closely integrated with religious independence for the Jews throughout history, but especially reflects the spirit of the Maccabees and the later revolutionaries who emulated them in the first century C.E.

The Baptist's growth (v. 80) reflects the influence of the narrative of Samson (Judg. 13:24–25) and Samuel (1 Sam. 2:21)—that is, growth as a warrior and as a prophet who anointed kings.

At this point the reader may be asking: why is all this belligerent material found in the Lukan infancy narratives if the rest of the Gospel pursues a nonviolent polemic? The reader may also legitimately ask whether this material speaks the mind of Luke. My answer would be that Luke is not only a historian and a theologian but also an artist. He seems to have used special sources for chapters 1 and 2, although the themes of the birth narratives do harmonize with the rest of the Gospel and Acts.[29] He allowed his sources to speak for themselves. They portrayed an ideology that was consonant with the military and revolutionary atmosphere of the first century C.E. This suited Luke's purpose in a significant way. He wished to show that Jesus had inaugurated an *entirely new* age,[30] and this is thrown into higher relief by the contrasting material in the infancy narratives. This hypothesis is, in part, supported by Conzelmann's division of salvation history into three epochs: that of Israel, that of Jesus, and that of the church. However, Conzelmann gives little consideration to the infancy narratives. My interpretation of this material allows it to fit neatly into the period of Israel.

The Birth of Jesus (Luke 2:1–20)

In Luke's Gospel the birth of Jesus is placed within the context of world history—at the time when Quirinius, the Roman governor, took a census of the Jewish people by order of the emperor. Enormous discussion has taken place over the question of the date of this census. The main difficulty lies in the fact that Quirinius took a census in 6 C.E. in Syria rather than 4 B.C.E. in Judea. Luke 1:5 dates the conception of John and of Jesus before 4 B.C.E., when Herod the Great died. Yet Luke 2:1–3 dates the birth of Jesus to ca. 6 C.E. This creates an almost insoluble problem, the details of which we cannot discuss here.

The answer seems to lie partially in the fact that Luke was not especially interested in chronology (cf. the two dates for the ascension according to Luke 24:50–53 and Acts 1:9–10). However, both 4 B.C.E. and 6 C.E. were very important in Jewish history. In 4 B.C.E. the death of the tyrannical and oppressive Herod the Great led to rebellions until Herod Antipas succeeded his father. In 6 C.E. Judea became a Roman province and tribute was imposed on the Jews by the Romans. At this date Judas the Galilean led a revolt on the grounds that submission to taxation was idolatrous. Josephus (*Ant.* 18:8) says that Judas sowed the seed from which sprang the war of 66–74 C.E.

I feel that Braunert offers the most reasonable explanation of this apparent chronological error on the part of Luke.[31] Braunert avers that both the death of Herod and the census taken in Syria caused widespread and protracted repercussions. Luke should have dated the birth of Jesus ten years earlier— that is, not 6 C.E. but 4 B.C.E. The source of the idea of the later date may be sought in the Jewish Christian community in Judea outside Jerusalem, a community that held political beliefs akin to those of the revolutionaries and hoped that Christ would be a powerful earthly ruler at his second coming. Luke is influenced by this early Christian group, which wished to associate the birth of Jesus with the rebellion instigated by Judas the Galilean. The birth of Jesus is, therefore, postdated because this date was highly significant for national history.

However, Luke turns the tables on that same Judean community and portrays Jesus in contrast to Judas and other revolutionaries. He carefully records that Joseph and Mary reported for the enrollment (Luke 2:1–7). He wishes to show that Jesus' family was never involved in the rebellion against Rome; it did not espouse the philosophy of Judas the Galilean and his followers. Some may think it curious that Mary should accompany Joseph, but evidence that women from the age of twelve were subject to registration has been discovered.[32]

The description of the birth of Jesus is very restrained. He was wrapped in swaddling clothes as is reported of Solomon, "I was carefully swaddled and nursed, for no king has any other way to begin at birth" (Wisd. 7:4–5). A nonbiblical Jewish source mentions the Messiah's being wrapped in swaddling clothes (*Ekah Rabbah* 1:51).[33]

The Shepherd Background and Jewish Messianic Expectation (Luke 2:8)

The presence of the shepherds gives the clearest allusion to the messianic character of the newborn child. Micah 4:8 reads:

And you, tower of the flock,
hill of the daughter of Zion,
to you shall it come,
the former dominion shall come,
kingdom of the daughter of Jerusalem.

This passage was interpreted messianically. The "tower of the flock" was interpreted to mean the sheepfold from which the King-Messiah would be revealed. Neirynck proposes that the shepherds of Bethlehem played a special role in late Jewish expectation of the Messiah; he refers to the *Targum of Jonathan* on Genesis 35:21, and also to Micah 4:8 and 5:1–3. Neirynck argues that the angel in verse 11 can be understood as proclaiming that the prophecy of Micah has been realized.[34] The word "today" (Luke 2:11) has a special Lukan overtone of eschatological salvation fulfillment (see Luke 4:21; 19:9; 23:43). In Luke chapter 2 the point is the fulfillment of the Micah prophecy, which, at the same time, provides an explanation for calling Bethlehem the city of David. In the Old Testament the "city of David" always refers to the hill of Zion in Jerusalem—that is, the residence of King David. Neirynck thinks that the setting of the appearance of the angel should remind us of apocalyptic visions.

It may also be observed that the Micah text has a military context. The one who delivers Israel from its enemies will come from Bethlehem (see also Mic. 5).

Jesus as Emperor (Luke 2:9–12)

The angel's announcement to the shepherds is in rhythmic prose and it echoes words and phrases from the Roman imperial cult. First, "good news" or "gospel" is a word used frequently with reference to the coming of emperors.

Secondly, their birth was referred to as "gospel." For example, we find in the Priene inscription: "The birthday of the god [Augustus] has marked the beginning of the good news [gospel] for the world!"

Thirdly, the emperors were also called "saviors." The title "savior" for Jesus is comparatively rare in the New Testament, but the term was used of God in the Old Testament, of the Roman emperors, and of Hellenistic rulers. It is, therefore, significant that it appears three times in the Lukan narratives (1:69, 71, and 2:11): salvation is associated with the coming One.[35] Elsewhere in the Gospels it is used only in John 4:42—the Samaritan woman's word to Jesus—and twice in Acts. The good news that the angel tells Luke's readers is that it is Jesus, not Augustus, who is savior. Yet the full meaning of savior, a spiritual not political meaning, remains to be revealed in the body of the Gospel; it is not explicit in the infancy narratives.

Fourthly, peace on earth (cf. Luke 2:14) was closely associated with the emperors. Indeed, the reign of Augustus was remarkable for the *pax Romana* (Roman peace) that it brought to the whole empire, albeit with the help of the Roman army.

Brown remarks that the imperial features add solemnity to the shepherd incident, particularly inasmuch as the reign of Augustus was remarkable for bringing peace.[36] Indeed, R. Gyllenberg sees the whole passage as an acknowledged or obvious parallel to the secular *pax Romana* and the savior, Augustus.[37] José Comblin defends a similar thesis but places it within the general background of a fuller interpretation of the theology of Luke.[38] In the Septuagint (the Greek translation of the Hebrew scriptures) Luke "read the promises about messianic peace which he understood to mean 'an Israelite peace,' in a historical, political sense as peace with all nations." Jesus came to bring that peace. In Luke 1–2 the narrative of the birth of the king of peace was an opportune place to develop such a thought pattern.

The Shepherds Greeted by an Army (Luke 2:13–14)

The Hellenistic and Roman armies were of vital importance to the Greek rulers and the Roman emperors. Hence it is not surprising that the Lukan infancy narratives associate the birth of Jesus with the appearance of a celestial army. After the words of the angel of the Lord to the shepherds there appears to them not a chorus or choir of angels but an *army*. In Luke 2:13 the word *stratia* means militia or battalion. It occurs only here and in Acts 7:42 and twice in the Septuagint (2 Chron. 33:3 and Neh. 9:6; cf. 1 Kings 22:19 and 2 Esdras 19:6, both LXX). It is true that all these three references are to the "host of heaven," but the host of heaven was thought of as the militia of the warrior God and the classical meaning of *stratia* is the same as that of *stratos*, army. It can be used for a naval force, a land force, or an expedition. In 2:13 Luke could have used *sabaoth*, the usual word for the hosts of Lord in the Septuagint (and the MT). However, the secular word might have been more understandable to his readers.

The phrase *plethos stratias*, usually translated "a multitude of the heavenly host," is more accurately "a large number of soldiers." Winter finds the following parallels to the army of angels in Luke 2 in nonbiblical Jewish literature:

> *Testament of Levi* 3:3; the strength of the ranks of soldiers
> *Pseudo Philo* 19:12; battalions of heaven
> *Slavonic Enoch* 17:1; armed troops serving the Lord
> *4 Esdras* 6:3; battalions of angels
> *2 Baruch* 61:2; the armies of the angels.[39]

In the books of Maccabees there are references to similar celestial apparitions, either of a single celestial being or several, who helped the Maccabees overcome their enemies. For example, in 2 Maccabees 3:24–25 a heavenly horseman appears and in 3:30 he is identified with the Lord; all are filled with joy and gladness (cf. Luke 1:14, but there is no verbal affinity). In 5:1–4 horsemen are seen in the air, and everyone hopes that these apparitions will turn to good. In 10:29–32 five comely men upon horses appear from heaven, and in 11:28 horsemen with white clothing and golden armor are seen. Although the word "angel" is not used, it is difficult to see what else could have appeared to the Maccabees except angels, save in 2 Maccabees 3:30 where the vision is specifically identified with the Warrior God. Where there are several beings they cannot all be Yahweh. In Jewish tradition angels do appear as equestrians.

In the infancy narratives of Luke the description of the appearance of the warrior Gabriel, once to Zechariah and once to Mary, the manifestation of the angel of the Lord (Luke 2:9), and the heavenly army (*plethos stratias*) in Luke 2:13 are more restrained, but not necessarily less militant than the Maccabean visions. The angel of the Lord can bear a sword (Num. 22) although the angelic presence is usually beneficent. Most probably the shepherds see a vision akin to the apparitions reported in 2 Maccabees. Josephus reports a similar phenomenon before the destruction of Jerusalem (70 C.E.):

> Again, not many days after the festival [the feast of unleavened bread] . . . there appeared a miraculous phenomenon, passing belief. Indeed, what I am about to relate would, I imagine, have been deemed a fable, were it not for narratives of eye witnesses and for subsequent calamities

which deserved to be so signalized. Far before sunset throughout all the parts of the country chariots were seen in the air and armed battalions hurtling through the clouds and encompassing the cities [*B.J.* 6:296-99; cf. Tacitus, *Hist.* 5:13].

Luke 2:8-20 includes ordinary persons, the shepherds, who have messianic expectations with nationalistic and martial overtones. It would have been persons such as these whom both the Maccabees and the revolutionaries recruited.

The angels sing a song, perhaps a proleptic victory song. Its literary form may be either a couplet[40] or a triplet. Brown demonstrates:

Glory in the highest to God
and on earth peace among men (persons) favored (by God)

or

Glory in the highest to God
and on earth peace
(and) among men (persons) of divine favor.[41]

In both, one sees the contrast or complementarity of God and humans—between heaven and earth and between glory (the divine effluence) and peace (harmony) on earth. Peace is not only cessation of battle but fulness of blessings brought with the messianic age (see Isa. 9:5f.; Mic. 5:4). In the Old Testament *shalom* (peace) can be wished on a well-conducted war (2 Sam. 11:7)—"peace to Joab, peace to the people, peace to the war." The gift of peace is given not so much to persons of good will (which is an old rendering) but persons upon whom the divine favor rests.[42] This meaning is clearly indicated in nonbiblical Jewish literature (*Ps. Sol.* 3:4; 8:39; 16:12; *1 Enoch* 1:8 [Gk.]; *Test. Levi* 18:13; *Shemoneh Esreh* 17).[43] More importantly, it is found at Qumran (1 *QH* 4:32f.; 11:9). It denotes those whom God has elected—the children of his good will—but it has a rather elitist ring to it.

The shepherds go to see what God has revealed to them. They see Mary, Joseph, and the child. All wonder, but Mary ponders these things in her heart. "Ponder" is a verb used to denote the discerning of mysteries (see Gen. 37:11; Sir. 39:2; Dan. 7:28; *Test. Levi* 6:2).

The Presentation of the Child Jesus in the Temple (Luke 2:21-38)

The narrative of the presentation contains three distinct motifs. First, the purification of the mother according to Leviticus 12:6. This emphasis on fulfilling the law of Moses further stresses the dutiful obedience characteristic of the persons in the infancy narratives. The second motif is the offering of the firstborn in the Temple. However, it was not necessary to bring the child to the Temple; the redemption ceremony could be performed locally. The fact that the parents bring the child to Jerusalem may suggest that he is offered or dedicated to the Temple as was Samuel (1 Sam. 1:11, 22, 28). However, this would not require an offering. (For the biblical texts on the consecration of the firstborn, see Exod. 34:19f.; Num. 3:11–13, 40–51; 18:15–18; Deut. 15:19f.) No ransom price is mentioned in our text. The third motif is the prophecies of Simeon and Anna.

Simeon

The third motif is the one of greatest interest to us. As in the case of the name of John and of Jesus (Joshua), the name Simeon (a variant of Simon) is both a Maccabean name and one that appears frequently among the revolutionaries of the first century C.E. In the Hebrew scriptures the name Simon occurs only once. In the Greek Old Testament it appears once, in Sirach (50:1, the great high priest Simon, son of Onias) and seventy-four times in the Maccabean literature. Simon was an outstanding Maccabean leader and it was from the time of Simon's "peace treaty" that the era of Jewish independence is dated (142–63 B.C.E.). In the words of the writer of 1 Maccabees:

> In the one hundred and seventieth year the yoke of the Gentiles was removed from Israel, and the people began to write in their documents and contracts, "In the first year of Simon the great high priest and commander and leader of the Jews" [13:41–42].

Simon was a religious zealot and performed violent actions to purify the country. He purified Jerusalem and "the Jews entered it with praise and palm branches, and with harps and cymbals, and stringed instruments, and with hymns and songs, because a great enemy had been crushed and removed from Israel" (1 Macc. 13:51). The peace and prosperity enjoyed under Simon's leadership is praised in a canticle in 1 Maccabees 14:4–15. Simon's good deeds were recorded on bronze tablets that were placed on pillars on Mount Zion (1 Macc. 14:25–49).

Josephus mentions twenty-nine men by the name of Simon. Of interest to our subject are: Simon, the son of Matthias; Simon ben Giora, a prominent freedom fighter and messianic figure; Simon, father of Eleazar; Simon, son of Ari; Simon, son of Judas the Galilean; and Simon, the brother of John of Gishala. All of them were revolutionaries. Thus Simon is a name frequently associated with the Maccabees and the first century revolutionaries.

The Consolation of Israel

Simeon is represented as waiting for the "consolation" of Israel. We have been accustomed to think of this as "comfort," but the Greek *paraklesis* can mean exhortation to battle (2 Macc. 15:12–16). Further, Simeon speaks of an oracle telling him that he would not "die" before he should see the Messiah. But the word he uses for "die" is also a metaphor employed for discharging soldiers after a victorious battle. Simeon represents himself as a watchman on sentry duty. He calls himself a slave and God a master (*despotes*). This terminology is found among the revolutionaries. Simeon states that his eyes have seen salvation, which he identifies with Jesus (Isa. 40:5, 52:10, Ps. 98:2, and 1 *QH* 5:12 also identify salvation with a person). Jones thinks that the author of the Nunc Dimittis has Psalm 98 (97) in mind:[44]

> He has remembered his steadfast love and faithfulness
> to the house of Israel.
> All the ends of the earth have seen
> the victory of our God [v. 3].

It is a celebration of victory when God vindicates the people.

The First Oracle (Luke 2:29–32)

Simeon remarks that this salvation has been prepared before the face of "all the nations." Although scholars disagree on the interpretation— whether the verse refers to Jews or gentiles—most think that it refers only to Jews, and that the gentiles will see and admire but not participate in the glory of the Lord (cf. Isa. 49:6 and 42:6).

The Second Oracle (Luke 2:34–35)

This canticle resembles an Old Testament grief oracle (lamentation). Behind the idea of Jesus as causing the rise and fall of many and being a sign of contradiction lies the text of Isaiah 8:14-15, which concerns Yahweh. The Hebrew text and the Aramaic translation are as follows:

And he [Yahweh] will become a sanctuary, and a stone of offense and a rock of stumbling to both houses of Israel, a trap and a snare to the inhabitants of Jerusalem. And many shall stumble thereon; they shall fall and be broken; they shall be snared and taken.[45]	And if you will not hearken, his *memra'* [word] shall be amongst your vengeance and for a stone of smiting, and for a rock of offense to the two houses of the prince of Israel, for a breaking, and for a stumbling, because the house of Israel hath been separated from them of the house of Judah who dwell in Jerusalem. And many shall stumble against them, and shall fall, and be broken and be snared and taken.

Both texts speak of God or his agent (his word) as executing vengeance. Simeon gives a similar prediction concerning Jesus. He appears to speak of two groups of persons: those who reject the Coming One and fall; and those who accept him and rise. However, it is also possible that he means that one group will be obliged to fall in order that it may rise (in resurrection). The reference to "rising" may reflect Isaiah 28:16 and Psalm 118:22, where there is a cornerstone upon which workers build. In the targum "stone" is replaced by "king."

Verse 35a refers to the sword that will pierce Mary's heart. The text is explained best by Ezekiel 14:17, where God allows a sword to pass through the land to cut off humans and beasts. But in our text the sword is not only one of judgment but also of discrimination; it reveals the thoughts of human hearts. As the leaders of Israel reject or accept Jesus, so their hearts are revealed.

Simeon, thus, has waited to see salvation ushered in by a political messiah who will be a source both of destruction and of redemption.

Anna Greets the Child (Luke 2:36–38)

The prophetess Anna from the tribe of Asher now appears. It is conceivable that, if revolutionaries counted male prophets among their members, there could also have been female prophets. Note that Anna speaks of those who were looking for the "redemption" of Jerusalem. When the revolutionaries were winning the war against Rome they issued coins with the inscriptions "for the redemption of Zion" and "freedom of Zion." Redemption, therefore, can be political or spiritual.

Anna is a second witness to the Lord Christ. Marshall points out that her name is the feminine form of Ananas (recall the high priests of this name in the first century C.E.). She seems to have lived for a total of 84 or 91 years as a widow. If the former number is correct, she would be as old as Judith (Jth. 16:23), who did not remarry after the death of her husband. She was revered for this (Jth. 8:4–8; 16:22f.). Further, Anna's prayer and fasting are similar to Judith's (Jth. 11:17; 1 Esd. 9:44). The description of Anna's widowhood may have influenced the concept of widowhood in the early church (Acts 6:1; 9:39; 1 Tim. 5:3–16), but the Judith typology is more germane to the Lukan infancy narratives. Anna is, therefore, a Judithlike figure and not necessarily pacifist.

Mary and Joseph can be compared to Hannah and Elkanah who brought Samuel to the sanctuary at Shiloh (1 Sam. 1:24–28). Simeon blessed Joseph and Mary (Luke 2:34) as Eli blessed Hannah and Elkanah. In Luke's Gospel Anna appears, and in the Book of Samuel there are women at the door of the sanctuary (1 Sam. 2:22). Finally, Luke's conclusion that Jesus grew strong and was filled with wisdom is parallel to Samuel. "The young child Samuel grew in the presence of the Lord. . . . Samuel continued to grow both in stature and in favor with the Lord and with the people."

Summary

Our examination of the infancy narratives has shown that the war angel, Gabriel, appeared to Zechariah and Mary. John the Baptist was to work in the spirit and power of the zealous prophet Elijah. The names Jesus (Joshua), John, and Simeon are names found among Jewish freedom fighters. The annunciation to Mary and the Magnificat have political and military overtones. The words of Elizabeth and Mary echo the beatitude pronounced over Jael and Judith. The shepherd verses have imperial overtones, and a heavenly army appears to them. When Jesus is presented in the Temple two persons appear, Simeon and Anna, who may have been anticipating a political leader.

From now on in his Gospel, Luke will take almost every opportunity offered him to show that Jesus, contrary to all expectations as seen in the infancy narratives, is a preacher with an urgent message to his generation and to the generations to come, the powerful message of nonviolent resistance and, more strikingly, loving one's enemy in word and deed.

Chapter 3

JOHN THE BAPTIST: TRANSITIONAL FORERUNNER

Although Luke's portrayal of John the Baptist has much in common with the other three Gospels, some interesting features peculiar to Luke seem to be in sharp contrast. In the infancy narratives the Baptist is depicted in the spirit of Elijah, with the further intimation that he will be like Jonathan the Maccabean.

Luke gives a more detailed account than Matthew and Mark of the preaching and work of John. Conzelmann believes that John belongs to the old era of Israel,[1] but it is probably better to see him as a transitional personage and, from our point of view, less militant than the contemporaneous revolutionaries but not as pacific as Jesus. John prepares for the nonviolent ministry of Jesus.

Luke opens his record of the ministry of John by giving the reader a detailed chronology, not only of the imperial (Roman) world, but also of the Jewish political situation. This introduction is similar to those found in other ancient histories. Luke mentions the geographical areas germane to his work, including the areas originally belonging to Herod the Great. He omits regions, such as Syria, that Jesus did not visit.

The Jewish pro-Roman leader who receives Luke's greatest attention is Herod Antipas, son of Herod the Great. He was tetrarch or ruler of Galilee and Peraea from 4 B.C.E. to 39 C.E., when he was deposed by Emperor Caligula. He is mentioned in Luke 3:19; 8:3; 9:7; 13:31; 23:7–15; Acts 4:27; 13:1.[2] All but one of these texts are peculiar to the Lukan writings.

Luke refers to two high priests, Annas and Caiaphas, although Annas had retired during Jesus' lifetime. The priesthood is to have considerable influence on Luke's account of the crucifixion, for in Luke it is the chief priests who are responsible for the death of Jesus; the Pharisees are not implicated. The high priests played an important part in the Jewish revolution and during the war.[3] They were usually pro-Roman and, according to Josephus, they continually tried to dissuade the people from revolting.

37

By giving details of Roman and Jewish history, Luke places John the Baptist's career and, indeed, the entire Gospel, against a historical background that is vitally important for understanding his special material and his non-violent philosophy. He is the first evangelist to write a history of Christianity, and he deliberately records it in line with secular history, and delineates the political stance of this new religion, especially with regard to war and peace.

John's calling is similar to that of the Old Testament prophets. The word of God came to him. His role is seen as a fulfillment of the prophecy in Isaiah 40:3.[4] This text is quoted by Mark and Matthew in the same context, but Luke significantly extends the quotation to 40:4-5, to include the important line: "and all flesh shall see the salvation of God." "All flesh" is a wider term than "people" *(laos)* or "nations" *(ethnē)* and is reminiscent of Genesis 1-9, the creation stories.[5] It could even include the animal kingdom but, more importantly, it would include women and slaves (and gentiles), who were usually regarded as property or chattels in the ancient world. By including this verse Luke looks forward to the account of Pentecost in Acts 2, where Peter tells the people that the prophecy of Joel is fulfilled and the Spirit will be poured out on "all flesh." Salvation will be for all classes and both sexes.

This universalism—salvation for all—though found in Isaiah 40-55, would not be acceptable to the revolutionaries who hoped for vengeance on and destruction of the gentiles. But at the very beginning of his Gospel Luke portrays the first of his *dramatis personae,* the Baptist, as announcing salvation to all creation. This bold proclamation sets the tone of the Gospel and of Acts—and is in stark contrast to what we have found in the infancy narratives.

Mark and Matthew suggest a likeness between the prophet Elijah and the Baptist in that they tell us of John's garments and his diet. He was clothed with camel's skin and a leather girdle and dined on locusts and wild honey. Because Luke does not want to portray John in the likeness of Elijah, he omits this description. He wants to deemphasize the Elijah-Phinehas image so much favored by the Maccabees and the revolutionaries and, indeed, clearly portrayed in the words of Gabriel to John's father Zechariah. This avoidance of Elijah-like characteristics is confirmed by the fact that in chapter 7 (parallel in Matt. 11) Luke omits Matthew's identification of John the Baptist with Elijah. Luke does not wish to present John as being impulsive or aggressive or to connect him with one who had been (Phinehas) or would be (Elijah) leader of a holy war. Thus, at the beginning of his Gospel, Luke has altered two points found in the infancy narratives: John should have the power and spirit of Elijah, and "salvation" would be a purely national event, a deliverance of Israel from its gentile enemies.

W. Wink remarks on the arresting difference between the portrayal of John the Baptist by Matthew and his portrayal by Luke.[6] Luke does not identify him with Elijah (contrast Matt. 11:14; 17:10; Mark 9:9-13). He does not mention resurrected prophets or Jesus' cry of dereliction on the cross, which was erroneously interpreted as his calling on Elijah (Mark 15:34f.;

Matt. 27:47). Only Herod and the crowd hold these mistaken views about resurrected prophets (Luke 9:7–9, 19–21). Luke omits five of Mark's references to Elijah, but has three peculiar to himself (Luke 1:17; 4:25–26). One comes from the infancy narratives, and the other portrays Elijah's good deeds on behalf of gentiles. Wink observes that for Luke, in the main part of his Gospel, Elijah does not have an eschatological role as in Malachi, Mark, and Matthew (and one may add Sirach).[7] For Luke, Elijah is the Spirit-filled prophet who is without honor in his native land. "Thus Luke divests John of the role of Elijah *redivivus* and keeps the tradition of Q that John only prepares for the Messiah."[8] Eschatological events do not occur with the ministry of John, according to Luke, but only after John.[9] Conzelmann believes that Luke deliberately distinguishes between the geographical domains of John and Jesus and that he attributes much more success to Jesus.[10]

Luke, rather than portraying John as the eschatological prophet, sees him as an itinerant evangelist (3:3, 18) and a teacher of ethics and prayer (11:1; 5:33). Wink concludes:

> Luke's greatest innovation in the use of traditions about John is the way he has incorporated John into his grand outline of redemptive history. . . . His work as preparer of the way marks the first stage in the central epoch of salvation-history, and therefore he receives a special niche in the Christian dispensation. It is because he commands such a prominent position in the history of redemption that Luke gives him such a prominent role in his Gospel.[11]

The Ethical Teaching of the Baptist (Luke 3:10–14)

Luke alone reports the teaching that John gave to three groups of persons: the crowds, the tax collectors, and the soldiers.

John's advice to the crowds initiates a subject that is important in Luke's Gospel: the correct use of wealth and possessions. John counsels his hearers to share their meager possessions. This advice should be seen against the social and economic background of Palestine in Luke's time, described above in chapter 1. Rhoads gives a short description of the dissension in the countryside under the government of the Roman Cumanus (48–52 C.E.).[12] It was aggravated under the procurator Felix (52–60 C.E.) who, although he captured Eleazar ben Dinai and other brigands, could not prevent the spread of banditry. It was during his time that the *sicarii* appeared and apocalyptic prophets multiplied. Matters were even worse under Albinus (62–64 C.E.). The last procurator, Florus (64–66 C.E.), was guilty of such enormities that brigands were treated with impunity and "throughout the countryside . . . all were at liberty to practice brigandage" (*B.J.* 2:278). Thus the social and economic situation shortly before Luke wrote his Gospel encouraged plundering rather than sharing goods or the necessities of life. John appears to be speaking to the poor about the bare necessities of life.

Horsley offers a perspicacious survey of ancient Jewish banditry with reference to the rebellions against Rome and the final war.[13] He suggests that bandits often symbolize the peasant sense of justice, as well as peasant religious ideals, and that sometimes millenarianism arises as a component part of this ideology.[14] For example, the Galileans were distressed when Herod the Great killed the brigand Hezekiah and his companions (*Ant.* 14:159; *B.J.* 1:204).[15] Horsley sees banditry as "the principal cause of the Jewish revolt against Rome."[16] In the light of such social disturbance one can readily understand Luke's inclusion of John's counsel to the crowds, perhaps lower- and middle-class persons. They are to share what little they have instead of robbing from others. Luke's counsel, then, is to be seen against the background of social banditry, the Robin Hood mentality of the first century C.E.

Even the tax collectors came to John. He did not tell them to give up their occupation; he accepted them on condition that they did not take more than was their due. It is most probable that these were Jewish tax collectors. A number of prominent tax (toll) collectors belonged to high priestly families. John's attitude toward tax collectors is significant because many Jews, especially strict Pharisees, would not accept tax collectors even when they repented, because they were unable to make adequate compensation to those whom they had defrauded. As a class they were hated, despised, and feared, but they were welcomed by John and Jesus. A fuller discussion of tax collectors and toll collectors is taken up in chapter 5, below. However, it should be emphasized that John's acceptance of tax collectors was extremely provocative, especially because John's ministry took place after the rebellion of Judas the Galilean; its repercussions endured long after the revolt failed.[17]

The economic and social background also illuminates John's attitude toward soldiers, the third group to whom he gave counsel. Luke reports that *even* (Greek *kai*) soldiers asked John what they should do. Jews were not obliged to join the Roman army, because such military service would involve so many conflicts with their religious traditions—for example, fighting on the Sabbath. However, there were many Jewish soldiers: those of Jewish governors—such as Herod Antipas, who had forces stationed in Peraea (*Ant.* 17:198f.)—soldiers who performed police duties, soldiers in the resistance movement, and those engaged in guerrilla warfare. The guerrillas carried on raids in order to provide for themselves and the poor. A good example of this phenomenon is the *sicarii* who retired to Masada. Rhoads suggests that their principal activity was harassment of both Jews and Romans in that region. At first they merely collected supplies but later, when the inhabitants of Engaddi (Engedi) were at Jerusalem for the feast of unleavened bread, they attacked the village, killed those who had remained behind, and carried away their booty to Masada (*B.J.* 4:401–4). Other militants joined them for similar raids on other villages (*B.J.* 4:404–5).

John advises the soldiers not to extort money by violence and not to "intimidate" civilians (cf. 3 Macc. 7:21). He tells them to be content with their provisions or, as some would translate it, with their wages *(opsōnion)*. Soldiers' wages were low because they could also rely on procuring spoils after battle. Caragounis sees a climax in John's advice to the soldiers: they are not to rob violently, not to accuse falsely, and they are to be content with their provisions (wages).[18] He notes that John's words to the soldiers are stricter than those to the tax collectors. The inference is probably that "the soldiers' conduct was much more insolent, exasperating"[19]—and more violent. Whether the injunctions are addressed to Roman soldiers or Jewish, they represent a condemnation of a depraved practice among soldiers, that of commandeering civilians' provisions either as they came from the market place or in their homes. John's advice is interesting in the light of Josephus's calling many of the freedom fighters "brigands." It would be inviting to see John's converts as reformed freedom fighters. Note that the soldiers are not told to give up their occupation.

Thus John gives counsel to three groups whose condition in life may have been worsened by economic straits. John checks any violent reaction to their circumstances, but he does not ask either the tax collectors or the soldiers to relinquish their occupations.

The Stronger One (Luke 3:15–17)

Only Luke and John (1:19–28) record that the Jews wondered whether John might be the Messiah. Luke makes this question the introduction to John's words about "the mightier one" who is to come after him. The question is important in Luke's time because of the messianic and prophetic expectations among the revolutionaries. Their prophets claimed they would perform signs and wonders, often similar to those that Moses performed in the wilderness. Josephus reports that Theudas expected to perform miracles analagous to those of the exodus event, such as dividing the Jordan *(Ant.* 20:97–99). Hengel suggests that Theudas may have considered himself a second Moses or a second Joshua, but he was not so much a prophet as a messianic pretender.[20] Under Felix (52–60 C.E.) deceivers and imposters arose who, under the pretense of divine inspiration, stirred up revolts to overthrow the state *(B.J.* 2:264–65). Their enthusiasm was contagious and throngs flocked to the desert awaiting signs of freedom *(semeia eleutherias)*. They met the same fate as did Theudas (Acts 5:36). An Egyptian prophet arose who led the people from the desert to the Mount of Olives *(Ant.* 20:169–71). They expected the walls of Jerusalem to fall down so that they could take possession of the city. Felix dispersed the followers of the Egyptian and the prophet himself disappeared. In Festus's time a "god appeared and led the people into the desert."

Against this background one can understand why it was important for Luke to demonstrate that John was not a messianic pretender or an eschatological prophet. Further, he performed no miracles. When he was asked whether he were the Messiah, John answered by referring to the status of Jesus. He refers to him as the mightier one *(ho ischuroteros)* who will come after him. The definite article shows that John is speaking about a special individual. "The mightier one" may not have a precise messianic connotation but it certainly is eschatological. Be it recalled that Jewish expectations envisioned several figures for the eschatological drama.

The reference to the mightier one occurs in all the synoptics but not in John's Gospel. This epithet is used frequently for God in the Septuagint—for example, 2 Kings 22:32f. It also refers to military strength. It is employed about thirteen times in the Septuagint for warriors *(gbr)*. Scobie cites W. Grundmann, who explains the term in the light of the only other New Testament passage in which the comparative form occurs, Luke 11:20–22.[21] This passage is peculiar to Luke; it reads:

> When a strong man *(ho ischuros,* the strong one), fully armed, guards his own palace, his goods are in peace; but when one stronger *(ischuro-teros)* than he assails him and overcomes him, he takes away his armor in which he trusted and divides his spoil.

Here the mightier one is definitely a warrior figure. Grundmann surmises that the phrase "and divides his spoil" (Luke 11:22) is based on Isaiah 53:12, "and he shall divide the spoil with the strong." He supposes that here Jesus claims to be both a conquering messiah and the suffering servant. But Scobie notes that there is no evidence that the term "the mightier one" was in use as a messianic title and it does not appear in the shorter forms of the saying found in Matthew 12:29 and Mark 3:27 (the discussion about the prince of demons, Beelzebub). However, he observes that the word "mighty" can be used of a person who has been given special powers by God (e.g., Isa. 9:6 and *Ps. Sol.* 17:43–44, "the anointed of the Lord . . . will be strong and stumble not . . . he will be mighty in his works." Presumably it could be used of a prophet, mighty in words and deeds.[22] Luke 11:20–22 appears to refer to the mightier one's overcoming of Satan.

Vermès, however, does discuss the messianic significance of "the mightier one" *(geber* = warrior).[23] He considers the Qumran writings, the Septuagint, and the Targumim. The *geber* born in travail is described in 1 *QH* 3:7–10. He is shown in a messianic light in 1 *QS* 4:20–22. Both Vermès and Brownlee (cited by Vermès) find a messianic interpretation of *geber* in the above texts and also in 2 Samuel 23:1, Zechariah 13:7, and Numbers 24:17, LXX (as also in the nonbiblical works *Test. Jud.* 24:1 and *Test. Naph.* 4:5). A messianic interpretation of the biblical texts is supported by the Targumim. These also portray the *geber* as the king, the anointed of God.

It seems, therefore, that the term "the mightier one" used by the Baptist is employed with a similar connotation. The one whom the Baptist expected was the mighty warrior (and king), probably one who could fight on both earthly and heavenly dimensions, as in the battle described in the *War Scroll*. This would be perfectly consonant with the Maccabean idea of the holy war, with the same idea among the revolutionaries, and especially with the role of the Messiah as leader in the eschatological war. Hence it is understandable that John did not dismiss soldiers from their occupation. They would play a vital part in the eschatological war, but they must be pure in morals.

For Luke and Matthew "the mightier one" will baptize with *a* holy spirit and with fire. Judgment by fire is a recurrent theme in both the Old and New Testaments and also in nonbiblical Jewish literature, especially that from Qumran. Originally the text may have read "with wind" (the same word as "spirit" in Hebrew and Greek) "and fire." This would mean judgment by sirocco (or hurricane) and fire. Later, in the light of Pentecost, Christians would understand a *holy* spirit.

Thus, although Luke's portrayal of John differs from Mark and Matthew in that he is not Elijah *redivivus* and his ministry extends beyond the bounds of the Sadducees, Pharisees, members of Qumran, and the revolutionaries, nevertheless John retains the expectation of a military figure in "the one who is to come." John's is a transitional role until Jesus, the nonviolent leader, inaugurates his own ministry.

Unlike Conzelmann, I do not place the Baptist in the period of Israel but rather on the threshold of the Christian era. His character and role are more moderate than what was predicted for him in the infancy narratives, but he does not take a nonviolent stance as does Jesus.

The Emissaries of John the Baptist (Luke 7:18–35; cf. Matt. 11:2–19)

We have further confirmation of John's expectations not being consonant with those of Jesus in the pericope about the messengers of the Baptist.

The material here seems to come from a source common to Matthew and Luke but Luke's version differs from Matthew's. He omits the reference to John in prison. He reports in greater detail how John sent two disciples (the required number for witnesses according to Jewish law) to Jesus. They were sent to the "Lord" *(Kurios)*. They repeat the exact words of their master and teacher, John. Then, most importantly, Luke reports that miracles took place when John's disciples were present so that they could witness to what they had seen as well as report what they had heard. This is in accord with Luke's method of balancing deed and word—for example, he records the miraculous catch of fish and then the calling of the disciples. The disciples of John, therefore, can give their master a double witness. According to the synoptic Gospels, John was imprisoned before Jesus began his ministry; therefore it is unlikely that he himself witnessed any of Jesus' miracles.

Jesus' answer consists of six parallel clauses followed by a comment. In Luke there are two groups of three clauses joined by *kai* ("and"). The reply refers to Jesus' ministry as a whole, not just to the miracles that John's disci-

ples have witnessed. Behind this poetic form are the following texts from
Isaiah: 29:18f., 35:5f., 61:1, and 26:19. Only the healing of lepers is not
found in these Isaian texts. What Jesus omits is the idea of judgment, which is
certainly present in all these texts, as shown below.

Isaiah 29:18f. is followed by:

> For the tyrant will be no more
> and the arrogant will have gone;
> All who are alert to do evil will be cut off [v. 20].

Isaiah 35:5f. is preceded by:

> Be strong and fear not!
> Here is your God,
> he comes with vindication;
> With divine recompense
> he comes to save you [v. 4].

Isaiah 61:1 is followed by:

> To announce a year of favor from the Lord
> and a day of vindication by our God [v. 2].

Isaiah 26:19 continues:

> Go, my people, enter your chambers,
> and close your doors behind you;
> Hide yourselves for a brief moment,
> until the wrath is past.
> See, the Lord goes forth from his place,
> to punish the wickedness of the earth's inhabitants;
> The earth will reveal the blood upon her,
> and no longer conceal her slain.

John, who foresaw a warrior leader, "the mightier one," who would baptize with wind (or spirit) and fire and sift the wheat from the chaff is per-
plexed that Jesus does not fulfil this role. Jesus shows no aggressiveness.
John had not foretold that Jesus would perform healing miracles. John and
his followers expected a different behavior from Jesus, a behavior that would
be more in keeping with leadership in a holy war and acts of zeal like those of
Phinehas and Elijah. Jesus does not seem to be fulfilling this role. In Jesus'
reply to John he not only asserts that it is his function to heal and help the
needy but, as in Luke 4:19, he omits any reference to political victory, divine
vindication, or punishment of the wicked, as found in all the Isaian texts that
lie behind his answer to John the Baptist.

Praise of John the Baptist (Luke 7:24-28; Matt. 11:7-19)

Again the source is Q; the wording of Luke and Matthew is almost identical. Jesus' praise of John is extravagant but justified. He fulfilled the prediction of Malachi 3:1 and 4:5 and prepared the way for God (not for the Messiah).

Luke also appends an important addition to Jesus' statement that the person "who is least in the kingdom of heaven is greater than he." He mentions (vv. 29-30) that the people and the tax collectors glorified God when they heard these words, but the Pharisees and lawyers who, unlike them, had not been baptized by John, rejected the purpose of God. This addition is explained by Luke's inclusion of John's baptizing tax collectors, the poor, and soldiers, as also by his concern over the burden of taxation and the agents involved.

Luke 7 also omits Matthew 11:12-15, where Matthew associates the time of John and the kingdom of heaven with men of violence and states that John is Elijah who was to come. Luke has a similar statement later in his Gospel (Luke 16:16) but does not mention men of violence.

The Baptism and Genealogy of Jesus (Luke 3:21-38)

Luke, unlike Mark (1:1-9) and Matthew (3:13-17), does not explicitly say that Jesus was baptized by John. In keeping with the infancy narratives Luke must continue to avoid showing that John might be superior to Jesus in any way. Thus we hear only that Jesus was baptized but Luke does not say by whom. According to the Gospel of Luke Jesus received a manifestation of the Spirit in a form more visible than in Mark and Matthew: it comes in "bodily form, as a dove."

It is after Jesus' baptism, not in the infancy narratives, that Luke records the genealogy of Jesus. Luke's genealogy extends back to Adam, the son of God, and thus Jesus' pedigree is placed in the context of the whole human race. This is in vivid contrast with Matthew, who traces Jesus' genealogy only back to Abraham and artificially divides the generations into the periods of the rise of the kingdom of David, the fall of the kingdom with the captivity in Babylon, and then the rise once again with Jesus. Luke's genealogy shows clearly that human beings were God's children before God elected the Hebrews, made a covenant with Abraham, and placed upon the patriarch and his children the obligation of male circumcision, a rite that kept many gentile male adults from fully becoming Jews.[24]

The Eschatological Aspect of Luke's Genealogy

Luke's genealogy consists of seventy-seven names, which fall into eleven groups of seven. The number seventy-seven would seem to suggest totality or perfection. Marshall observes that the most significant names fall at the beginning or end of the groups.[25] Reading in reverse order, including Jesus (v. 38), back to verse 23, these names are:

Adam	Enoch
Methuselah	Shelah
Eber	Abraham
Isaac	Admin
Aminadab	David
Nathan	Joseph
Judah	Joshua
Er	Salathiel
Zerubbabel	Mattathias
Maat	Joseph
Jannai	Jesus

Marshall also believes that the groups of eleven have a symbolic meaning: they may reflect a division of history into eleven weeks; the twelfth week would be the messianic era. Therefore, with the birth of Jesus, world history comes to a climax. M. D. Johnson quotes 4 Ezra 14:10ff.:

For the age has lost its youth, and the times begin to grow old. For the age is divided into twelve parts, and nine of its parts have already passed, as well as half of the tenth part; so two of its parts remain, besides half of the tenth part. Now, therefore, set your house in order.[26]

Johnson points out that 2 Baruch 53–74 has fourteen periods, not twelve, and also some manuscript variants have seventy-two or seventy-three names, not seventy-seven as in the Lukan genealogy. Nevertheless, Luke may have known the Ezra tradition and the genealogy does seem to be associated with the eschatological era.

Genealogies may not seem very interesting today but they were of vital interest in antiquity.

The Purposes of Genealogies

Johnson finds the purposes of the Old Testament genealogies to be the following:[27]

(1) To demonstrate the relationships between Israel and the surrounding nations by using a tribal classification—for example, the "Table of Nations" (Gen. 10) is to show that the whole earth was peopled from the three sons of Noah.

(2) The genealogies of the priestly tradition in the first five books of the Bible link together isolated traditional elements concerning Israelite origins.

(3) Genealogies are also used to "establish continuity over those periods not covered by material in the tradition."

(4) Genealogies "served as the vehicle for chronological speculation concerning the 'Great Year' or 'world cycles' "; in other words, they can be a medium for eschatological thought.

(5) Some genealogies in 1 Chronicles may have been composed from material from military leaders: census lists are military in purpose and content. Military leadership in the tribes may have been hereditary.

(6) Genealogies were also used to give persons legitimacy in their office or link them with a hero in previous history. Pedigrees for both religious and political leaders are found.

(7) In Ezra and Nehemiah genealogies are significant for proving purity of descent, "holy seed."

(8) Genealogies were also used to trace continuity in the people of God after a national disaster—for example, the exodus or the Babylonian exile.

(9) Genealogies are most frequently used with regard to the priestly circles. The Toledoth Book "was organized around a group of pivotal figures culminating in Aaron, thus exhibiting a sense of movement within history toward a divine goal." Johnson quotes Lefèvre, who calls genealogies a work of art.[28]

This helps us understand that the genealogies of Jesus in Matthew and Luke are not to be taken literally but rather to be studied to find their purpose. Johnson concludes: "This means, in essence, that the genealogical form could be used as an alternative to narrative or poetic form of expression, that is, as one of several methods of writing history and of expressing the theological and nationalistic concerns of a people."[29]

Johnson cites Jeremias to the effect that the use of patriarchal names cannot be traced back to the sixth century B.C.E.[30] The first appearance of the names Joseph, Judah, and Simeon are found in Ezra, Nehemiah, and 1 Chronicles. Levi is first found among the Maccabees and in the New Testament. Further "Jesus" was not a popular name until Ptolemaic and, especially, Roman times. The Lukan genealogy would seem, therefore, to incorporate theological reflection.

Johnson believes that the significance of the Lukan genealogy is to be gleaned from three operative concepts. First, ancestry from David does not seem to be important to Luke (in contrast to Matthew). For him Jesus is primarily the Son of God. Luke's genealogy is the only one to trace ancestry to God. Johnson comments:

Jesus is the Son of God, not through the categories of pre-existence or physical (or metaphysical) relationship between Father and Son, but through the line of Old Testament patriarchs and post-biblical historical figures. In this way, Luke historicizes the title, emphasizing the continuity of the Son with the Old Testament and with Judaism. The Lukan genealogy would, therefore, be a prime example of Luke's consciousness of the continuity of history in the midst of seeming discontinuity.[31]

Secondly, Luke is interested in representing Jesus as *the* prophet. His genealogy does not go back to the royal line of Judah (through Solomon) but proceeds from the third son of David, Nathan. Johnson remarks:

> This deviation from the kings of Judah is highly significant since the genealogy not only rejects the royal line, but also fails to incorporate any OT genealogical data between Nathan and Zerubbabel. . . . It is entirely possible that *Luke's tendency to avoid any political overtones in his prescription of Christianity that might worsen the church-state relationship lies behind his rejection of the royal line:* Jesus is the Davidic Messiah, but not through the OT royalty, and *therefore his Messiahship is not to be considered as opposed to the legally ordained rulers of the state* [italics added].

Beginning with Zechariah 12:12, where the house of David and house of Nathan are mentioned separately, and continuing in nonbiblical Jewish and Christian writings, the third son of David, Nathan, is identified with the prophet Nathan.[32] These texts show that some Jews expected the Messiah through Nathan, not through Solomon. Aptowitzer thinks the pedigree from Nathan instead of Solomon was an anti-Hasmonean polemic.[33] This would certainly be consonant with Luke's nonpolitical stance.

Johnson finds the key to the Lukan genealogy in Luke's emphasis on prophecy in the person of Jesus, his contemporaries, and in the early church. Thus it is understandable that Luke derives Jesus' pedigree from Nathan, not Solomon. In this way Jesus is not presented as a royal-political messiah.[34]

I should like to add two considerations to Johnson's second point. (1) Luke does not call David "king." This is in contrast to Matthew who emphasizes it at the center of his genealogy (Matt. 1:6). (2) Scholars have suggested that the fourteen multiplied by three in Matthew's genealogy is the numerical value of the name "David." This would be arresting to Jewish readers. It is omitted by Luke.

Sahlin notes that there are priests mentioned in the genealogy of Luke.[35] This is the third operative concept: Luke wished to show Jesus as priestly Messiah. I may add that this would be consonant with Jesus depicted as Melchizedek or the prophet who announces him (see chap. 4, below), with Jesus' priestly prayer for forgiveness of unwitting sin when being fastened to the cross (see chap. 8, below), and with the final priestly blessing that Jesus gives before his ascension in Luke 24:50.

Abel remarks that to give support to Johnson's thesis we must find evidence for a prophetic-messianic theme in first-century Judaism.[36] Abel believes Johnson is correct. The warnings against false prophets in the New Testament and Josephus's witness to several prophetic and messianic personalities during this time prove it. Evidence is found also in the esteem given to prophecy in certain Jewish circles (*B.J.* 2:159) and among the members of Qumran. Prophets were not anointed, but they could be called "anointed" when the office of high priest and prophet were combined, as in Hasmonean times (*Test. Levi* 8:2–15; 18:2–12). He thinks that the genealogy might have originated from Jewish-Christian groups such as the Ebionites who rejected the genealogy of Matthew.

Jeremias contends that there were genealogies for lay nobility belonging to certain families who brought wood to the Temple.[37] A woman was obliged to know her genealogy for five generations if she wished to marry into a priestly family. Candidates for public office also were obliged to prove the purity of their pedigree. The Davidic family was the most important one among the laity; thus its pedigree would be kept meticulously. One of the messianic pretenders of the first century C.E., Menahem ben Hezekiah, claimed to be of Davidic ancestry (*J. Ber.* 2:4, 5a, 18). Jeremias continues:

> For more than a hundred years members of the family of Hezekiah, the chief robber in Roman times, distinguished themselves time and time again by their mutinies and pretensions to the throne; this too makes it seem probable that this family was of royal descent.[38]

With regard to the genealogy in Luke's Gospel, Jeremias gives a fairly favorable critique. In some details Luke is correct where 1 Chronicles is wrong. For example, whereas there is some doubt about the preexilic names in the Lukan genealogy, the postexilic names appear to be fairly accurate. We must take into account the fact that the royal family records were carefully kept, as were many of the contemporary lay genealogies, and thus one may assume that "Luke, or his source, may have preserved authentic material, at least for the last few generations before Joseph."

Luke's genealogy is important (1) in highlighting a special epoch in world history; (2) in implicitly including the gentiles in salvation by going back to Adam; (3) in revealing prophetic and, perhaps, priestly figures among Jesus' ancestors; (4) in tracing Jesus back to Nathan, not Solomon; and (5) in emphasizing the continuity of Israel at a time of national crisis. The most important aspect is Jesus' pedigree through Nathan the third son of David, which considerably reduces the political threat that direct association with Solomon would bring. The threat is diminished, too, by Luke's accepting the identification of Nathan, the son of David, with the prophet Nathan. Thus when Jesus first appears as an adult, Luke shows him as a prophetic, not military or political, figure.

The Imprisonment of John the Baptist (Luke 3:19–20)

Just as Luke never explicitly states that John baptized Jesus, so Luke diminishes the importance of John by omitting the detailed account of his imprisonment and death through the rash oath made by Herod Antipas to the daughter of Herodias (Matt. 14:3–12 and Mark 6:17–19). Luke reduces what he knew about John's imprisonment to two verses, and does not even mention his death.

This is all the more surprising if Hoehner is correct that the story of the death of the Baptist recorded by Mark and Matthew came from Joanna, the wife of Chuza, the financial minister of Antipas, who is mentioned in Luke 8:3 and 24:10, or from Manaen, the friend of Antipas, who appears in Acts 13:1.[39]

We are able to explain Luke's omission by viewing the life of John the Baptist in a political context. Herod Antipas committed incest when he dismissed his first wife, the daughter of the Nabatean king, Aretas, and married Herodias, who was his niece and one of his brothers' wives. This action was not only scandalous but politically dangerous in the eyes of the Jews. We learn this not only from the New Testament but also from Josephus, who says of John:

> . . . he was a good man and had exhorted the Jews to lead righteous lives, to practice justice toward their fellows and piety toward God, and so doing to join in baptism. . . . When others too joined the crowds about him, because they were aroused to the highest degree by his sermons, Herod became alarmed. Eloquence that had so great an effect on mankind might lead to sedition, for it looked as if they would be guided by John in everything that they did. Herod decided therefore that it would be better to strike first and be rid of him before his work led to an uprising, than to wait for an upheaval, get involved in a difficult situation, and see his mistake (*Ant.* 18:116–19).

Josephus concludes by stating that John was imprisoned in Machaerus and put to death by Herod Antipas. Thus Josephus gives us an insight that the Gospels omit: Herod saw a political, revolutionary danger in John. Although it has been questioned whether this Josephus passage is genuine, it is mentioned by both Origen and Eusebius, early Christian writers.

Manson believes that John's preaching had a political overtone in that it envisaged the Messiah whose role was to terminate foreign power over Israel. He thinks Antipas saw danger in John's attracting the lower classes but the upper classes remained aloof. Hoehner, although not agreeing with Manson about the Messiah, does feel that the story of the Baptist's imprisonment and death has political overtones.[40] Antipas might have believed, and rightly so, that religious fanaticism, compelling others to observe the Torah, was more dangerous than political ardor. Peace with the Nabateans was important politically, because it was a buffer state, and, economically, for control of the trade routes.[41] John's rebuke of Antipas "was not only embarrassing but politically explosive."[42] Josephus reports that the Jews believed that the destruction of Herod's army by Aretas, the Nabatean, was an act of divine vengeance for his murder of John the Baptist (*Ant.* 18:116–19).

There are also two passages from the Slavonic version of Josephus about John.[43] One, after describing John, states that he promised the Jews that "there would be granted to them a king who would set them free and subject all who were not obedient, but he himself would be subject to no one."[44] The passage also tells how he was interviewed by Archelaus and the teachers of the law, and that he enraged Simon the Essene.[45] In both of these passages John's Elijah-like clothing (omitted by Luke) is described.

In the second passage Josephus tells how John interpreted a dream of the tetrarch Philip, and Philip died the same day. The passage continues:

And his [Philip's] kingdom was given to Agrippa, and his wife Herodias was taken by his brother Herod. But for this reason all who were learned in the law abhorred him, but dared not accuse him to his face. That man alone, whom they called a wild man, came to him in wrath and said: "Forasmuch as thou hast taken thy brother's wife, thou evil man, even as thy brother has died a merciless death, so wilt thou too be cut off by the heavenly sickle."

Although these passages may not be original they do reflect an early tradition that saw John in a political role.

Luke, on the other hand, completely passes over the long narrative about Herod and the dancing girl given in detail by Mark (6:17–29) and Matthew (14:3–12). Perhaps Luke does this because he feels that the whole episode might revive the hatred felt for Herod and not serve the Lukan theme of nonviolence and reconciliation. In the light of the political importance attached to John in nonbiblical sources, it is very striking that Luke, who is interested in history and politics, should divest John of all political significance and strictly curtail Herod's role in his death. Luke may also have been reluctant to show any affinity between Elijah's danger at the hands of Jezebel and John's danger at the hands of Herodias. Luke does not even report John's death.

Summary

Luke's portrayal of the Baptist shows him as a transitional figure, moving beyond the period of Israel, yet not quite entering into the period of Christ. The beginning of the main part of the Gospel has a universalistic note. Luke has removed John's likeness to Elijah, emphasized that he is not the Messiah, and presented him as an itinerant preacher and ethical teacher. Yet John still expects a warrior messiah. Luke passes over the fact that John baptized Jesus and places emphasis on Jesus' genealogy, which follows his baptism. This genealogy is an artistic construct showing Jesus' place in human history and in the divine eschatological scheme of God. In contrast to the infancy narratives, it portrays Jesus, not as the successor to the throne of David, but rather as prophet and priest descended from Nathan, who, later, was identified with the prophet of the same name. Luke omits the murder of John the Baptist by Herod because nonbiblical tradition portrays John as a political figure. When John sends his disciples to question Jesus about his credentials, Jesus replies by quoting from Isaiah, but he carefully avoids any reference to vengeance on or oppression of the gentiles. Thus Luke has toned down considerably the political roles of John and Jesus. This portrayal of John prepares us for the appearance of Jesus, who will play a role that is far less aggressive and political than that of his forerunner.

Chapter 4

JESUS' REJECTION BY THE NAZARETH ASSEMBLY

In the desert after his baptism Jesus conquered the temptation to be an international political leader. He also refused the role of wonderworker as claimed by so many itinerant preachers and magicians in the ancient world.[1] He did not satisfy his own hunger by turning stones into bread.

According to Luke 4:14–15 he returned to Galilee "in the power of the Spirit"—a detail mentioned only by Luke. Luke omits any reference to John the Baptist; he does not report a visit to Capernaum, although it is implied in verse 23; he makes no mention of the tribal territories or of "a great light" dawning on "Galilee of the gentiles" (peculiar to Matt. 4:13–16). Luke alone at this point records the spread of Jesus' fame.

After this short summary, Luke introduces Jesus' first homily in Nazareth, his Galilean hometown, not far from the military stronghold of Sepphoris, which had shifted between Roman and Jewish control.[2] Most scholars agree that Galilee was rife with revolutionaries and apocalyptic thinkers, although this has been challenged recently by Freyne.[3] Luke 4:16–30 may be based on Mark 6:1–6 (cf. Matt. 13:53–58) but Luke's account is so much longer and contains such important theological points that there is reason to believe he may have had a separate source.[4] Mark and Matthew do not report that Jesus read a passage from scripture.

What is so arresting is the prominence that Luke attributes to this event in Jesus' life. If we study the Matthean and Markan context of this pericope and especially its place in the arrangement of their Gospels, we note a striking difference (Matt. 13:54–58; Mark 6:1–6a). Matthew and Mark report many activities of Jesus before his return to Nazareth. Indeed Matthew has ten chapters (not including the infancy narratives) and Mark has five, contrasted with Luke's single chapter (not counting the infancy narratives) before this event.

Luke effects a dramatic change. He makes the Nazareth event the very beginning of Jesus' ministry, and indeed an event that shows that Jesus' policies and ideology will have a radical and not altogether pleasing effect on his hearers. In this pericope Luke is able to foreshadow the major principles of Jesus' (or Luke's) theology. Jesus speaks as an anointed prophet; his mission is directed to the poor and the oppressed; it is a ministry of healing and illumination, on the physical, psychological, and spiritual levels; he proclaims a year (time) of favor for both Jew and gentile; and he will repudiate hatred and vengeance. His ideology will be found to be inimical to that of many of his contemporaries, especially the revolutionaries, and will lead to repeated rejection and finally a martyr's death. Thus the Nazareth pericope sets the stage for the public life of Jesus and prepares the reader for its unique character.

The Text from Isaiah and Jesus' Commentary (Luke 4:16–30)

Our text apparently contains the earliest extant description of a synagogue service. Jesus performs the office of "lector." It is not clear from the passage whether he or the synagogue attendant chose the section of scripture for reading. However, we know it was from Isaiah 61, although Luke quotes only two verses.

When we examine the quotation (although Jesus must have read a longer passage than that recorded by Luke) we find that the words are not precisely those of the Hebrew text of Isaiah 61. Jesus' text is a fusion of Isaiah 61:1–2 and 58:5d–6. From the latter text comes the claim "to set at liberty the oppressed." There was no standard Hebrew text of the Bible at the time of Jesus, and thus either Jesus had a text different from ours or he added the phrase about the oppressed. Either way, the phrase is important against the background of the oppressed status of Israel vis-à-vis Rome and the Herodian dynasty.

Isaiah 61, according to the Lukan passage, (1) presages an anointed prophet who possesses the Spirit; and (2) predicts an anointed prophet who preaches to the poor; (3) announces the release of prisoners; (4) promises restoration of sight to the blind; and (5) proclaims the acceptable year of the Lord.

For Luke, Jesus is the anointed prophet and this scriptural passage predicts the quintessence of the whole ministry of Jesus, while proclaiming liberty to the oppressed (Isa. 58). The healing of the blind is probably to be taken in a spiritual sense, even though Jesus himself did heal the physically blind. Only once was a blind person, Tobit, healed in the Old Testament. He was not congenitally blind (recall John 9:32, where the disciples say that they had never known one blind from birth to be healed).

We understand Isaiah 61:1–2 in the light of Jesus' entire ministry, but the congregation at Nazareth would see the text in a different light. It would kindle their political hopes. The original context of Isaiah 61 is the Babylonian captivity in the sixth century B.C.E. The text encourages the Jews in exile and those who remained in Judah under political subjugation to hope for peace and independence from Babylon. The exilic and postexilic prophets, such as Second Isaiah, Third Isaiah, and Ezekiel, anticipated a new state of Israel in which foreigners would serve the Hebrews and Hebrews not serve foreigners (see Isa. 61:5-7).

The text would be heard in a similar way in the first century C.E., but the expectation would be release from Roman, not Babylonian, domination.

The Jubilee Year

This Isaiah text was also one of the passages selected for reading at the commencement of the jubilee year. A jubilee occurred every forty-ninth year and was, in effect, a special sabbatical year. During the jubilee year:

(1) Everyone was to return to their own landed property.

(2) Debts were to be canceled.

(3) Land was to return to its original owner(s) or family. Originally, the land was equally distributed according to the number of persons in each tribe. The jubilee law was a return to this ideal.

(4) Slaves were to be freed.

(5) The land was to lie fallow, but the poor could harvest any spontaneous growth.

(6) Prisoners were to be released.

The jubilee was "good news" to the poor, slaves, debtors, and other oppressed persons who could rejoice in their freedom. There was a redistribution of wealth and everyone was put on equal footing. Thus a jubilee year was indeed an acceptable year to all the types of oppressed persons. Luke portrays Jesus as proclaiming the inauguration of such an era.

The primary biblical text legislating the jubilee year is found in Leviticus 25:9-17. Scholars are not certain how often, or to what extent, it was actually put into practice.

To substantiate a jubilee year we need to examine sabbatical years. North finds proof for sabbatical years in five texts from Josephus and one Old Testament passage:[5]

(1) The Samaritans are excused from tribute during the sabbatical year (*Ant.* 11:340).

(2) "As the siege was thus dragging on, it came time for the idle year, a seven-year period observed as a sabbath-repose by the Jews" (*Ant.* 13:234 [=*B.J.* 1:60]).

(3) The Jews are relieved from tribute during the seventh year in the reign of Gaius Caesar (*Ant.* 14:202-6).

(4) The Jews are suffering from hunger and lack of provisions because it was the sabbatical year (*Ant.* 14:475).

(5) The same sabbatical year is alluded to in the passage: "The seventh year, which came round at that time, forced them to leave the land unworked,

because we are forbidden to sow the earth in that year'' (*Ant.* 15:7). This sabbatical year seems to have been from October 38 B.C.E. to October 37 B.C.E.

(6) In 1 Maccabees 6:49, 53, we read that Judas the Maccabee was in trouble because "there were no victuals in the city . . . because it was the seventh year."

Gordon, discussing Ugaritic sabbatical cycles, says that the land lay fallow every seventh year so that the next seven would be fertile.[6] The gods died every seventh year. On account of the jubilee the forty-ninth and fiftieth years were fallow so that the next jubilee cycles would be productive.

Strobel postulates that the date of Jesus' sabbatical year was 26–27 C.E., which was the fifteenth year of the reign of Tiberius.[7] Therefore Luke 3:1 may be working with a relevant tradition. The sabbatical year 26–27 C.E. would be in the course of ten jubilee periods and, this being so, the apocalyptic hope with reference to Daniel 9:27 would be aroused.[8] Strobel believes that in view of the dominant messianic week prophecy of Daniel 9:24ff., a failure to count up the jubilee years (using the number of sabbatical years) would be highly unlikely. The early Christian tradition cannot be set aside. The date of John the Baptist's ministry and the important phrase in Mark 1:15 ("the time is fulfilled") may point to a jubilee year. Eusebius (*H.E.* 7:174) refers to the jubilee year of 28–29 C.E. Strobel says that a jubilee year can be argued from Josephus (*Ant.* 12:374).

However, with regard to Luke 4 we may be facing the same phenomenon as in the date of Jesus' birth: Luke is not interested in a precise chronology but in theology and the social background. In the light of these findings Luke's Jesus might well have been proclaiming the inauguration of a jubilee year.

Melchizedek

From the Qumran writings we can see a dramatic change in the concept of the jubilee. This is especially evident in a fragment called 11 *Q Melchizedek*. Although the text is difficult to decipher, we can gain some information from it. The fragment concerns the jubilee in the last days, the eschatological jubilee. During this year (or epoch) several events occur: (1) all persons return to their own landed property; (2) debts with other Hebrews are remitted; (3) the priest named Melchizedek appears.

We meet him in Genesis 14 as a person to whom Abraham paid tithes and who is called "priest of the Most High God" and king of Salem (Jerusalem). He also figures in Psalm 110, where he appears as both priest and king.

In the Qumran fragment he is an eschatological figure and he brings the people out of captivity (cf. Luke 4:18; "to proclaim release to the captives"). He also atones for the sins of the sons of light, who appear to be the same as the men of the lot of Melchizedek. They are distinguished from the men of the lot of Satan (called Belial). This jubilee is called the "year of good favor, for

Melchizedek.'' At this time ''he by his strength will judge the holy ones of God in the interests of a reign of justice.'' Melchizedek seems to be a supernatural figure, for he is said to be ''in the midst of the Elohim (gods)'' when he gives judgment. He also takes a throne on high.

However, Melchizedek is not merely a benign personage; he also comes to exact vengeance for God and probably to slaughter the enemies of Israel. Thus the Qumran community changed the social concept of the jubilee to an eschatological and apocalyptic one.

M. P. Miller demonstrates that, although Isaiah 61:1-2 is never quoted directly, it stands behind the text of 11 *Q Melchizedek* and may be seen to provide key words at crucial points.[9] The text of 11 *Q Melchizedek* deals with Leviticus 25:13 and Deuteronomy 15:2, which concern the jubilee and sabbatical year, respectively. The motifs of release and restoration are put in an eschatological context. Melchizedek comes to inaugurate the tenth and final jubilee year. He proclaims a message to captives.

Thus in 11 *Q Melchizedek* the three major texts from the Torah, the prophets, and the writings are drawn together and their meaning is revealed with reference to Isaiah 61:1-2.[10] Although 11 *Q Melchizedek* is not in structure a *pesher* (interpretation) or midrash (commentary) on Isaiah 61:1-2, the text is, as it were, telescoped in those verses.

It is important to note here that interest in the figure of Melchizedek in Christian circles began approximately in the second century C.E., but it is found earlier in Philo and in rabbinical circles. Therefore, hearing the Isaiah passage, the Nazareth congregation might well have been alerted to the coming of Melchizedek.

In 11 *Q Melchizedek* the concept of release is counterbalanced by judgment on Belial (Satan). Melchizedek's role is based on Isaiah 61:2. It is to proclaim both the ''year of the Lord's favor'' and also the ''day of judgment of our God.'' Melchizedek's two functions are ''to exact vengeance of the judgments of God'' and to bring the good news to the pious. He, or a prophet, is the one anointed by the Spirit (cf. Isa. 61:1ff.).

However, just as prominent as good news is the day of vengeance (*yom naqam*; Isa. 61:2). This is also emphasized by Qumran:

> And these are the norms of conduct for the man of understanding in these times, concerning what he must love and *how he must hate. Everlasting hatred* for all the men of the Pit because of their spirit of hoarding! . . . But he shall be a man full of zeal for the Precept, whose time is for the *Day of Vengeance* [1 *QS* 9:21-23; italics added].[11]

Dupont-Sommer comments:

> Entirely detached from concern for material things, the sectary is zealous only for the fulfillment of the Law and defers all his hope and

all his need of justice to the Day of Vengeance. He lives in constant expectation of this Day when he will be rewarded and the wicked punished.[12]

With the text above one may compare 1 *QS* 10:17–21, which contains part of the resolve of the perfect sectary, who will abstain from taking vengeance himself because he has so much confidence that the Day of Vengeance will be brought about by God.

> As for the multitude of the men of the Pit,
> I will not lay hands on them till the *Day of Vengeance;*
> but I will *not withdraw my anger far from perverse men,*
> I will not be content till He begins the Judgment.
> I will be without malice and wrath towards those that are converted
>   from rebellion,
> but *merciless* to those that have turned aside from the way;
> I will *not comfort them* that are smitten until their way is perfect
> [1 *QS* 10:19–21; italics added].[13]

Sanders also compares 1 *QM* 7:3–7 where the sectarians must be unblemished in body for the eschatological battle and so prepared for the day of vengeance.[14] Thus in 11 *Q Melchizedek* one sees the importance of Isaiah 61 for the members of Qumran. The texts quoted are an excellent witness to religious hatred.

Fitzmyer notes that elements from Leviticus 25 (on the jubilee year) run through 11 *Q Melchizedek*. Melchizedek's special role is to be associated with the divine judgment during the eschatological jubilee year, which "seems to refer to the end of the 490 years, or 'seventy weeks of years' of Daniel 9:24–27."[15] Melchizedek is associated with this, as well as divine judgment, a day of atonement, and a year of jubilee.[16] He enjoys a special place in the heavenly court. He is a heavenly figure of redemption.[17]

Commenting on line 6 of 11 *Q Melchizedek*—"And he will proclaim release to them"—Fitzmyer finds an allusion to Isaiah 61:1 and to Jeremiah 43:8 or Leviticus 25:10. He compares it to Luke 4:18 where Jesus is the anointed of Yahweh, "performing that which the expected figure in this text is to perform."[18] Then, in line 9—"He has decreed a year of good favor for Melchizedek and for . . ."—Fitzmyer finds another echo of Isaiah 61:2 and he compares it to Luke 4:18.[19] It is in line 13—"And Melchizedek shall exact the vengeance of the judgments of God (or 'El)"—that Melchizedek clearly appears as "an instrument of the execution of divine judgment"; his role is associated with "the day of vengeance of our God" (from Isa. 61:2).

F. L. Horton has written an entire book on the Melchizedek tradition.[20] He explores the Old Testament texts in which Melchizedek appears: Genesis 14:18–20 and Psalm 110, which may be a Maccabean psalm, perhaps relating to Simon Maccabee's acclamation as governor and high priest by his people.

However, Horton argues against this because of the prophetic element in the psalm. He dates it to the early period of David's reign. Horton agrees with Van der Woude that the date of 11 *Q Melchizedek* must be in the first half of the Christian century, about 50 C.E.[21] He agrees with Sanders[22] that "In 11 *Q Melchizedek* the great high priest . . . is made not only a deity . . . in the heavenly court, but is set over all other *elohim* (gods) as king, judge, and redeemer, in the final great eschatological drama." But Horton does not think that Melchizedek is the anointed one; the anointed one is a prophet who announces the reign of Melchizedek.[23] Horton thinks that we may have a myth of *deus descendens* (god descending) but the document has no hint of a reascent.[24]

If 11 *Q Melchizedek* is to be dated about 50 C.E., then its influence on Luke 4 is obviously editorial—that is, it could not have influenced Jesus, but it could have influenced Luke's depiction of Jesus. It is not impossible that Luke and John were both influenced by the interest in Melchizedek.

Jesus' audience, hearing the proclamation of Isaiah 61, would listen with expectancy and possibly with hope for the eschatological year of vengeance to begin. There may have been revolutionaries in the congregation, and they may have hoped that Jesus would join forces with them. However, they were to be disappointed.

Isaiah 61 is important, therefore, for understanding the jubilee year. From biblical and Qumran texts we know that both the sabbatical and the jubilee years began on the day of atonement. Therefore, Isaiah 61 is significant for the theology of atonement—that is, reconciliation between humankind and God and between human beings themselves. Jesus not only proclaims the jubilee but also atonement. Indeed, his whole ministry is reconciliation through nonviolent means. Jesus comes to announce clemency and reconciliation, not slaughter and vengeance.

We may summarize our findings so far. In the synagogue Jesus read from Isaiah 61. This text is associated with the day of atonement and with the inauguration and theology of the jubilee year. It is possible, and perhaps probable, that Jesus proclaimed a jubilee year, which fell between 26 and 28 C.E. According to calculations made from Daniel 9:24ff., by both Christians and Jews, this would be the eschatological jubilee year. On this occasion pious and aggressively zealous Jews, such as we find in Qumran, anticipated a divine, supernatural intervention. God would usher in a period of prosperity for the Jews and a day of vengeance (and slaughter) for the ungodly. Among God's agents would be the prophet anointed by the Lord and also Melchizedek. The latter would be responsible for blessing the good and punishing the impious. He would function as a warrior. Hatred and anticipated punishment for one's enemies was characteristic of groups such as we find at Qumran and also various groups of revolutionaries and zealots such as Phinehas, Elijah, and Judith. Thus when Jesus read Isaiah 61 in the synagogue, the congregation probably expected him to announce the vengeance on their foes, especially the Romans, which vengeance was seen as a preliminary step toward the time of salvation. The wrath of God must consume all evil before the dawn of redemption or time of favor can be ushered in. Recall John the Baptist's prediction that the "stronger one" would baptize with (wind and) fire.

Luke 4 and the Anointed Prophet of 11 Q Melchizedek

It has been noted that it is more accurate to identify the prophetic messenger in 11 Q Melchizedek with the figure in Isaiah 52:7 rather than with Melchizedek himself or with an anointed king or priest. De Jonge and Van der Woude point out that 11 Q Melchizedek gives no explicit reference to the priesthood of Melchizedek.[25] "He is so much 'God's warrior' that his priestly activities remain completely in the shadow." But 11 Q Melchizedek, line 18, "gives the first instance in the Qumran literature of a singular use of that expression [anointed] to denote a prophet."[26] He may be the prophet like Moses mentioned in Deuteronomy 18:15 and early Jewish messianic proof texts. De Jonge and Van der Woude discuss the use of Isaiah 52:7 and 61:1f. in the New Testament. They observe that euaggelizō ("proclaim good news") is frequent in Luke; ten times in the Gospel and fifteen times in Acts. They draw attention to Matthew 11:3 (Luke 7:19), which deals with the deeds and words of Jesus and implicitly refer to him as the euaggelizomenos ("messenger with good news"). They find an allusion to Isaiah 61:1 in Matthew 5:3 and Luke 6:20, and to Isaiah 61:2 in Matthew 5:4 and Luke 6:24.[27] However, they state:

> One of the most important passages for our purpose is the Lukan story of Jesus' preaching in Nazareth (Luke 4:18–30) which starts with a quotation from Isaiah 61:1–2. According to the evangelist this passage of scripture obviously gives a good characterization of Jesus' work and God's intentions with it. Very important is it that here also the first sentence of Isaiah 61:1 is quoted and that Jesus states explicitly: "Today this scripture is fulfilled in your hearing" (v. 21).[28]

De Jonge and Van der Woude observe that, although there is no mention of Christos ("anointed") in the passage, Jesus' words occasion a "fierce 'christological' debate" in the Nazareth congregation.[29] The Galileans are amazed that the son of Joseph should make such an extreme claim, but Jesus answers simply that no prophet is acceptable in his own country. De Jonge and Van der Woude compare Luke 4:18–30, with its emphasis on Jesus' gracious, healing work, and Acts 10:36–38, where the anointed one is described in a similar way.[30]

However, they find an important contrast between Luke 4 and 11 Q Melchizedek. In the New Testament all the emphasis is on God's grace in Jesus. What was alarming to the Nazareth congregation was Jesus' omission of the day of vengeance from Isaiah 61:2. In fact, Jesus stops in the middle of a sentence. Further, if all of Isaiah 61:1–9 were to be read, then Jesus omitted all that was hostile to the gentiles. Similarly in Acts 10:36–38 all the attention of the writer is on peace, good works, and healing. In Luke 4 salvation is to be extended to the gentiles, but in 11 *Q Melchizedek* salvation is destined for a small group of Jews.[31] De Jonge and Van der Woude have already drawn attention to the fact that in 11 *Q Melchizedek* the destruction of evil begins the time of salvation that had been announced in Isaiah 61:1f.[32]

It would seem to be the absence of a reference to the day of vengeance and to the destruction of the evil among the gentiles that disturbs the synagogue congregation at Nazareth. Most interpreters are of the opinion that Jesus' words at first kindled admiration among his hearers, but that they turned against him when he pointed out that a prophet is not acceptable in his own country and when he cited the examples of Elijah and Elisha, both of whom healed gentiles, and lodged and dined with them.[33] The congregation members reached such a pitch of anger that they drove Jesus out and tried to throw him over a cliff to assassinate him, but he escaped from their midst. However, one major difficulty arises with this interpretation. It is strange that a congregation should change from great admiration to murderous intent in such a short time.

Several scholars have sought a solution to this difficulty. We shall look at the work of two of them. In 1939 B. Violet argued that the understanding of Luke 4:22 depends on the correct interpretation of *emarturoun*, which is usually translated "spoke favorably" of him, and *ethaumazon . . . logois tes charitos*, which is usually rendered "they marveled at the appealing discourse that came from his lips."[34] Violet suggests that the word *ethaumazon* in the second clause means not only "wonder" but "be astonished" in the Septuagint. He shows that it can express a deep bewilderment (for example, Isa. 52:5; Sir. 11:21; 26:11; Luke 1:21; 2:33; 20:26; Acts 3:12). It can mean to be dumbfounded or "stricken with annoyance or horror." Further, *marturoun* does mean witness but it does not necessarily mean witness in a favorable sense.[35] It is used in this way in Susanna 41. It can also be taken in a neutral sense but probably in this text it means to "witness against him." Violet then opted for a Semitic background to most of the passage.[36] Through this scriptural passage Jesus is announcing the jubilee year and the fulfillment of messianic promises. His words are not full of "charm" but full of "grace." But his audience was filled with horror at his words of grace *toward the gentiles*, and all witnessed against him and said, "Is not this Joseph's son?" There is no reversal of feeling but hostility from the beginning. Violet, however, does not really explain why the congregation should be angry throughout.

Jeremias added to Violet's thesis.[37] He saw this pericope against the background of the hostility toward the gentiles that obtained in Palestine during Jesus' and Luke's lifetime. The attitude of the Jews was affected by the oppression that they had long suffered under foreign nations, by their fear concerning mixed marriages, and by the fact that many gentiles appeared to be godless, sinful, violent, and wicked—and yet, from the political and social point of view, they flourished. We must remember that the revolutionaries themselves were intensely nationalistic.

This enmity toward the gentiles is reflected in popular eschatology. In the minds of many, the Messiah would be one who would deliver the Jewish people from foreign oppression, establish a Jewish kingdom, and take vengeance upon the heathen. However, some did hold a universalistic approach: they believed that certain gentiles would participate in the future glory. Neither the Qumran community nor the revolutionaries appear to have espoused a universalistic approach.

Jeremias notes that the passage is remarkable for the apparent sudden change of attitude on the part of Jesus' audience, first spellbound by his words and then driving him from the synagogue with the intent to murder him. Jeremias first considers the words in verse 22, *kai pantes emarturoun auto* ("and all wondered at him"). The pronoun may be a dative of advantage or of disadvantage. Thus the clause may mean "they bore witness in favor of him" or "they bore witness against him." The interpretation depends upon the translation of the following words in the same verse: *kai ethaumazon epi tois logois tēs charitos tois ekporeuomenois ek tou stomatos autou. Thaumazein* can mean both "admiration" and also "astonishment" toward something strange, but in this context Jeremias draws attention to the fact that *hoi logoi tēs charitos* in Semitic language does not mean "words full of charm" but "words of (God's) mercy." Thus he would render the phrase, "they were all astonished that he spoke of the mercy of God" (toward the gentiles). The reason for this astonishment on the part of the congregation was the fact that Jesus broke off his reading of scripture in the middle of a sentence. The text was from Isaiah, and the words "to proclaim the acceptable year of the Lord" are followed by "and a day of vengeance of our God" (Isa. 61:2). The audience was outraged because Jesus omitted the day of vengeance. Thus Jeremias would render the whole sentence: "they protested with one voice (*pantes emarturoun auto*) and were furious (*kai ethaumazon*) because he (only) spoke of God's year of mercy (and omitted the words about the messianic vengeance)."

In the light of 11 *Q Melchizedek* and other texts from Qumran and also from the activities of the freedom fighters, we can understand much more clearly why the omission of the day of vengeance would infuriate the congregation.

This would be a typical revolutionary or religious zealot reaction. It was inherited from the Maccabees and was felt to be justified by them. It is against this background, which breathed a relentless, vengeful holy wrath against the pagans, and the increased expectation of a second coming of Melchizedek, who would wreak divine vengeance on the gentiles, that the Lukan pericope as a whole must be understood. Thus Jeremias illustrates a crescendo of hostility from the congregation.

Its attitude was aggravated because Jesus alluded to the miracles of Elijah and Elisha, which the prophets performed for the benefit of the gentiles. As

Jesus has referred to himself as a prophet (Luke 4:24), he deliberately placed himself in the tradition of Elijah and Elisha, but not Elijah-Phinehas as the revolutionaries conceived him.

This aspect is further elucidated by L. C. Crockett.[38] He argues that the references to Elijah and Elisha anticipate Jewish-Christian relationships in Luke's Gospel and Acts. He reproduces the texts and shows the parallelism in structure. Contrasting the Old Testament accounts of Elijah and those of Sirach 48, the *Biblical Antiquities* of Pseudo Philo, and Revelation 11:6, he argues that Luke knew of the Elijah traditions alive in his time.

Luke mentions the famine in the time of Elijah. It was only in Samaria, not over all the earth (Luke 4:25). It is parallel to another famine in Acts 11:28; Luke intentionally linked the two famines. It is significant in his scheme of prophecy and fulfillment. The famine brings disparate peoples together. The gentile Christians from Antioch sent relief for the Jewish-Christians.[39] It is important to note that Elijah is sent to the widow at Sarepta "in order to be fed there."[40] Therefore this passage in Luke is pertinent to the questions in the early church: (1) Should Jews and gentiles dine together? (2) What is the relationship between Jews and gentiles in the new era, that of the church? Both Naaman and Cornelius (Acts 10:1–11:18) are commanders and Cornelius may be modeled on Naaman.[41] The raising of the widow of Naim's son may be influenced by Elijah's raising of the widow's son.

Although Luke 4:16–30 is an illustration of Jesus' ministry, it is also a dramatic portrayal of his rejection. M. Miyoshi finds a parallel to Jesus' rejection by the Samaritans and his rejection by his own people at Nazareth.[42] The attitude of Jesus toward vengeance is similar in both passages. But Miyoshi shows that there is a difference in the pericopes. In Nazareth Jesus stands among his fellow citizens. In the Samaritan pericope he is with his disciples. However, in all Jesus' rejections he is seen as a prophet.[43] The Nazareth pericope is a model for the mission of the church as well as for the ministry of Jesus. The pericope contains many of the themes that will appear in Luke-Acts. It is Jesus' "keynote" address pertinent to his own words and deeds, and to those of his church as well. For Luke, the opening words of Jesus' public ministry are ones of forgiveness and healing, not wrath and destruction. Thus his theology is in stark contrast to that of the revolutionaries.

Luke 4:16–30 is the basis of his entire Gospel and a prelude also to Acts, especially in regard to the gentile mission. Dillersberger, cited by Elias, states, ". . . it is a stroke of genius on the part of St. Luke to put this event at the beginning, for it lets us see, as in a picture planned by a master, the whole revelation which Jesus made to men in this 'acceptable year of the Lord.' "[44]

Moreover, in the view of our study of nonviolence in the third Gospel, Luke 4:16–30 clearly shows Jesus adopting an ideology that is in vivid contrast to the freedom fighters of the first and second century C.E. and their expectation of the warrior, Melchizedek.

We might also tentatively add that Jesus' program contrasts with that of Simon bar Giora, a prominent revolutionary figure during the 66–74 C.E.

war. Simon (Simeon) attacked the houses of the rich estate owners (*B.J.* 2:652) and freed many slaves. He had first won his spurs in the successful battle at Beth-Horon against the Roman, Cestus Gallus (66 C.E.). According to Josephus, Simon captured the Roman baggage and engaged in banditry, although this may be Josephus's way of saying that Simon engaged in military operations with other revolutionaries. Simon's opponents obliged him to retire to Masada with the *sicarii*; when he left them he conducted a terrorist campaign throughout the country. Simon occupied part of Idumea. In April 69 C.E. he entered Jerusalem and took control of a large portion of the city, although the partisans of John of Gischala opposed him. When Titus, the emperor's son, approached the city they united but were overthrown by Rome. At first, Simon hid underground among the ruins. Then he emerged wearing white tunics and covered with a purple mantle. This frightened even the Romans. The purple may have suggested messianic expectations and the white the idea that he thought of himself as a martyr.

Simon was executed in Rome at the climax of the celebration of the military triumph of Vespasian and Titus. This suggests that he was a very special figure. The Romans may have regarded him as the leader of all the revolutionaries. Indeed, he had more troops than did his opponents—about fifteen thousand at the beginning of the siege. His soldiers were well disciplined and well organized. He was invited to leadership in Jerusalem by both the priests and the people. This may imply that his leadership had some legal basis. He was certainly seen as an eschatological leader and possibly as king-messiah. He was renowned for his bravery and audacity. He was distinguished by his antipathy toward the rich, his championship of the poor, and his liberation of slaves.

Did the Nazareth congregation hope that Jesus would be another Simon bar Giora? If so, its adverse reaction to Jesus' nonviolent approach to the gentiles is understandable. This, of course, would be a Lukan redaction because Simon lived after Jesus' time.

Thus Luke 4:16–30 shows Jesus beginning a new age in which there will be clemency and succor, not vengeance toward the enemies of the Jews.

Chapter 5

THE STRATEGIC ROLE OF TAX COLLECTORS IN LUKE'S GOSPEL

According to Luke's chronology, the birth of Jesus coincided with an important rebellion against Roman taxation by Judas the Galilean and Zadduk the Pharisee and their followers. Taxation was one of the major causes of the Roman-Jewish War from 66 to 74 C.E. Hence one can readily understand why taxation and toll and tax collectors were hated by the Jews. Jesus' approach to tax collectors is part of his nonviolent, philo-echthrological ministry.

In order to understand their position, it is necessary to give a survey, however brief, of tax collecting in the Roman Empire as it affected Palestine. This, in turn, will enable us to realize the scandal Jesus caused by consorting with persons considered to be traitors.

When Pompey conquered Palestine (63 B.C.E.), he required the Jewish people to pay tribute. The responsibility for the collection of this tribute was placed in the hands of the high priests (*B.J.* 1:154–58; *Ant.* 14:73–76). A few years later, after some disorders in 57 B.C.E., the governor of Syria, Gabinius, divided the Jewish people into five districts for the purpose of tax collecting (*B.J.* 1:167–70; *Ant.* 14:89–91). It was at this juncture that the Jewish people came to know the Roman *publicani*, public servants of the Roman Empire who collected the required taxes from towns and communities. They were not members of ancient aristocratic families, who usually served the state on a voluntary basis (without remuneration). The *publicani*, tax gatherers, worked for their own financial gain, frequently more than they deserved. They were often cruel and belligerent. Thus in 57 B.C.E. the Jews had a further alien and unjust practice with which to cope.

However, ten years later an important change took place. Caesar, in view of service given to him by the Jewish leaders Hyrcanus II and Antipater, changed the taxation in Judea in their favor. He reduced the taxes, remitted taxes in the sabbatical year, and returned the city of Joppa to Hyrcanus, although the latter was obliged to pay a certain amount of grain and harbor dues for the city. In 44 B.C.E. Caesar abolished tax farming by the *publicani* both in Judea and in Asia. The taxes were probably collected by Hyrcanus and Antipater. Thus some of the burden was lifted from the Jews.

When Herod the Great came to the throne (37 B.C.E.), he was obliged to pay tribute for Idumea and Samaria, but this was rescinded in 30 B.C.E. by Augustus, and thus his kingdom was relieved of Roman taxes. He does not seem to have farmed out tax collection. However, Herod Antipas resumed the practice.

It was in 6 C.E. (Luke's date for the birth of Jesus) that taxation again became a matter of fierce controversy. Archelaus, one of the successors of Herod the Great, was deposed, and Judea became a Roman province subject to tribute. The governor took charge of the taxes, although the money was actually paid into the public treasury rather than the imperial treasury.[1] However, in the eyes of the Jews, they paid taxes to Caesar (Mark 12:14ff.; Matt. 22:17ff.; Luke 20:22ff.). Jewish authorities helped to collect the revenue. Taxes were heavy and both Syria and Judea complained. Tacitus says that the provinces of Syria and Judea, burdened with taxes, continually begged for tribute reductions.[2]

Two principal taxes were collected: (1) the *tributum agri*, the agricultural (land) tax, which was paid partly in kind and partly in money, and (2) the *tributum capitis*, the poll tax. However, it does not seem that these taxes were farmed out, but that the Sanhedrin was held responsible for their payment. In addition indirect taxes—for instance, on goods in transit, on all purchases and leases in Jerusalem (*Ant.* 17:205; 18:90)—had to be paid. Cities and dependent kingdoms also levied tolls on their borders.

Customs were collected by the *publicani* ("publicans") who leased the customs for a fixed annual sum. If they collected more, as they usually did, it was to their gain. Taxes were also farmed out to the highest bidder (see *Ant.* 12:169). Those who leased taxes had their network of subordinates. Murders and burning of villages in order to exact taxes were not uncommon.

The coins of Augustus and Tiberius had the orb and the image of Nikē (Greek goddess of victory) on them.[3] Images of the staff, or scepter, and the eagle were also used on coins. The orb was "an open denial of God's omnipotence."[4] The Jewish sages forbade the images of a staff, a bird, a ball, a bowl, a sword, a crown, and a ring.[5] Thus the handling of foreign coinage presented a difficulty to the Torah-abiding Jew, who felt it violated the First Commandment, the prohibition of making images.

Although there are some exceptions in rabbinic literature, in general tax collectors were hated by the people, and neither they nor their families were allowed to act as witnesses, or to give to the charity fund (*B.K.* 113a). Even upon repentance, they were not always received as *haberim* ("brothers") by the Pharisees (*Bek.* 31a). If they entered a house, especially if they were accompanied by a gentile, that house was declared unclean (*Hag.* 26a). One talmudic source says that to meet a tax gatherer is like meeting a bear (*Sanh.* 98b), and another lists them with "confiscators, extortioners, and collectors of customs." In a word, they were ostracized (*Shebu'oth* 39a).

The Revolt of Judas the Galilean

The year 6 C.E. was a turning point. It was in that year that the Romans incorporated Judea into the empire as a province and appointed Coponius as its first prefect. A new legate, Quirinius, came to Syria. It was his responsibility to take a census of the people to levy taxes according to the Roman practice. He began this in 6 or 7 C.E. He met opposition from many sides, although the high priest Joazar persuaded the people to submit. Judas the Galilean, most probably the son of Hezekiah, a Hasmonean and social bandit whom Herod the Great captured, joined with a Pharisee named Zadduk and preached rebellion in the name of religion. From this rebellion arose the revolutions that sparked the political and social unrest that eventually ended in a holy war against Rome in 66 C.E. The freedom fighters kept alive the spirit of the Maccabees.

Although these freedom fighters were not of uniform belief, they appear to have agreed on five principles: the avoidance of idolatry; the acceptance of one master, God alone; male circumcision; fulfillment of the Torah; the priority of Israel over the gentiles.

They believed that as long as there was idolatry in the world, there was divine wrath (*Sanh.* 10: 6; *Sifre Dt.* 96; cf. 1 Macc. 3:8). These religious zealots prohibited any kind of images and idols. Some even regarded looking upon them, or falling under the shadow of an idol, as sinful (*Shabbath* 6:10; *Tosephtah Shabbath* 6).

Josephus reports that the revolutionaries in 6 C.E. would call no one lord except God, even if they would be tortured or killed for their belief:

> They have a passion for liberty which is almost unconquerable since they are convinced that *God* alone is their leader (*hegemona*) and master (*despotēn*). They think little of submitting to death in unusual forms and permitting vengeance (*timorias*) to fall on kinsmen and friends if only they may avoid calling any man master [*Ant.* 18:23; cf. *B.J.* 2:118].

With regard to the law of circumcision, it was said that these rebels would slay any uncircumcised gentile who listened to a discourse on God and God's laws, unless he were prepared to undergo the rite (cf. *Sanh.* 59a). They worked for the reestablishment of the state of Israel free from any foreign oppression, and saw both guerrilla warfare and organized battle as a duty of the holy war.

Hippolytus, writing at a later date, gives us further details apparently about these same rebels (*Ref. Haer.* 9:26). He says that they never touch, carry, or look upon a coin with an image on it. They do not enter towns lest they should walk under the shadow of statues. They are prepared to kill men unwilling to undergo circumcision.

Judas the Galilean is an excellent example of these patriots. He reprimanded his countrymen as cowards for consenting to pay tribute to a pagan state and for tolerating earthly masters. Josephus says of him and Zadduk:

[They] maintained that this census would lead to nothing less than complete slavery, and they called upon the people to vindicate their liberty. They argued that, if they succeeded, they would enjoy the consequences of their good fortune, and if they failed, they would at least have the honor and glory of having shown a greatness of spirit. Moreover, God would surely assist them in their undertaking if, inspired by such ideals, they spared no effort to realize them [*Ant.* 18:4–5].

Kennard identifies this Judas with the one who seized the opportunity to aspire to kingship in Galilee (*B.J.* 2:56).[6] Josephus directly connects the revolt under Judas the Galilean with the question of taxation and the subsequent fall of Jerusalem. He says of Judas:

A Galilean named Judas incited his countrymen to revolt, upbraiding them as cowards for consenting to pay tribute, and tolerating mortal masters, after having God for their Lord. This man was a sophist who founded a sect of his own, having nothing in common with the others [*B.J.* 2:118].

The last statement is modified in *Antiquities* 18:23, where Josephus says that Judas's sect is a fourth philosophy and similar to the Pharisees.

Black remarks that the capture of the archbrigand Hezekiah by Herod, and the smoking out of the brigands, also by Herod, throw light on Judas's rebellion.[7] Black quotes Dalman who observes:

. . . in the Maccabean period these [caves of Rubela] were already places of refuge for the strict Jews who adhered faithfully to the Law. . . . In the year 38 B.C. the place was used, as Josephus puts it, by "robbers," whom Herod caused to be "smoked out" . . . [and] who were certainly the remnant of the armies of the last Hasmonean prince, Antigonus.[8]

After the death of Herod, Judas seized the royal palace and the armory at Sepphoris in Galilee. When Josephus says that he aspired to royalty (*B.J.* 2:56), it could imply that the family of Hezekiah was a branch of the Hasmonean house. However, it was Judas's rebellion against the census, some years later, that gave him a place in history. Farmer suggests that Judas might have been descended from the Maccabees and that this may account for his aspiration to royalty.[9]

If Black and Farmer are correct in their hypotheses, the descendants of Hezekiah carried on the resistance movement after Herod's conquest of

Palestine. They provided a "Hasmonean" opposition to the Herodian party and to the Romans themselves. If so, Judas the Galilean is an important link in the "dynastic" chain of pure Jewish national leaders and thus his rebellion is important not only as an anti-Roman but also as a Hasmonean demonstration. However, he is remembered chiefly for his opposition to the sacrilegious census and taxation, which were considered signs of slavery. It is not without importance that Agrippa's speech to the Jews before the outbreak of the war accused them of insurrection and nonpayment of taxes (*B.J.* 2:402-5). These were the same accusations brought against Judas.

Applebaum adds further important reflection on Judas.[10] He observes that the influence of Judas was greater because the census was against the Jewish theology of the land—that is, the land belonged to Yahweh and therefore the land tax was sacrilegious. Although Julius Caesar's treaty with Hyrcanus II exempted the country from tax in the sabbatical year, it is possible that this provision was abolished in 6 C.E. This would explain the Jewish support that Judas received and would help to heighten the odium in which tax collectors and toll collectors were held.

In sum, Judas the Galilean's revolt apparently continued the Maccabean-Hasmonean struggle against foreign control of Palestine, and had repercussions up to the war against Rome beginning in 66 C.E. Judas, seemingly, aspired to (Davidic) kingship. He and his followers deemed it idolatry to pay taxes; for them it was equivalent to acknowledging Caesar as Lord. They held the land to be sacred, the possession of Yahweh. Tribute should be paid only to God as the owner of the land. Only God was permitted to take a census; a human census was sacrilegious, although one might count shekels or passover lambs. God's final census would be an eschatological one. Judas may have objected to the nonexemption of sabbatical years from taxation. His rebellion, which may have been directed toward reestablishing a theocracy, bore the characteristics of a holy war. It should be seen against the history of the Maccabees when taxation was also a volatile issue.

With the ascendancy of Simon the Maccabee in 142 B.C.E., the Jews had achieved both tax exemption (1 Macc. 13:39; *Ant.* 13:213) and national autonomy. In view of this great accomplishment they began a new chronology (1 Macc. 13:42). Simon minted coins that bore new dates and a legend in Hebrew. 1 Maccabees observes:

> Thus the yoke of the Gentiles was removed from Israel, and the people began to write in their documents and contracts, "In the first year of Simon the great high priest and commander and leader of the Jews" [13:41f.].

It should be added that this Simon appeared in the Temple and in his palace with all the signs of royalty (1 Macc. 15:32). With him a new dynasty began, the priestly house of the Hasmoneans; his grandson, Aristobolus I (104 B.C.E.), was the first to declare himself king in name.

Thus tax exemption and political autonomy are very closely linked. Judas may have hoped for an achievement similar to that of Simon the Maccabee.

When Luke involves himself in the subject of tax collectors, he is touching on an inflammatory political issue highly pertinent to the theme of loving one's enemies.

Another important issue that arose before Luke wrote his Gospel was particularly provocative to the Jewish people. After the war (70 C.E.) the half-shekel tax levied for the Temple in Jerusalem had to be paid instead to the Roman emperor for the pagan temple of Jupiter Capitolinus. This was pure discrimination against the Jews: there were many non-Jewish temples in the Hellenistic world whose worshipers were not under such an obligation. This tax must have been seen as sacrilegious and outrageously unjust by the Jews. It may well have agitated the Lukan churches but was not an issue at the time of Jesus.

Tax and Toll Collectors in Luke's Gospel

In the light of these events and perhaps others similar to them, Luke's treatment of tax collectors is remarkable. Mark has only two references to tax collectors, one of them being the call of Matthew (Levi; Mark 2:13-17). Matthew has nine references but, except that to the Matthean (10:3), they are general statements. In Luke we find singular and important narratives about tax collectors.

Luke's references are carefully placed. First, he reports that Joseph and Mary went to Bethlehem to comply with the census stipulations. Thus they are not shown as sympathizers of the revolt under Judas the Galilean. Luke records that Jesus was born at the time of the census.

Secondly, Luke recounts John the Baptist's advice to tax collectors. He does not tell them to give up their occupation but merely to exact no more than what was just. Thus we know of John's disposition toward reformed tax collectors. Not all Jews received converted tax collectors back into the community because restitution to those whom they had wronged was so difficult.

Thirdly, Luke records the call of Levi. Presumably he is the same person as Matthew in the Matthean Gospel (although Levi is not named among the apostles in Luke 6:12-16 or Acts 1:13). Levi was probably collecting tolls on goods entering the domain of Herod Antipas. Mark and Luke call Matthew "Levi," which might suggest that he came from a priestly family. We know that many priests in Jerusalem and their relatives engaged in tax collecting.

The Call of Levi (Luke 5:27-32; Mark 2:13-17; Matt. 9:9-13)

Luke's account of the call of Levi is much more elaborate than that of Mark or Matthew. As in their Gospels the pericope is appropriately placed after the healing of the paralytic, which demonstrates Jesus' authority to forgive sin. The call of a tax collector would imply the acceptance of a great sinner.

Mark (2:13-17) contents himself with a simple description of Levi, the son of Alphaeus, sitting at the customs desk, of the many who followed Jesus, and of his dining with sinners and tax collectors. When the scribes and Pharisees complained about Jesus' association with sinners, he told his disciples that it was the sick who needed a doctor, that he came to call sinners, not the righteous.

Matthew's account (9:9-13) is very similar, although the wording is not identical. Matthew does not mention the name Alphaeus, or say that many followed Jesus. He calls Jesus "teacher" and he adds the quotation from Hosea 6:6 about God's desire for mercy, not sacrifice. Luke's account is much more graphic.

Both Matthew and Mark say that Jesus was passing by (*paragōn*) but Luke omits this, as if to suggest that Jesus went out deliberately to look for Levi. Luke uses a stronger verb (*theaomai*, cf. 23:55; Acts, 3 times for) "to see": it can mean "see in a supersensual sense." It suggests that Jesus discerned the character of Levi. Whereas Mark and Matthew merely say that Matthew arose and followed Jesus, Luke says that Levi *left everything* and rose up and followed him. We may compare the conditions for radical discipleship in Luke 9:57-62, where the disciples leave everything to follow Jesus.

In Matthew and Mark the tax collectors recline with Jesus, but it is not said who is the host. In Luke it is obvious that Levi is the host. Among even orthodox Jews one could dine with gentiles in one's own home because the purity laws would be observed. Dining in the house of a "sinner" was an entirely different matter. One could not be certain that the ingredients of the meal had been tithed, an animal had been killed according to kosher principles, dishes for meat and dairy produce had been kept separate, and the persons themselves who prepared the meal were in a state of purity. These were only a few of the purity laws.

Thus Jesus' acceptance of the invitation is scandalous. It places him and his disciples in a condition of ritual impurity, which was often associated with the demonic. Levi's meal for Jesus is the first of many in Luke's Gospel.

The meals described in Luke's Gospel have theological significance. They comprise: (1) Levi's meal (5:27-32); (2) the meal where the sinful woman enters (7:36-50); (3) the feeding of the five thousand (9:10-17); (4) Mary and Martha's hospitality (10:38-42); (5) the meal where Jesus criticizes the Pharisees (11:37-54); (6) the occasion of Jesus' teaching about seats at a banquet and the parable of the great supper (14:1-24); (7) Zacchaeus's hospitality (19:1-10); (8) the passover (22:4-38); (9) the Emmaus meal (24:29-43). All of them have their own contribution to make to Lukan theology. Seven of them fall in the prepassion life of Jesus.

The first meal is a "great banquet" (*dochē megalē*). Every meal was of religious significance for a Jew because it established an ontological union between the diners. The word *dochē* is used for important banquets in the

Old Testament (Gen. 21:8, Isaac's weaning; Gen. 26:30, the covenant meal between Abimelech and Isaac; Dan. 5:1, King Balshazzar's feast for a thousand of his lords). In the New Testament it is used only here and in Luke 14:7-14.

The most arresting feature about Luke's depiction of this first meal is his redaction of his source. He has changed Matthew's and Mark's "many" to a "large crowd of tax collectors and others" (v. 30). Mark and Matthew call these others "sinners" and neither one gives the impression of so many being present. We may have to think in terms of a hundred guests or more.

Who were the tax collectors and "sinners" ("others") who attended the banquet? Both Jeremias and Donahue argue convincingly that the Gospels speak, not about tax collectors, but toll collectors.[11] The tax collectors gathered the land and poll taxes, and the toll collectors gathered "the myriad of minor taxes, sale taxes, customs taxes, taxes on transport," and the like. There was more hostility toward the toll collectors (*mokhesin*) than toward the tax collectors (*gabba'im*).[12] Toll collectors were to be found at the commercial centers.[13] At this banquet Jesus dines with toll collectors, known for their injustice and chicanery. But others were present as well. Jeremias, discussing "sinners" and despised trades, has compiled lists of suspected or despised occupations that would ostracize those who practiced them and deprive them both of civic and religious privileges.[14] These ostracized persons would be called "sinners."

These lists are germane to the discussion of our text because most of the trades in lists 1 and 4 and some in lists 2 and 3 pertain to persons dealing with goods in transit: the type of persons with whom toll collectors frequently came into contact. Many of them may have been present at the great banquet. Trades involving transport were thought to be open to dishonesty.[15] Shopkeepers were thought to cheat their customers.[16] Physicians were accused of attending the rich and neglecting the poor.[17] Butchers were suspected because they might sell blemished or otherwise nonkosher animals.[18] Dung-collectors must have worked on the roads and at market places. Copper-smelters and tanners were regarded as repugnant.[19] The traders mentioned in list 3 were suspected of associating with women and hence of falling into immorality.[20]

The greatest stigma was attached to those in list 4. These trades were reputed to be based on deceit and dishonesty; their practitioners were precluded from all civic and political as well as religious rights. They were fiercely hated. This helps us realize the enormous implications of Jesus' calling a toll collector to be one of his intimate disciples, "and announcing the good news to publicans and 'sinners' by sitting down to eat with them."[21]

If we are correct in seeing not only toll collectors but other ostracized persons and perhaps their families gathered together at this great banquet, we can but conjecture at the offense Jesus caused his contemporaries. Perhaps the best contemporary analogy would be Christians sitting down to dine with members of the mafia. As Donahue observes, ". . . if the controversy mirrored a setting in Judea prior to A.D. 44 or a church concern after 44, Jesus' fellowship with toll collectors could be interpreted as fellowship with virtual *traitors*'' (italics added).[22]

The Ostracized

1 *Kidd*. iv. 14	2 *Ket*. vii. 10	3 *b. Kidd*. 82a	4 *b. Sanh*. 25b
1. Ass-driver	1. Dung-collector	1. Goldsmith	1. Gambler with dice
2. Camel-driver	2. Copper-smelter	2. Flax-comber	2. Usurer
3. Sailor	3. Tanner	3. Handmill cleaner	3. Pigeon-trainer
4. Carter		4. Pedlar	4. Dealer in produce of the sabbatical year
5. Herdsman		5. Weaver	5. Herdsman
6. Shopkeeper		6. Barber	6. Tax collector
7. Physician		7. Launderer	7. Publican
8. Butcher		8. Blood-letter 9. Bath attendant 10. Tanner	

Both this and the rebellion over taxation in 6 C.E. by Judas the Galilean and his followers might well have been a very important contribution to the mounting hatred of Jesus, which eventually led to his crucifixion.[23]

Ellis suggests that the feast may have been a farewell dinner for Matthew's colleagues.[24] There might even have been a covenant character to the meal. Some of Jesus' followers may have been among the publicly shunned guests.

The deeds of a master, not only his words, were followed by his disciples. Daube observes, "So powerful is a master's position that an action he condones may be imputed to him just as much as one he initiates."[25]

The Question about Fasting (Luke 5:33–39; Mark 2:18–22; Matt. 9:14–17)

Levi's meal could be a quasi-*haberim* (brothers') meal welcoming converts. This is a point made by W. Grundmann, who further suggests that the pericope put after it probably comes from the table talk at the banquet.[26] Luke also seems to connect the sayings about fasting and the old and new wineskins more closely with the calling of Levi than do Mark and Matthew.

Voluntary fasting was practiced by the Pharisees and the disciples of John the Baptist, but Jesus declared that the time of his ministry is like a wedding celebration: fasting would be out of place. The new wine of the gospel cannot be contained in the old skins of Judaism (or perhaps even of John the Baptist). There is an indirect reference to Jesus' death; the bridegroom will be taken away; *then* there will be fasting. "Bridegroom" in the Old Testament is used to describe God but not the Messiah (Hos. 2:18, 21; Ezek. 16; Isa. 54:5–8; 62:5; Jer. 2:2). Jesus makes a provocative statement here: he implicitly equates himself with God.

Luke turns the simile concerning the cloth and wine into parables. In Luke the cloth is torn from a new garment, which is foolish. The new spirit requires new forms. It is important to note that the *neos* (new) for wine denotes new in time, whereas *kainos* (new) for the skins means new in quality. Both symbolize the form of the new era, differing in quality and quantity from the old (Luke 16:16). The three parables depict persons unwilling to abandon their old habits. Their teaching makes the contrast between toll collectors (and "others") and the scribes and Pharisees much greater. Verse 39 is peculiar to Luke; it intimates that those who have the old wine do not even attempt to try the new. In the Gospel of Luke this table talk shows that a new age has begun with the acceptance of tax collectors and sinners.

Thus, the first public meal for Jesus is hosted by a person who would be equivalent to a member of the mafia in contemporary society. Jesus begins his ministry by dining with the dregs of society and entering into fellowship with them. He declares that a new age (symbolized by the new wine and wineskins) has begun. For Luke the new age is Jesus' ministry.

The Parable of the Pharisee and the Tax Collector (Luke 18:9–14)

This pericope is part of Luke's answer to the question, "Who will be found faithful when the Son of Man comes?" It is also a good example of his teaching on the qualifications for entering the kingdom of God and is an extension of his teaching on discipleship. It is a striking instance of faith and humility triumphing over legalism and false piety. It stands as the climax of the journey section, the non-Markan segment of Luke's Gospel (9:51–18:14).

In the parable, the Pharisee is represented as going beyond the requirements of the law in the Hebrew scriptures. Jesus' purpose in telling the parable seems to be to "bring about a new social and religious valuation" of the requirements of the law.[27] However, the Talmud is aware of hypocritical Pharisees, as is seen in *Sotah* 22b where seven types of hypocritical Pharisees are mentioned. There is a similar but less abrasive prayer than that of Luke's Pharisee in the hymn scroll from Qumran: "[I give Thee thank]s, O Adonai, for Thou hast not cast my lot among the congregation of vanity and hast not set my decree in the assembly of hypocrites" (1 *QH* 7:34).

Jeremias asserts that "details of language and content reveal the parable as belonging to an early Palestinian tradition."[28] There is a severe judgment on the Pharisee because he "trusted in himself." Verse 14b contains a generalizing conclusion that expresses a favored gospel theme: the eschatological reversal of existing conditions. It is in the form of an antithetic parallelism, describing God's dealings at the last judgment; God will humble the proud and exalt the humble (cf. the Magnificat).[29]

The Pharisee describes the rest of humankind as robbers, swindlers, and adulterers. Jeremias observes that the phrase "tax collectors and sinners" is paralleled by other similar combinations:[30]

tax collectors	and	robbers
"	"	prostitutes
"	"	gentiles
"	"	swindlers
"	"	adulterers
"	"	toll collectors
"	"	money changers
"	"	thieves
"	"	murderers

These combinations infer that "sinners" are persons whose immorality is notorious, whether because of their way of life or their occupation. Luke's parable paints a realistic picture.

The tax collector's prayer may have been one of despair. Perhaps he realized he could not reach full repentance, because he would be obliged not only to give up his profession but to make restitution for his ill-gotten gains plus one fifth. But God forgives the tax collector and not the Pharisee. Jeremias states: "Such a conclusion must have utterly overwhelmed its hearers. It was beyond the capacity of any of them to imagine. What fault had the Pharisee committed, and what had the publican done by way of reparation?"[31] The tax collector is like the repentant psalmist in Psalm 51, and God is the God of those in despair, as in the same psalm.

In the prayer of the Pharisee we find the synonyms used for tax collectors: "extortioners, unjust . . . even like this tax collector." The tax collector echoes the words of Matthew's Gospel (not Luke's) at the end of the pericope of the calling of Matthew, "I desire mercy, not sacrifice" (cf. Targ. Ps. 57:2; 53:3; 56:2, 18).

It may be significant that both the Pharisee and the tax collector (v. 10) "go up" (*anabainō*), literally, from the lower city to Mt. Moriah on which the Temple stood, and that the tax collector goes down (*katabaino*) justified. Both verbs would be meaningful to Luke who shows the anabasis (going up) and the katabasis (going down) of Jesus in the Gospel, beginning with the journey section and ending with the passion. But the most important verse is 14b, for "He who exalts himself will be humbled and he who humbles himself will be exalted" forms an important part of the whole Lukan concept of *analēmpsis* (going up) in Luke 9:51. The tax collector goes through the anabasis and the katabasis required of the true disciple, just as Jesus suffers and is exalted.

This parable stands at the end of the non-Markan material in Luke. I concur with the many scholars who see it as the end of the journey portion in Luke. Who was found faithful when the Son of Man came? A tax collector!

Zacchaeus (Luke 19:1–10)

The narrative of the chief tax collector, Zacchaeus, is the last story in the pre-Jerusalem ministry of Jesus. The Galilean ministry proper begins with the calling of Levi, a lesser tax official; it concludes with a tax-collection overseer. Of the Zacchaeus story Marshall states:

It is a supreme example of the universality of the gospel offer to tax collectors and sinners, with Jesus taking the initiative and inviting himself to the house of Zacchaeus. In doing so Jesus was certainly responding to the interest shown in him by Zacchaeus, but the decisive action, contrary to all that would be expected at the time, stemmed from Jesus.[32]

W. P. Loewe finds that this pericope condenses much that is peculiarly Lukan in the rest of the Gospel.[33] He singles out: the vocabulary; tax (toll) collectors, who appear in contrast to the self-righteous; the rich, who are indifferent to the poor; the themes of seeking (11:9, 10; 12:31; 11:30; 9:9), seeing (2:12, 29, 30; 3:6; 9:9; 19:3; 23:8), today (2:11; 23:43), and *dei* ("it is necessary"; 2:49; 4:43; 9:22; 13:33; 17:25; 22:37; 24:7, 25–27, 44); son of Abraham (1:55, 73; 3:8–9); and the mission of the Son of Man to save what is lost.

Loewe finds the Zacchaeus pericope to be strategically placed, for it is associated with the healing of the blind man at Jericho. Both pericopes answer the question posed in 18:8, "But when the Son of Man comes, will he find any faith on earth?" The answer is: the tax collectors and the blind will be found faithful.

The Zacchaeus incident also brings the theme of toll collectors to a climax. Jericho itself is a significant city for the conversion of Zacchaeus because tolls would be collected here on goods coming to Judea from Perea, and travelers to Jerusalem, Bethel, and the north could hardly avoid it. Zacchaeus was probably the head of a large group of toll collectors; as such his conversion would be public, controversial, and highly influential.

Zacchaeus gave half his possessions to the poor, although the rabbis advised that one-fifth was sufficient. He was also prepared to pay fourfold anyone whom he had deceived. This was the penalty imposed on robbers. Normally a tax collector who confiscated anything wrongfully was obliged to restore only double the value of the goods. Further, if the complaint was not lodged within a year, simple replacement was adequate. If force had been used, a threefold restitution was required. Zacchaeus, therefore, goes far beyond the demands of the law.

The crowd, complaining because Jesus goes to dine with a sinner, would be justified by contemporary standards: tax collectors and toll collectors were classed with robbers and usurers (*B.K.* 94b; cf. *B.M.* 8:26) because of their extortions. And they were considered unclean because they associated with gentiles. They were the direct opposite to the Pharisaic *haberim*. Inasmuch as Jesus dines "at his house," we should probably envisage a large assembly: family, colleagues, subordinates, slaves, and probably soldiers, who were also used to exact taxes.

Jesus' announcement to Zacchaeus that "salvation has come to this house" resumes the theme of salvation in the infancy narratives. However, it is a completely different salvation: not conquest of an enemy, political freedom, and reversal of fortune on this earth for the rich, but fellowship with a converted rich sinner.

The Zacchaeus pericope forms a grand finale to the theme of toll collectors in Luke's Gospel and Zacchaeus's hospitality is Jesus' last recorded meal before the passover.

Jesus has prepared his audience for this teaching by the parables of the lost sheep, the lost coin, and the prodigal son (Luke 15). All these were told when toll collectors and sinners were drawing near to Jesus—and the Pharisees and the scribes murmured (Luke 15:1–2). All three parables show that Jesus claims that in his actions the love of God to the repentant sinner is made effectual. This, indeed, is preaching good news to the "poor" (Luke 4:18).

The parable of the prodigal son is far bolder than the parable of the sheep or the parable of the coin. It shows that sinners are not only sought and accepted but that they receive honor, responsibility, and authority.

Luke, by making his toll collectors both so prominent and so attractive, seeks to allay resentment, agitation, and rebellion over the question of taxes on the part of the first-century Jews and perhaps in his own church. The tax and toll collectors, who practiced violence, and to whom violence was shown, are now invited into the kingdom of God.

This is the Lukan Jesus' indirect answer to Judas the Galilean and his followers, and also to the revolutionaries who refused to pay taxes in 66 C.E., thus contributing to the causes of the war. All three synoptic Gospels report the incident about giving tribute money to Rome (Luke 20:20–26; Mark 12:13–17; Matt. 22:15–22). On this occasion Jesus gave an ambiguous answer but certainly not a definitely negative one.

Luke's treatment of tax and toll collectors is his answer to the psychological, spiritual, and social violence shown to them by Jesus' contemporaries.

It is a very practical way of implementing the sermon on the plain (Luke 6) and the teaching of Jesus about doing good to those who hate or maltreat you.

Chapter 6

JESUS' PEACEABLE APPROACH TO THE HATED SAMARITANS

Go nowhere among the Gentiles, and enter no town of the Samaritans, but go rather to the lost sheep of the house of Israel [Matt. 10:5f.].

Jesus gave his disciples this directive on the occasion of their first mission. At the time, Samaria extended over about a third of Palestine. The inhabitants seem to have been hellenized and fairly prosperous.[1] Josephus notes the abundance of sweet water, the fertile land, and dairy produce.[2]

Jesus' prohibition makes him appear a bigoted racist. However, many orthodox Jews would have nothing to do with either Samaritans or gentiles. Our concern here is with the Samaritans. Recall John 4:9:

The Samaritan woman said to him [Jesus], "How is it that you, a Jew, ask a drink of me, a woman of Samaria?" For the Jews have no dealings with the Samaritans.

Luke not only omits the statement from Matthew (above), but he includes special material about Samaritans: Luke 9:51–56, where Jesus is refused hospitality by a Samaritan village and yet declines to take revenge on it, unlike Elijah (2 Kings 1:9–16); the parable of the good Samaritan (Luke 10:29–37); the story of the grateful Samaritan leper (17:11–19); and finally the conversion of the Samaritans by Philip the Evangelist and their reception of the Holy Spirit through the imposition of hands by Peter and John from Jerusalem (Acts 8).

The novelty and audacity of speaking well of the Samaritans cannot be understood fully without a survey of the history of the hostilities between the Jews and the Samaritans throughout Jewish history, especially during the first century C.E. It was a history of continual conflict and violence between these two peoples.

79

The Jews and the Samaritans

After the death of Solomon, the Hebrew Kingdom was divided into two, Judea in the south and Israel in the north. In the eighth century B.C.E. the Jewish Northern Kingdom of Israel (later Samaria) was subjugated by the Assyrians. Many inhabitants were deported, and Assyrian immigrants took up residence in the Northern Kingdom. This caused syncretism in culture and religion and led to mixed marriages. From the eighth century, the Jews in Judah, the Southern Kingdom, regarded the inhabitants of Israel, the Northern Kingdom, as impure and unacceptable as coreligionists.

In the sixth century B.C.E. came the next major crisis, after the exile of the Jews from Judah to Babylon. The Babylonians conquered Jerusalem in 587 B.C.E. After about seventy years, the Jews were permitted to return to their land under the Persian king, Cyrus. They were also allowed to rebuild the Temple. The Samaritans asked to be allowed to help in its reconstruction. The Judeans refused to allow this because they considered the Samaritans impure. This caused sharp conflict. The Samaritans tried to stop the rebuilding of the Temple (Ezra 4:4; 1 Esdras 5:72; cf. *Ant.* 11:87–88). They even wrote to Darius, the Persian king, and accused the Jews of building fortifications in Jerusalem (Ezra 6:1; 1 Esdras 5:23; *Ant.* 11:97). Eventually they contrived plots against the Jews, killed many, and made an attempt on the life of Nehemiah. So great was the disturbance that the Jews were filled with terror and almost abandoned their work on the Temple (Neh. 4:7 [Hebr., 4:1]; 2 Esdras 14:7; cf. *Ant.* 11:174).

In the fourth century B.C.E. there was further controversy. Josephus reports that in the time of Alexander the Great (d. 323 B.C.E.) the Samaritans courted his favor and asked for relief from tribute during the seventh year. Josephus remarks:

> For such is the nature of the Samaritans, as we have already shown somewhere above [*Ant.* 9:291 and note]. When the Jews are in difficulties, they deny that they have any kinship with them thereby indeed admitting the truth, but whenever they see some splendid bit of good fortune with them, they suddenly grasp at the connection with them, saying that they are related to them and tracing their line back to Ephraim and Manasseh, the descendants of Joseph [*Ant.* 11:340–42].

Josephus records that Alexander allowed them to build their own temple (*Ant.* 11:322–24). They constructed it on Mount Gerizim, on the model of the one in Jerusalem. This was contrary to Jewish law, which forbade a temple outside Jerusalem. Therefore, there was increased bitterness and rivalry between the Jews and the Samaritans. This conflict over the two temples is mentioned in John 4:19–26.

According to the Samaritan chronicles, the Samaritans experienced various fortunes and vicissitudes under Alexander, but they do report that they were allowed to build their temple and that a covenant was made to protect them. Further, Josephus informs us that Alexander took many Jews and Samaritans to Egypt (*Ant.* 12:7). He states that the Jews and the Samaritans in the Egyptian city of Alexandria quarreled about their respective temples and speeches were made for both sides (*Ant.* 13:74-79). The decision was made in favor of the Jews. The Samaritans, together with their advocates, were put to death. This shows that conflict and violence went beyond Palestine itself.

Alexander's empire was divided when he died. The temple on Mount Gerizim remained. Josephus sarcastically remarks, "And whenever anyone was accused by the people of Jerusalem of eating unclean food or violating the Sabbath or committing any other such sin, he would flee to the Shechemites (Samaritans), saying that he had been unjustly expelled" (*Ant.* 11:346-47).

In the second century B.C.E. the Jews suffered cruel persecution from the Hellenistic ruler Antiochus Epiphanes. This was just before the uprising of the Maccabees in 175 B.C.E. (1 Macc. 1:44). Josephus gives us information which is not found in the Old Testament. He reports that when the Samaritans saw the persecution of the Jews under Antiochus Epiphanes, "they would no longer admit that they were their kin or that the temple of Garizein [Gerizim] was that of the Most Great God, thereby acting in accordance with their nature, as we have shown [*Ant.* 9:291]; they also said they were colonists from the Medes and Persians, and they are, in fact, colonists from these peoples" (*Ant.* 12:257-64). They sent a letter to Antiochus stating that they were not Jews and asking him that their temple on Mount Gerizim should be known as that of Zeus Hellenios. Antiochus granted their request. Paganizing their temple would scandalize the Jews and alienate them still further from the Samaritans.

At the same time matters were not improved vis-à-vis the Maccabees. Apollonius, the governor of Samaria, took his soldiers and set out against Judas Maccabee. But Judas engaged him in battle and defeated him (1 Macc. 3:10; cf. *Ant.* 12:287).

In the second century, Hyrcanus, the Jewish leader (135/4-104 B.C.E.), conquered several cities including Shechem and Gerizim, where the temple stood. This was the time of the vital break between the Jews and the Samaritans. Hyrcanus marched against Samaria, attacked and besieged it vigorously "because of the injuries which, in obedience to the kings of Syria, they had done to the people of Marisa, who were colonists and allies of the Jews." The Samaritans were subdued by famine "to such a state of need that they were forced to take for food even things that are not used for that purpose." They called for help from abroad but in vain. Finally they surrendered (*Ant.* 13:273-79).

Hyrcanus had captured the city of Samaria after besieging it for a year, "but not content with that alone, he effaced it entirely and left it to be swept away by the mountain torrents, for he dug beneath it until it fell into the beds of the torrents, and so removed all signs of its ever having been a city" (*Ant.* 13:280). The Samaritan chronicles give another version of the destruction of their city by Hyrcanus.

Such a brutal and complete destruction of the city of the Samaritans by a Jew could only fearfully aggravate the hostility between the two peoples.

In the first century B.C.E., in Roman times, Pompey rebuilt several cities including Samaria (*Ant.* 14:75). Indeed, Josephus lists Samaria as one of the towns liberated by Pompey from the rule of the Jews (*B.J.* 1:156). He also reports that Gabinius, the Roman (57–58 B.C.E.), restored order in several cities including Samaria, which is one of the towns where "colonists [were] gladly flocking" (*B.J.* 1:166). This brought in even more pagan influence, and made the Samaritans appear pro-Roman.

Further, in the same century, the Samaritans were not only pro-Roman; they were also pro-Herodian and hence despised by Herod's Jewish opponents who wanted a purebred Jew for the throne.

In 37 B.C.E., three years after Herod the Great had been proclaimed king in Rome, he besieged Jerusalem. Josephus reports that "to ensure that there should be no shortage in the immediate future, he instructed the inhabitants of the district of Samaria, that city having declared in his favor, to bring corn, wine, oil, and cattle down to Jericho" (*B.J.* 1:299). The Jews sent orders to hold up the convoys and gathered forces above Jericho, but Herod thwarted them and also sent his Roman army to winter quarters in Idumea, Galilee, and Samaria. Herod also rescued his mother and other relatives and sent them to Samaria (*B.J.* 1:303). Then, to add insult to injury, "leaving his most efficient lieutenants to superintend these works, he went off himself to Samaria to fetch the daughter of Alexander, son of Aristobolus, who . . . was betrothed to him. Thus, so contemptuous was he already of the enemy, he made his wedding an interlude to the siege" (*B.J.* 1:342–44). After the wedding he returned with larger forces to Jerusalem. He made a brutal conquest of Jerusalem in 37 B.C.E.

Later Herod founded the city of Sebaste, formerly Samaria, and also built a temple to Caesar there. The inhabitants enjoyed a privileged constitution (*B.J.* 1:403). He considered making a third rampart against the entire nation out of Samaria for he believed that this place would give him "no less security against the country [than the others], since it was only a day's journey from Jerusalem and would be equally useful for controlling affairs in the city and in the country" (*Ant.* 15:292). Herod fortified Samaria and brought settlers there (*Ant.* 15:296–98). Thus Samaria was placed in a position of antagonism vis-à-vis the anti-Herodian Jews.

In the first century C.E., Samaria again appears pro-Roman. Josephus informs us that Varus, a Roman governor, quelled disturbances in Palestine. He pursued his march into Samaria; but he spared the city because it had taken no part in the general tumult (*B.J.* 2:66–71). Josephus makes a similar statement about Samaria's pro-Roman tendencies (*B.J.* 2:96), saying that the ethnarchy of Archelaus comprised the whole of Idumea and Judea, and the district of Samaria, "which had a quarter of its tribute remitted in consideration of its having taken no part in the insurrection."

Summary

Thus the deep hatred of the Jews toward the Samaritans in the first century is perfectly understandable, and it can be seen that the history of the relationship between the Jews and the Samaritans was continually acrimonious. There were major conflicts in the eighth century, under the Assyrians; in the sixth and fifth, under the Babylonians and the Persians; in the fourth, under Alexander the Great; in the second, under Antiochus Epiphanes, and in relationship to the Maccabees, and the Hasmoneans under John Hyrcanus; and in the first century, under the Romans and Herod the Great. The most bitter resentment must have occurred when Hyracanus I destroyed Samaria in such a brutal fashion.

However, relationships could not have improved when the Samaritans showed pro-Roman tendencies or failed to oppose Rome. Josephus makes repeated references to this attitude. The Jews despised especially the hellenization and romanization of their rivals. Matters were only aggravated by Herod the Great's use of Samaria and his hellenization of that city. His Samaritan wedding during the siege of Jerusalem must have inflamed the Jews with indignation.

The Samaritan Profanation of the Jerusalem Temple

There are two more incidents from the first century that must be mentioned. In their light, Luke's amicability toward the Samaritans can be seen as an audacious and threatening move on his part. He worked for healing between alien peoples.

The first incident took place when Coponius was procurator (6–9 C.E.). Samaritans secretly joined the Jewish passover pilgrims in the Temple and committed an egregious sacrilege. They placed human bones in the porticoes and in the sanctuary and thus defiled the Temple. Corpses and bones were the most unclean of all objects in the eyes of the Jews. A priest attended only the funerals of his nearest relatives. Anyone who touched a corpse or bone was obliged to take a ritual bath and remain unclean for twenty-four hours. Thus the Samaritan action was about the worst desecration possible. Josephus remarks that the priests excluded everyone from the Temple—a most unusual step (*Ant.* 18:29–30).

Although Josephus passes over this episode without further comment, it must have been highly offensive and provocative to the Palestinian Jews and to those who were attending the festival from the Diaspora. Carcopino[3] would connect this incident with an inscription in Palestine that forbids the removal of buried bodies from one place to another.

The Samaritan Provocation at Ginae

The second incident was even more volatile. It led to a year-long bloody conflict between the Jewish masses and the Samaritans, and was one of the major causes of the Jewish-Roman war (66–74 C.E.).[4] Because it could have been the chief reason for Luke to wish to reconcile Jew (and Christian) and Samaritan, it is necessary to describe it in detail.

Josephus reports (*B.J.* 2:232–35) how during the time of the Roman governor Cumanus (48–52 C.E.),[5] at a village called Gema (Ginae),[6] which was situated in the great plain of Samaria on the border between Galilee and Samaria,[7] the Samaritans of the village murdered one of a large company of Jews on their way to Jerusalem for the festival of passover. Enraged by this incident a great crowd of Galileans assembled, intending to make war on the Samaritans. The Jewish authorities, however, tried to negotiate with Cumanus and beseeched him to punish the murderers in order to avoid hostilities. Cumanus, belittling their cause, dismissed the Jewish leaders. When word of the murder reached Jerusalem, the masses abandoned the passover feast and hurried to Samaria without any generals in command and without listening to the magistrates. They chose as their leaders Eleazar, son of Deinaeus, a "brigand," and Alexander.[8] The Jewish crowds massacred the inhabitants of Gema without distinction of age and burned down their village.

Cumanus, taking with him a troop of cavalry from Caesarea, went to avenge the Samaritans. He imprisoned many of Eleazar's followers and also slaughtered a considerable number. The magistrates of Jerusalem, still hoping to avert war, hastened to the Jewish insurgents and, dressed in sackcloth and with ashes on their heads, implored them to return home and not to bring down "the wrath of the Romans on Jerusalem, but take pity on their country and sanctuary, on their own wives and children; [for] all these were threatened with destruction merely for the object of avenging the blood of a single Galilean."

If Josephus is correct, it is very important to note that the Jewish leaders predicted dire consequences if the masses continued their fight. It was not merely a local affair; at stake were the country and the sanctuary. The crowds did disperse but many turned to robbery, raids, and insurrections. The leading Samaritans went to Tyre and urged the Roman Umidius Quadratus, governor of Syria, to punish the Jewish revolutionaries. The Jewish leaders also had recourse to Quadratus and maintained that Samaritans were the cause of the riots, but they said that the blame lay with Cumanus, who failed to take action against them.

Quadratus, after some delay, went to Caesarea where he crucified all the prisoners whom Cumanus had taken. Then he went to Lydda where he heard the Samaritans again. He beheaded eighteen Jews who were accused of having participated in the fighting. He sent the high priests Jonathan and Ananus and other Jewish leaders, together with some Samaritans, to Caesar. He also sent Cumanus and Celer, the tribune, to Rome to give an account of their conduct to the emperor, Claudius. Then he left Lydda and went up to Jerusalem. The Jews were celebrating the feast of unleavened bread quite peacefully. The second reference to the feast of unleavened bread must mean that all these events extended over a whole year, from one passover to the next.

At Rome, even though several eminent persons supported Cumanus, Caesar was won over by Agrippa's appeal for the Jews. The emperor condemned the Samaritans and ordered three of the most prominent men to be executed. Cumanus was banished. Celer, the tribune, was returned to Jerusalem where he was dragged round the city and then beheaded.

Yet throughout this year-long fighting, the Jews had been the unjust victims of oppression, and the Romans had, to a large extent, given support to the real aggressors, the Samaritans. It was quite providential that Agrippa II was in Rome to justify the Jews and win their acquittal.

Josephus gives another account of these important events in his *Antiquities of the Jews,* 20:118–36. There are some significant differences.

Antiquities was written later than the *Jewish War* and might be more representative of popular, contemporary thought among Jews and Jewish Christians in the time of the early church. The grievances against the Samaritans are expressed far more acutely. This may have inspired Luke to write with the hope of reconciling the two peoples.

Josephus informs us that it was a custom for the Galileans to pass through the Samaritan territory on their way to Jerusalem. According to *Antiquities,* not one, but "a great number" of Galileans were slain in a full-scale battle. We are told that Cumanus was bribed by the Samaritans so that no vengeance would fall on them. The Galileans urged the Jewish masses "to assert their liberty," an exhortation that sounds more like revolt against Rome than pure vengeance on the Samaritans. For they added further, ". . . slavery was in itself bitter, but when it involved insolent treatment, it was quite intolerable." In *Antiquities* Josephus describes Eleazar as a "brigand (*lestēs*) who for many years had had his home in the mountains." The Jews are said to have burned and sacked several Samaritan villages. The appeal of the leaders in Jerusalem is more graphic; Josephus writes: "They urged them [the masses] to picture to themselves that their country would be razed to the ground, their temple consigned to flames, and they themselves with their wives and children reduced to slavery." He says that "from that time the whole of Judea was infested with bands of brigands" (revolutionaries). He describes the Samaritan attitude as decidedly pro-Roman:

> They professed to be indignant not so much *because of the treatment that they themselves had received as because of the contempt that the Jews had shown for the Romans.* For the Jews, they said, should have

appealed to the Romans to decide the matter, if indeed the Samaritans had done them an injustice, and not, as they had now done, have over-run the Samaritan country, as though they did not have the Romans as their governors [*Ant.* 11:340–42; italics added].

There is some confusion in the texts about the fate of the Jewish and Samaritan leaders under Quadratus. *Jewish War* 2:241 refers to all the prisoners, presumably both Jews and Samaritans, or only Jews, who were imprisoned by Cumanus. *Antiquities* says that he crucified some of the Samaritans and some of the Jews, who were part of the rebellion, but another source speaks of his crucifying only the Jews. Tacitus (*Ann.* 12:54) states that Quadratus put to death the Jews who had killed Roman soldiers. However, in all these accounts it would appear that the Jews received greater punishment than did the Samaritans.

Finally, *Antiquities* 20:130, after reporting that Quadratus gave a second hearing to the Samaritans, says that he was informed by a certain Samaritan that a Jewish leader named Doetus with four other revolutionaries (*neoreristai*) had "instigated the mob to revolt against the Romans" (*Ant.* 20:130). Quadratus put these men to death. Further, Josephus, speaking of the hearing at Rome, reports that Caesar's friends and freedmen "displayed the greatest partiality for Cumanus and the Samaritans," but Agrippa the Younger persuaded Agrippina, the wife of the emperor, to give the case a thorough hearing. Eventually, Emperor Claudius decided in favor of the Jews.

D.M. Rhoads, after discussing this whole incident, observes:

> . . . this incident, which took place around 51 C.E., was a turning point in the Jewish relationship with Rome, for the assertion of liberty and the direct clash with Roman soldiers in Judea stirred up all the dissatisfied elements throughout the countryside.[9]

It is highly unlikely that Luke was ignorant of these domestic battles. Inasmuch as the Samaritans played an important part in provoking the war with Rome, doubtless when the Jews were defeated by the Romans their hostility would be magnified.

This is why Luke (and John) speak positively about the Samaritans and show Jesus conducting himself in a way diametrically contrary to his fellow Jews. Even in the face of the lamentable quarrels between Samaritans and Jews, Luke's Jesus does not share his people's hostility in the slightest degree.

The Samaritans in Luke's Gospel

The Samaritans are introduced at a key point in Luke's narrative: where he leaves his Markan source and begins his central section (9:51–18:14), which describes Jesus' journey from Galilee to Jerusalem.[10] The journey begins with

Jesus' strong resolve to go up to Jerusalem to face his death, knowing, however, that it will be followed by his exaltation (resurrection and ascension). The special Lukan material ends with the parable of the humiliation and justification of the toll collector (18:14). Thus, just like the strategic position of the homily in the Nazareth pericope (Luke 4), which shows Jesus' non-violent policy, so the Samaritan episode is also thrown into prominence. It is necessary to investigate this Lukan central section to elucidate more clearly Jesus' attitude to the Samaritans.

The journey begins on an unusually awesome note that is impossible to reproduce adequately in translation:

> When the days *drew near (were fulfilled)* for him to be *received up*, he set his face to go to Jerusalem. And he sent messengers ahead of him, who went and entered a village of the *Samaritans*, to make ready for him; but the *people would not receive him, because his face was set toward Jerusalem*. And when his disciples James and John saw it, they said, "Lord, do you want us to bid *fire come down from heaven and consume them?*" But *he* turned and *rebuked them*. And they went on to *another village* [Luke 9:51–56; italics added].

Here we have in four sentences five important Lukan themes: time of fulfillment; "received up"; the Samaritans; Jesus' determination to go to Jerusalem; and James and John's expecting Jesus to desire miraculous vengeance on the inhospitable Samaritans.

As C.F. Evans has shown, Luke has begun this section (9:51–18:14) and his record of Jesus' journey up to Jerusalem by choosing his words carefully and producing "an especially solemn note by an unusually strong concentration of biblical idioms."[11] Very significant is Luke's use of "were fulfilled" (*sumplerousthai*), which, as Evans avers, ". . . is perhaps chosen here as a sonorous word fitting an important moment; it recurs with this meaning only, and perhaps significantly, in identical words . . . [in] the story of pentecost." By this word Luke suggests that the moment of eschatological fulfillment of the divine plan is approaching. Jesus begins to accomplish his exodus, going out to his death (Luke 9:31) in Jerusalem. In concert with this, Luke portrays his attitude to the age-old enemies of the Jews, the Samaritans.

The next pregnant word is "received up" (*analēmpsis*). This has a three-fold meaning: (1) to travel up; (2) to be lifted up on the cross and die; (3) to be lifted up in glory; the ascension. The time of Jesus' passion is approaching, and, like the servant of the Lord in Isaiah 53, he sets his face resolutely to accomplish God's will.

The concept of being "received up" (assumption or ascension) is associated with two important biblical personages: Moses, who died but, according to Jewish tradition, was assumed into heaven, and Elijah, who did not die, but was carried heavenward in a chariot with fiery horses.

The Bible tells us about the assumption of Elijah (2 Kings 2:9–12), and, interestingly enough, there is a nonbiblical Jewish work called the *Assumption of Moses.*

Scholars think that originally the latter was two works: the *Testament of Moses,* written in Hebrew between 7 and 29 C.E., and the *Assumption of Moses,* written in Greek also in the first century C.E. A few allusions to it are found in Acts 7:36 (Stephen's speech); Jude 9, 16, 18; and in the nonbiblical writings of Clement of Alexandria, Origen and some other Greek writers, and 2 Baruch.[12] Luke and his readers could have known this work and recognized the analogy between Moses and Jesus, especially as Luke emphasizes the prophetic side of Jesus' character throughout his Gospel.

Luke used the key word found in the title of the *Assumption of Moses,* "received up" or "assumption" (ascension, in Luke 9:51), and recorded important teachings by Jesus prior to his death, just as Moses is portrayed as giving instructions to his successor Joshua (Greek, "Jesus") before his death. As we have seen above, Joshua (Hebrew) is Jesus (Greek). For the majority of Luke's readers, Moses' instructions were given to Jesus, the son of Nun.

C. F. Evans proposes that this travel narrative of Luke has affinity to the *Assumption of Moses.* The title (assumption, *analēmpsis*) is precisely the word that Luke uses of Jesus' being received up (9:51). Like Luke's central section, the *Assumption of Moses* concerns not only the mysterious death of an important prophet, Moses, but also gives a series of addresses and injunctions delivered to Joshua (Jesus) as his successor. Evans concludes:

> This might go some way toward explaining why the evangelist, after an introduction in solemn biblical tones, chose to place under the head of an approaching *analēmpsis* (assumption) not only the Passion, Resurrection, and Ascension of Jesus in or near Jerusalem, but also a mass of teaching delivered in the course of a journey thither.[13]

Evans compares and contrasts the central section of Luke's Gospel and the Book of Deuteronomy, laying them out in parallel columns.[14] Luke's teaching mitigates some of the severity found in Deuteronomy and, most importantly for us, the attitude toward foreigners.

In Deuteronomy 7 God gives instructions to his people to utterly destroy all foreigners, to make no covenant with them, to have no mercy, and not to enter into marriage with them lest they turn the Hebrews away from true worship. God's people should dash to pieces their altars and burn their images. John Hyrcanus, who destroyed Samaria, and the Jews who took vengeance on the Samaritans at Ginae conducted themselves according to the deuteronomic ethos.

However, it was not Jesus alone who mitigated these precepts. To some extent we see this in books such as the *Assumption of Moses.* For if Evans is right in seeing the "going up" (*analēmpsis*) of Jesus as analogous to Moses' assumption, it seems that he has omitted an even closer analogy between the apocalyptic book now named the *Assumption of Moses* and this central section of Luke. In his introduction to the translation of this text, R. H. Charles proposes that this work was composed by a Pharisaic quietist who designed it as a protest against "the growing secularization of the Pharisaic party through its fusion with political ideals and popular Messianic beliefs."[15] The writer attempted to inspire his readers to obedience to the law, and he looked for the establishment of the theocratic kingdom and the triumph of Israel over its foes. But he was not a revolutionary: he does not make a call to arms but counsels observance of the law and repentance while the people awaits a personal intervention of God on its behalf. He does not bring into prominence or praise the Maccabean military leaders; instead, his heroes are a group of martyrs, Eleazar and his seven sons.[16] Charles adds:

> It adds no little to the interest of the book that it was written during the early life of our Lord, or possibly contemporaneously with his public ministry, and that its conception of spiritual religion as opposed to an alliance of religion with politics generally or with any specific school of politics was essentially one with his.[17]

If this book has influenced Luke, then it is of extreme interest to us. It supports the antirevolutionary or antipolitical polemic in Luke, but Luke's Jesus goes beyond the *Assumption of Moses*. Moses did not undergo the suffering that was Jesus' destiny before his exaltation (assumption). Although there is no aggressive behavior on the part of human beings toward the heathen in the *Assumption of Moses*, it does portray God exacting vengeance:

> For the most high will arise, the Eternal God alone,
> And He will appear to punish the gentiles,
> And He will destroy all their idols.
> Then thou, O Israel, shalt be happy,
> And thou shalt mount upon their necks. . . .
> And they shall be ended. . . .
> And thou shalt look from on high
> and shalt see thy enemies in gehenna.
> And thou shalt recognize them and rejoice. . . .
> [*Assump. Moses* 10:7–10; cf. Rev. 14:9–11]

In sharp contrast we shall note Jesus' geniality toward Samaritans, which is a prelude to his acceptance of gentiles, the climax of his ministry of reconciliation.

In his central section Luke follows the ideology of the *Assumption of Moses* but goes a step further. God in Jesus Christ will show marked clemency to the enemies of the Jews. Luke, at the beginning of this section, deals with enemies who are particularly offensive to the Jewish people, the Samaritans.

Jesus' Clemency toward the Inhospitable Samaritans (Luke 9:51-56)

Luke is the only evangelist to record Jesus' journey through Samaria on his way to Jerusalem and to show how the Samaritans refused his hospitality. Jesus showed no resentment at all.

Jesus' conduct is exactly the opposite to that of the Jews who had followed the same path to Jerusalem during Cumanus's governorship and passed through Ginae. It is true that Jesus' followers were not murdered. Nevertheless, Jesus' example would appear extremely startling to his Jewish contemporaries and the Christians in the Lukan communities.

This is thrown into higher relief by the fact that Jesus is accompanied by James and John, who are called "sons of thunder" or "sons of rage" in Mark 3:17. They were probably religious zealots (recall Simon the zealot). They appear to have expected a theocratic messianic kingdom and hoped for influential positions at the right and left hand of Christ in his glory (Mark 10:35-45; Matt. 20:20-26). Significantly, this passage is omitted by Luke and by John. When the Samaritans refuse Jesus, these zealots innocently ask the Lord whether they are to bid fire to come down from heaven to consume them. Some ancient witnesses add "as Elijah did." Obviously the disciples are still thinking of Jesus in the character of Elijah, who called down fire three times upon the Samaritans (2 Kings 1:2-16). According to the best manuscripts, Jesus merely turned and rebuked them. However, some ancient manuscripts add: "And he said, 'You do not know what manner of spirit you are of; for the Son of Man came not to destroy men's lives but to save them.' "

This pericope is not only in contrast to 2 Kings but also strikingly different from John the Baptist's prediction (according to Luke and Matthew) that the Coming One would baptize with fire. W. Wink is correct when he says that Luke rejects the eschatological (or should we say "apocalyptic"?) role of Elijah popularized by Malachi: 4:5f. and Sirach 48:10.[18] Flender argues that the rejection of the spirit of Elijah in this passage also contains a rejection of the political messiahship associated with Elijah *redivivus*.[19]

In the great journey toward Jerusalem (Luke 9:51-18:14) Jesus moves toward his death and ascension even as Elijah made a journey before his ascension (2 Kings 2). Flender observes that by introducing the heavenly exaltation in Luke 9:51, Luke removes the political associations in the tradition that he is using.[20] Jesus' destination is still Jerusalem, but he will receive a heavenly exaltation, not an earthly kingdom.

Jesus proceeds in the spirit of Moses and Elijah but in a refined, nonapocalyptical, nonaggressive view. Thus the solemn journey to Jerusalem begins with an explicit and active denial of the *lex talionis* (law of retaliation; Exod. 21:23–25), which we find in 2 Kings and in the *Assumption of Moses*. The supercession or reversal of the *lex talionis* will be elaborated in Jesus' teaching, especially in the parables during this journey. This is especially pertinent to the subject of nonviolence.

The whole passage is an antithesis to the entire history of the relationship between Jews and Samaritans, especially in the first century C.E., and in particular to the notorious episode in 51 C.E. at the village of Ginae.

Most significantly, the whole pericope is a challenge to the Lukan church, which may well have had vivid reminiscences of the governorship of Cumanus and the year-long struggle with the Samaritans. After Quadratus had dampened the conflict between the Samaritans and the Jews, he went to Antioch (*B.J.* 2:224). Luke was probably in communication with the Christians at Antioch and may have been accurately informed about Cumanus's actions.

We might also mention a theory of A.R.C. Leaney.[21] He notes Luke's reference to the days of the Son of Man (Luke 17:26). He proposes that these days are: the transfiguration, the resurrection, the ascension, and the parousia (second coming). In the account of the first three, Luke has the identical phrase: "behold, two men." The two men at the transfiguration are Moses and Elijah. Leaney suggests that they also appeared at the resurrection and the ascension, and will appear at the parousia. This thesis would explain why Luke has a Moses-Elijah motif running through his Gospel. However, his Jesus surpasses both these men by his explosive teaching on nonviolence and kindness toward enemies.

The Good Samaritan (Luke 10:25–37)

All Luke's Samaritan texts are placed within the central section of his Gospel. As Enslin notes, Mark gives no reference to the Samaritans or Samaria, and Matthew has only the prohibition (Matt. 10:5).[22] The rest of the New Testament, except for Acts and John 4, does not mention Samaria. Luke's incidents are highly significant for his purpose in Luke-Acts—namely, to show that the Samaritan mission was the beginning of the gentile mission and was part of the divine plan.[23] Enslin notes that the pericope discussed above stands at the beginning of the journey to Jerusalem with its accompanying ministry. It is parallel to the rejection at Nazareth, which stands at the commencement of the Galilean ministry. There is an Elijah motif in both. He finds a verbal affinity between this pericope and the Septuagint reading of 2 (4) Kings 1:10–12. He proposes that it is "intended as a deliberate and conscious answer to Matthew 10:5." It is an anticipation of the mission of the seventy, which is also in the central section and is "a deliberative counterfoil to the sending of the Twelve in Galilee."

The important and provocative pericope about the good Samaritan follows the mission of the seventy (seventy-two), a mission that symbolizes the evangelization of all the nations of the world (counted as seventy in antiquity). The good Samaritan pericope in Luke introduces the theology of the mission to the gentiles. It does so in Acts 8. A mission to the gentiles would have been totally unacceptable to most revolutionaries.

The pericope of the good Samaritan may be compared to Mark 12:28–34 and Matthew 22:23–40, which concern the two precepts of charity, but the parable is typically Lukan. The question asked by the lawyer—"Who is my neighbor?"—was one that arose in rabbinical circles. The discussion was far from frivolous. Orthodox Jews—for example, the members of Qumran and the strict pharisees—could seriously question whether those who did not observe the law meticulously were actually "brothers" ("sisters") or "neighbors." Thus it is understandable why the lawyer set out to test Jesus (v. 25). It should also be obvious why only Luke extends the incident to include the Samaritan story. Even "liberal" Jews might not have countenanced Samaritans as neighbors.

Luke appears to have produced a parable from narrative material found in Mark, just as he used the story of the woman who anointed Jesus, and appended to it the parable of the two debtors (Luke 7:36–50). We can, however, ask whether this pericope does actually contain a parable. There is no mention of the parabolic term as elsewhere in Luke—for example, Luke 12:16 and 15:3. In the light of the whole phenomenon of brigandage described above and the incident at Ginae (Gema), it is very possible that the story is a real incident or that there had been numerous incidents similar to what is described here. In view of the historical events, I maintain that Jesus relates or builds upon a genuine happening. For robbers on that road, see Josephus (*B.J.* 4:475).

We must notice, too, that Luke is not only dealing with Samaritans but also with "robbers" (*lestai*), Josephus's words for revolutionaries. Thus the teaching is doubly pertinent vis-á-vis the Jewish-Roman war. It teaches compassion for those who were attacked by revolutionaries—for example, the *sicarii*. It demonstrates that a hated foreigner, a Samaritan, can be compassionate. It is contrary to Josephus's repeated statements that the Samaritans took sides with the Jews when they prospered and disowned them when they were in trouble.

I. H. Marshall thinks the lawyer may have chosen the phrase "the one who showed mercy" to avoid actually naming the despised Samaritan.[24] By his answer, the lawyer shows that being neighborly means showing mercy. Implicitly he seems to deem racial considerations to be irrelevant. Jews were forbidden to receive works of love from non-Jews.[25]

In this Lukan pericope both the giving and receiving of mercy transcend national and racial barriers. With authority Jesus commands the lawyer to go away and begin to emulate the Samaritan's example.

Sellin also believes we are dealing with a real event. He thinks that the story may show an anticlerical thrust.[26] In 1882 Halevy tried to argue that the Samaritan was an addition to the text because the relationship between the Jews and the Samaritans was so hostile.[27] Montefiore argues that the original series would be priest, Levite, and Israelite.[28] He thinks that the reference to the Samaritans destroys the logical order. Linnemann observes that priests were not in good standing in the time of Jesus.[29] This is well known from the class conflict of the first century (see chap. 1). She argues that the priest and the Levite might be chosen because they represent Israel, but it was the Pharisees who represented the people rather than the priests. Sellin argues that both opinions are right if one considers not only the time of Jesus but also the time of Luke.[30] He thinks that the point of the parable rests on a contrast between the Samaritan and the Jew.[31] However, I should add that this does not preclude an anticlerical touch. Jesus is claiming that the Samaritan was more of a neighbor to the Jew than were his own priests and Levites.

It is striking that Luke places this narrative as an answer to the lawyer who asks how he will inherit eternal life. C. F. Evans sees Luke 10:25–27, the lawyer's question and Jesus' answer, in the context of the Shema (Deut. 6:5) and Leviticus 19:18.[32] This is followed by Moses' exhortation to the Israelites to have complete devotion to God so that they may inherit the land (Deut. 6:18) and so that they may live (Deut. 6:24). Evans sees the narrative about the good Samaritan (Luke 10:29–37) in contrast to Deuteronomy 7, which commands Israel to destroy the foreigner and to have no mercy on him (Deut. 7:22), "lest he corrupt you from the true worship of the one God. If you do this the Lord will keep you from all evils, and will lay them on those who hate you" (Deut. 7:15). This seems to enhance the importance of the pericope considerably.

J.D.M. Derrett points out that it may be highly meaningful that the Samaritan pours oil and wine into the wounds of the Jew.[33] No Jew was permitted to purchase or use oil and wine obtained from Samaritans; such products were considered nonkosher. We now know, according to the Temple Scroll, that there was a special feast for new wine held on the Jewish feast of weeks, or Pentecost, and also a feast of new oil.[34]

Sellin, as well as Evans, thinks that the "parable" should be considered from an ethnological, not an ethical and christological, point of view.[35]

G.V. Jones states, "The parable is not a pleasant tale about the traveler who did his good deed: it is a damning indictment of social, racial, and religious superiority."[36] Crossan sees the focal point of the story to be not only just or good deeds but the "*goodness* of the *Samaritan*."[37] The story challenges the hearer to place together two incompatible words: "Samaritan" and "neighbor." The whole thrust of the story demands that the hearer say what cannot be said: "good Samaritan." "The original parabolic point was the arrival of the kingdom of God upon the hearers in and through the challenge to utter the unspeakable and to admit thereby another world which was at the very moment placing their own under radical judgment."

Thus Luke's narrative of the good Samaritan marks a significant, highly provocative, and novel step in the mission of Jesus. Luke's teaching, which commands a new attitude to the Samaritans, must have been something that the early Christians found difficult to embrace. In the light of the Cumanus incident preceding the war, the narrative dramatically illustrates Jesus' command to love one's enemies and to do good to them. Indeed, the whole incident illustrates Jesus' teaching in the sermon on the plain (Luke 6:27–49), which gives clear instruction about his followers' duty toward their enemies.

The Samaritan Leper (Luke 17:11–19)

The curing of the ten lepers, one of whom was a Samaritan, was another incident that occurred as Jesus was traveling to Jerusalem between Samaria and Galilee. If Luke has redacted the healing of the leper reported in Matthew 8:1–4 and Mark 1:40–45 (but see Luke 5:12–16), then his addition of the Samaritan is very striking.

Jesus' command to the lepers to show themselves to the priests is remarkable when compared to the healing of the leper in Mark 1, Matthew 8, and Luke 5 (see above). In these texts Jesus bids the leper to report to the priest but also to offer the prescribed sacrifice, which, presumably, would take place in the Temple. In Luke 17:11–19 there is no mention of the sacrifice. We may ask whether this was out of courtesy and sympathy for the one Samaritan. His temple had been brutally destroyed by the Jew, Hyrcanus, in 129 B.C.E. Therefore, he could not offer sacrifice. His nine companions go to Jerusalem to Herod's temple. The Samaritan returns to give thanks before the new temple, Jesus. This pericope, therefore, shows some affinity to John 4:1–42 (the only other pro-Samaritan passage in another canonical gospel): "But the hour is coming, and now is, when the true worshipers will worship the Father in spirit and truth, for such the Father seeks to worship him" (John 4:23). For Luke the grateful Samaritan leper is one of the true worshipers.

A Pro-Samaritan Prediction of Jesus (Luke 23:30)

The pericope about the wailing women will be discussed in chapter 8, below, but it is appropriate to add one note here. When Jesus speaks to the women who mourn his suffering and death, he predicts suffering for Jerusalem. However, his words have a more poignant echo vis-à-vis Jewish and Samaritan hostility and especially the brutal and complete destruction of Samaria by John Hyrcanus or even by the Assyrians in the eighth century B.C.E. Jesus' words are based on a quotation from the Septuagint of Hosea 10:8, which is found in essence in the Hebrew text:

> Samaria's king shall perish, like a chip on the face of the waters. The high places of Aven, the sin of Israel [the Northern Kingdom], shall be destroyed. Thorn and thistle shall grow up on their altars; and they shall say to the mountains, Cover us, and to the hills, Fall upon us [10:7–8].

The quotation suggests that the Samaritans wish to escape tribulation by hiding in the caves of the hills and mountains, or they wish an earthquake to destroy them so that their suffering will be ended. For our purpose it is sufficient to note that Jesus boldly accommodates a text predicting the fall of Samaria and uses it against Jerusalem! It does not seem to be a question of retaliation but rather a warning that the purebred Jew may suffer a fate similar to that of Samaria in the days of the Assyrians. Repentance is necessary for all, regardless of race.

Luke brings his Samaritan theology to a close in Acts 8 where he records the conversion of the Samaritans and their reception of the Holy Spirit through the Jerusalem apostles. The unique aspect of this text is that the Holy Spirit is not given with the reception of baptism. It is perhaps best to explain this in the words of F. D. Bruner:

> It was evidently not the divine plan, according to Luke's understanding, that the first church outside Jerusalem should arise entirely without apostolic contact. . . . The Samaritans were not left to become an isolated sect with no bonds of union with the apostolic church in Jerusalem. If a Samaritan church and a Jewish church had arisen independently, side by side, without the dramatic removal of the ancient and bitter barriers of prejudice between the two, particularly at the level of ultimate authority, the young church of God would have been in schism from the very inception of its mission.[38]

Luke, as historian and theologian, understood perfectly the momentous innovation involved in accepting "heathen" enemies into the covenant of baptism.

Chapter 7

DISCIPLESHIP AND PACIFISM

This chapter discusses some aspects of wealth and poverty, of discipleship, and of Jesus' teaching against vengeance. The material should be read in the light of the social, economic, and political situation of first-century Palestine as sketched in chapter 1. The discussion here is confined to material peculiar to Luke unless Lukan redaction of Mark or Q shows obvious nonviolent polemic.

The Parable of the Rich Fool (Luke 12:13–21)

This parable, found only in Luke, appears to interrupt Jesus' teaching on fearless confession, which is addressed to his disciples. However, it touches on important aspects of discipleship: there should be no covetous desire in a disciple and it is impossible to foresee the future or forestall sudden death. The man in the parable is so concerned about material comfort that he fails to consider eternal happiness. The parable is followed by Jesus' teaching on care and anxiety (Luke 12:22–34; cf. Matt. 6:19–21, 25–33). It is a Lukan gem surrounded by material from Q.

The parable must not be divorced from the request that prompts it. A man in the crowd says to Jesus, "Teacher, bid my brother divide the inheritance (possession or property, *kleronomia*) with me." He is concerned about family inheritance, probably of considerable size. Among both the Maccabees and certain revolutionaries there was a quasi-dynasty in effect and possessions passed from father to son. For example, Hezekiah, the chief "brigand," was succeeded by Judas the Galilean, and after him two sons, crucified by the Roman procurator Tiberius Alexander (46–48 C.E.); then arose another son, or grandson, Menahem, who played a leading part in the early days of the revolt of 66 C.E.; and the leader of the *sicarii* at Masada, in 74 C.E., Eleazar, was also a descendant of Judas the Galilean. Josephus reports that Judas aspired to royalty and wealth:

This Judas got a large band of desperate men at Sepphoris in Galilee and there made an assault on the royal palace, and having seized all the arms that were stored there, he armed every single one of his men and *made off with all the property* that had been seized there. He became an object of terror to all men by *plundering those he came across in his desire for great possessions and his ambition for royal rank (epithumia meizōn pragmatōn kai zelosei basileiou tenes)*, a prize that he expected to attain not through the practice of virtue but through excessive ill-treatment of others [*Ant.* 17:271–72; italics added].

Even allowing for Josephus's prejudice, we might surmise that there was some truth in his statement that Judas aspired after riches and kingship. Hengel[1] thinks that perhaps Eleazar and Menahem had originally thought of a double sovereignty, one that would combine the priesthood and the kingship, as we find among the Qumran community and during the Bar Kochba revolt. Brandon suggests that there may have been a dynastic structure to the Jerusalem church first led by James, the brother of the Lord, and then by Symeon, another relative of Jesus, "a cousin of the Savior" (Eusebius, *H.E.* 3:11).[2]

Did the early church writers fear that, just as the Maccabean revolt, which had begun as a purely religious movement, eventually developed into a priestly and wealthy "monarchy," and as the many revolutionaries also fell prey to this temptation, so might the church? We cannot assume that all primitive Christians were nonviolent or poor. In fact, the reiterated teaching against abuse of wealth (and also ambition and rivalry) in a multitude of passages in the New Testament would seem to indicate that these vices were problems.

This might be the reason why only Luke relates the parable of the rich fool, including the Q material on God's providence and a certain indifference to material needs (Luke 12:22–31; cf. Matt. 6:19–21, 25–33). Then he follows this teaching with three verses peculiar to himself (Luke 12:32–34), telling the disciples that *their father* will give them the *kingdom* (cf. the *basileia*, kingship, in the Josephus quotation above) and that they are to sell their possessions and provide themselves treasure in heaven. In other words, he emphasizes a spiritual kingdom and heavenly treasure, in contrast to the aspirations of the later Maccabees, the Hasmoneans, the Herodians and the Romans themselves.

The section is completed by the pericope in verses 35–38, again found only in Luke. This passage, which concerns the householder and the thief, seems to introduce a different subject altogether, but it does not. "House" is a synonym for dynasty and "thief" can apply to illegitimate leaders of the community (John 10:1). However, what is of interest in the Lukan pericope is not so much the theme of watching and waiting for the master but the fact that the master girds himself and makes the servants sit down at the table and comes to serve them.

It seems to me that this pericope and the washing of the feet in John (13:3–17) is in direct contrast to the Baptist's idea of "He That Cometh" whose sandals the Baptist is not worthy to carry. Luke's "He That Cometh" is *himself* a servant. However, John goes beyond Luke and records that Jesus washed his disciples' feet.[3] In antiquity clothing was a manifestation, or even an extension, of one's personality. Hence Jesus' teaching and action is highly challenging. The concept of the Son of Man serving others, as depicted here and in John 13, must have been astonishing, almost unbelievable, to the disciples. They would be accustomed to think of a Son of Man (v. 40) as he is described in Daniel 7:13f.:

> . . . and behold, with the clouds of heaven
> there came one like a son of man,
> and he came to the Ancient of Days [God]
> and was presented before him.
> And to him was given dominion
> and glory and kingdom,
> *that all peoples, nations, and languages*
> *should serve him* [italics added].

The Son of Man, according to Jesus, came not to be served but to serve (Matt. 20:28; Mark 10:45; Luke 22:24–27). This is in direct contrast to politico-religious leaders at the time of Jesus and the Lukan church.

Thus in the parable of the rich fool, in the statement that God will give the disciples a kingdom, and in the teaching that the Son of Man will conduct himself like a servant, Luke clearly demonstrates that the disciples must not aspire after wealth and prestigious positions, as did Maccabees, the Hasmoneans, and some of the revolutionaries. These pericopes form part of Luke's answer to the social, political, and economic problems in Palestine at the time of the writing of his Gospel, although they do not have a particular historical event behind them.

The Galileans Killed by Pilate, the Persons Killed by a Falling Tower, and the Parable of the Fig Tree (Luke 13:1–9)

Jesus' audience expects him to react to the news about the slaughtered Galileans with indignation, or with a statement that death was due to sin, but Jesus' attitude is one of nonviolence and he teaches that all should repent.

The Galileans appear to have been killed at the feast of the passover, for they were preparing their own offerings. Blinzler suggests several occasions that may have been the one in question.[4]

(1) The episode may be one mentioned by Josephus (*B.J.* 2:169–74; cf. *Ant.* 18:55–59). Under cover of darkness, Pilate brought into Jerusalem standards that bore the effigy of Caesar. When daylight came, the Jews, both in the city and in the country, were in consternation. They went to Pilate at Caesarea to ask him to remove the standards. They prostrated themselves before him for five days. On the sixth day he took his seat in the stadium, surrounded the Jews with troops, and would have killed them. They "extended their necks" and volunteered to die for their laws. Pilate was over-

come by their zeal and ordered the removal of the standards. This occurred about 26 C.E. However, this incident did not occur in the Temple and there was no slaughter.

(2) Luke 13:1-3 might refer to an attack by Pilate on some Samaritans (*Ant.* 18:85-87). A "false prophet" told the Samaritans that he would reveal to them the sacred vessels hidden on Mount Gerizim. Many assembled to ascend the mountain but Pilate cut them down with cavalry and heavily armed infantry. He was sent to Rome by Vitellius to answer for this incident. This occurred in 36 C.E. However, it involved Samaritans, not Jews (Galileans).

(3) Archelaus, Herod's son, went to Rome to have his claim of kingship confirmed by Caesar. After the mourning for his father, a number of Jews organized mourning for the Jews who had taken down the golden eagle placed by Herod at the gate of the Temple. Herod had massacred them (*B.J.* 2:648-55). Archelaus was exasperated by this demonstration but attempted to appease the Jews. At the feast of passover the mourners attempted to gain recruits and distributed food to the people. Archelaus's troops were sent but they were stoned and the crowd returned to the sacrifices. Archelaus then sent his whole army and slew about three thousand while they were engaged in the ceremonies. (*Ant.* 17:206-18 gives a more detailed account.)

Luke may have confused Pilate and Archelaus, but the incident is consistent with what we know of the character of Pilate. He may have perpetrated a slaughter similar to the one perpetrated by Archelaus. There is, however, no confirmation of it in secular sources.

C. B. Caird associates this incident, the following one, and the parable of the fig tree with the mission of Jesus:

> In the mounting hostility to his own mission, in the strange relations between Jew and Gentile, in frequent outbreaks of patriotic frenzy, and in the growing severity with which these outbreaks were repressed, Jesus read the signs of the times, which he believed to be equally legible to others. . . . The urgency of the need is brought out in the three paragraphs which follow. . . . The victims of the tragedy, whether it is due to the vindictive severity of Pilate or to unforeseeable accident, must not be regarded as outstanding sinners especially singled out for divine retribution, but provide nevertheless a reminder that the whole nation is heading for more comprehensive disaster. Like the unfruitful fig tree which is given one last chance to respond to special treatment, Israel must use the respite which God in his mercy has given her to bring about a national reformation, or to find that there is a limit to the divine forbearance.[5]

It is not clear why Jesus was informed about this Galilean event. But it would seem that the informants expected him either to side with the Galileans or speak against the Roman authorities, or they expected him to do both.

Jesus, however, takes a pacifist attitude and turns the occasion into one for an exhortation to general repentance. The same impartial judgment awaits Jews and gentiles alike. But it is very important for our study that only Luke records this incident. He is anxious to resolve any problems concerning Jesus' political stance and to show his nonviolent attitude.

Jesus confirms his point by citing the example of the eighteen persons who were killed when a tower fell. Siloam was a reservoir supplying water from Gihon to Jerusalem (Isa. 8:6; John 9:7, 11). The tower may have been part of the fortifications.

The accident may be associated with the building of an aqueduct by Pilate (*B.J.* 2:175–77; *Ant.* 18:60–62). Pilate financed it with sacred money known as *corbonas* (sacrifices). When the Jews protested, he ordered his soldiers to beat them with cudgels. Some died and some were trampled to death. The Jews were outraged because the money, which Jews from Palestine and the Diaspora contributed for these sacrifices, was used for secular purposes (See *Shek.* 3:2).

Jesus' point is that persons who suffer natural catastrophes are not greater sinners than others. All need repentance before the last judgment (or before the destruction of Jerusalem).

The parable of the fig tree (Luke 13:6–9) reinforces the theme of repentance. The fruit symbolizes the people of Israel, or perhaps the teachers of Israel. Fig trees bear fruit every year, but this one had produced nothing for three years.

Jeremias sees in this parable "one more respite for repentance . . . even as he [God] can again, in the last extremity, suspend the fulfilment of his holy will and shorten for the sake of his elect the time of Antichrist's power (Mark 13:20)."[6]

Jeremias also explains that the first three years' growth of the tree was sacred; the owner may take the fruit only in the fourth year. In the parable he comes in the sixth year and complains that the fig tree has been barren for three years plus the three that he was not allowed to use (Lev. 19:23). It was barren, yet it was taking nourishment from the ground. A fig tree does not usually need care; thus the gardener's offer was exceptional.

There is a somewhat similar and popular tale in the story of Ahiqar, where a tree that bears no fruit, even though it is planted near water, asks to be transplanted. The owner says, "When you stood by the water you bore no fruit; how then will you bear fruit if you stand in another place?" The owner refused the fig tree's request.

But Jesus' parable ends in an entirely different way, even though he may have known the other story. The request for more time is granted. Jeremias asks whether the gardener symbolizes Jesus, who obtains a reprieve from judgment upon Israel, barren for so long.

Another important aspect of the parable is that it is peculiar to Luke but it may be a redaction of Markan and Matthean material. Mark and Matthew report Jesus' cursing of the fig tree when he goes to Jerusalem to face his death. Such a destructive act would be disconsonant with the character of Luke's Gospel and it would be understandable if he had converted it into a parable with an optimistic outlook. Instead of cursing the tree, God gives it time for repentance.

Thus in Luke 13:1–9 there are three themes pertinent to repentance but also germane to the theme of nonviolence. Jesus urges his hearers not to think in terms of vengeance because of Pilate's (or Archelaus's) treatment of the Galileans; not to consider those who suffer natural catastrophes greater sinners than themselves; and, finally, to imitate the forbearance of God symbolized by the gardener in the parable of the fig tree. Most importantly, however, one must notice that Jesus shows no sign whatsoever of hatred or vengeance when he is told of Pilate's cruelty to his compatriots. Once again all this teaching strikes at the root of religious fanaticism, such as we find in the first century, which was ready to punish sinners, speedily and without mercy, and take revenge on their sins.

Table Etiquette (Luke 14:1–14)

The parable about table etiquette (vv. 7–11) is inserted within the mention of Jesus' meal with one of the leaders of the Pharisees (v. 1), the healing of the person with edema (vv. 2–6), and Jesus' teaching on table etiquette (vv. 12–14). We note that the meal is attended by leaders and doctors of the law. It is probably a meal after a synagogue service, perhaps even in Jerusalem, or a meal modeled on the Greek symposium—a dinner with extended academic debate. Recall that some of the leading revolutionaries were sophists or doctors of the law (e.g., Judas the Galilean) as were the Maccabean leaders, Judas and Matthias.

It seems both impolitic and impolite for Jesus to criticize his fellow guests. Perhaps, however, we are not to think of a private dinner party but of a confraternity-type dinner, at which there would probably be edifying conversation or teaching (akin to the Greek symposium).

The advice Jesus gives in the parable (vv. 7–14) is contrary to the regulations in the *Rule of the Community* from Qumran:

This is the rule for an assembly of the Many. Let each man sit according to his rank! Let the priests sit in the first [place], and the elders in the second, and then the rest of all the people; let them sit according to their ranks [1 *QS* 6:8–9].

Jerome Murphy-O'Connor has shown how the Qumran community lost its flexibility and became disciplinary and hierarchical.[7] The revolutionaries, too, were concerned with rank. The parable is told, not only to teach social etiquette (cf. Prov. 25:6–7), but to inculcate a spiritual truth: recognition evades those who seek it.

Jesus' teaching about the choice of guests is also contrary to prevailing norms. Biblical law (e.g., Deut. 14:28; 16:11, 14; 26:11f.) provides for the alien, the orphan, and the widow, but does not include the handicapped. In 2 Samuel 5:8 the blind and the lame are mentioned as enemies of David; at Qumran the handicapped are not allowed in the assembly (1 *QSa* 2:10). The excluded comprise those in ritual impurity, those with physical diseases, those paralyzed in their feet or hands, the lame, the blind, the deaf, the dumb, those with a blemish (perhaps lepers), and aged persons who totter. All these may not enter the community. If they have anything to say, they are questioned privately. The reason for their exclusion is that the angels of God are in the assembly and a handicapped condition would bring ritual impurity with it.[8]

Thus Jesus' teaching corrects the strict, inflexible religious teaching that held that disease was due to sin and, therefore, excluded the handicapped. Jesus not only includes such persons but invites them to an important banquet (*doche*, the same word used of Levi's banquet in Luke 5).

How this teaching is germane to nonviolence will be seen in the next section.

The Great Supper (Luke 14:15–24)

This parable is found also in Matthew 22:1–14 and in the *Gospel of Thomas* 64. The Lukan and Thomas versions are shorter and may reflect the original story more closely.

The story is best explained in conjunction with a similar tale that Jesus may have known. A rich tax collector, Bar Ma'jan, died and was given a lavish funeral. A poor scholar also died, but no one attended his funeral. When an explanation was demanded, it was said that although the tax collector had not lived a pious life, he did do one good deed just before his death. "He had arranged a banquet . . . for the city councillors . . . but they did not come. So he gave orders that the poor . . . should come and eat it, so that the food should not be wasted."[9] The invitations were refused by those who scorned the tax collector's way of life; thus the poor attended. It may be that Jesus did not scruple to use this story, originally about a tax collector, to illustrate both the anger and the mercy of God. Jeremias comments:

> The incredible seriousness of the conclusion could not be better expressed. We must picture to ourselves how Jesus' audience would smile at the description of the insolence with which the *parvenu* was treated, and of his consequent rage; we must imagine them breaking out into audible laughter at the depiction of the upper ten with scornful glances watching from their windows the curious stream of seedy guests moving toward the gaily bedecked custom-house. How shocked they must have been when Jesus, the master of the house, decisively declared, "The house is full, the number is complete, the last place is occupied; close the doors, none henceforth may be admitted."[10]

The parable of the great supper clearly concerns salvation—the rejection of the pious and the acceptance of the poor. It is complementary to Jesus' conduct in dining with tax collectors and sinners.

However, more germane to our subject of nonviolence are the following points. If Luke is using a source that he shared with Matthew, he has removed violent features and introduced a novel, oblique, but meaningful reference to the concept of holy war.

Luke omits certain violent features. He does not make the host a warlike king (Matt. 22:2). He omits, too, the brutal behavior of the servants (Matt. 22:6). Although he describes the host as angry (Luke 14:21; cf. Matt. 22:7), he does not say that he sent his troops to destroy the murderers and burn their city (Matt. 22:7). Further, he does not report the incident of the man without a wedding garment and his being cast into outer darkness (Matt. 22:11–14). If Luke is writing against an apocalyptic, revolutionary background, these omissions are perfectly understandable: Luke's Jesus is not to be associated with violence and retribution.

Moreover, Luke's additions are significant. The context of the Lukan parable is different. Matthew's comes after the parable of the wicked tenants. Luke's comes after Jesus' lament over Jerusalem and his prediction that its house will be taken away (Luke 13:34–35). Further, as Caird remarks, the parable is "called forth by a remark of conventional piety from one of Jesus' fellow guests: 'Blessed are those who are entitled to attend the great banquet of the kingdom of God.' "[11] This is found only in Luke (v. 15). Behind this statement may lie the Jewish concept of a great feast to be held when the messianic kingdom is established on earth. Such ideology is reflected in the idea of the millennium, the messianic earthly kingdom, found in Jewish literature and in Revelation 20:4–10. Its inauguration is usually pictured as following a battle.

Further, the excuses offered by the guests in Luke resemble the dispensations given to certain men in the event of war. In Deuteronomy 20:5–9 the officers of the Hebrew troops are required to say to the people:

> What man is there that has built a new house and has not dedicated it? Let him go back to his house, lest he die in the battle and another man dedicate it. And what man is there that has planted a vineyard and has not enjoyed its fruit? Let him go back to his house, lest he die in the battle and another enjoy its fruit. And what man is there that has betrothed a wife and has not taken her? Let him go back to his house, lest he die in the battle and another man take her.

The officers then tell the fearful and fainthearted to return home.

It is interesting to note that these regulations were implemented under the Maccabees:

> And he [Judas] said to those who were building houses, or who were betrothed, or who were planting vineyards, or who were fainthearted,

that each should return to his home, according to the law [1 Macc. 3:56].

The Mishnah (*Sotah* 8:1–7) is more explicit. It extends the biblical dispensations by stating specifically what kind of houses or "barns" are included; that planting five trees is sufficient for exemption; marriage with either virgins or with widows qualifies one for exemption. Those who return home provide water and food and repair the roads. From the Mishnah it would seem, therefore, that the biblical law could be extended or modified. Comparison of the biblical text with the Mishnah makes it less surprising that Luke's parable refers to some excuses not found in the biblical text, such as purchasing a field and five yoke of oxen (note the number "five").

The *Gospel of Thomas* gives additional excuses: "I have money to collect from merchants"; "I have bought a house and it needs a day's attention"; "My friend will marry and I must take care of the feast."

The most interesting point the Mishnah adds is the following:

What has been said applies to a battle waged of free choice; but in a battle waged in a religious cause all go forth, even the bridegroom out of his chamber and the bride out of her bridechamber [*Sotah* 8:7].

The revolutionaries certainly regarded the war against Rome as a holy war.

The import of Jesus' words seems to be, "You waived these dispensations in your holy war but you offer them as excuses when an invitation to the (nonviolent) banquet of the kingdom of God is offered to you." In the parable Jesus suggests that the same urgency and waiver of dispensations associated with a holy war must be applied to the pursuit of the kingdom of God.

Luke, therefore, has "turned the tables" and used holy-war principles in the cause of the kingdom.

Further, the guests who take the place of those who were first invited may also be viewed in contrast to war regulations. For example, in the Qumran *War Scroll* we read:

And no lame man, no blind, nor crippled, nor having in his flesh some incurable blemish, nor smitten with any impurity in his flesh, none of these shall go out with them into war. They shall all be volunteers for the battle and shall be perfect in spirit and body and prepared for the Day of Vengeance [1 *QM* 7:4–6].

Here, too, Luke has reversed the principles of holy war in the interest of the kingdom.

When the servants go out the first time, they collect those who would be precluded from the Qumran community and from the holy war. When the servants go out the second time, they constrain those from the highways and hedges to come in. Edersheim observes that the first servant is told to go into the "(larger) streets and the (narrow) lanes of the city"; the scene is depicted in the city, "the professed habitation of God."[12] Thus it can be assumed, according to Edersheim, that the first guests were the chief citizens and that the lame and blind symbolize the publicans and sinners. But the second sending out of the servants is beyond the city—that is, "outside the theocracy," "to those who travel along the world's great highway, or who have fallen down weary, and rest by its hedges; into the busy, or else weary, heathen world." Thus this reference is to the heathen world and this is made clearer because the servants go into the hedges. There were no hedges around the fields of the Jews (*B.B.* 4a). Probably, these people from the world's highway have not heard of the master of the house and this is why the servants were obliged to urge them to enter. The revolutionaries and Pharisees would be extremely angry with the idea of the heathen entering the kingdom (but see Matt. 8:10–13 and parallels).

Thus, in the parable of the great banquet, Luke (1) omits the violent elements that were present, presumably, in Matthew or his source; (2) he takes the regulations for the holy war and makes them apply to the requirements of the gospel and the kingdom; and (3) he admits into the kingdom and to the banquet the handicapped, who were precluded from the holy war and from the Qumran community.

Demands of Discipleship (Luke 14:25–33)

Disciples must be ready to carry their cross for the sake of the kingdom. Here Luke does not qualify cross by "daily" as in Luke 9:23. The cross (crucifixion) was the fate that always threatened revolutionaries; two thousand were crucified near Jesus' home during his youth. Brandon even avers that "carrying one's cross" was a revolutionary slogan adopted by Christians.[13] It was, indeed, a destiny that was very real for anyone, man or woman, who rose up against the Romans.[14]

This saying is not peculiar to Luke but its insertion in this context is found only in Luke. The evangelist expressly states the alternative to holy war chosen by Jesus himself.

Jesus illustrates the seriousness of discipleship by two analogies: the person building the tower, and the king preparing to go into battle.

Purgos ("tower") can mean a farm building or even an extensive, ornate building. Josephus describes Phasael, one of Herod's towers (*B.J.* 5:168). It contained "sumptuous apartments including a bath, in order that nothing might be wanting to impart to this tower the appearance of a palace (*basileion*)." "Tower" could also have a military connotation and, most probably, it does so in this context. It would fit in better with the exhortation to renunciation, the carrying of the cross, and the king preparing for war. Jeremias quotes a parable in the *Gospel of Thomas* (98) that makes the same point as the ones about the tower and the king.[15] It "draws upon the stern reality of the Zealot movement":

Jesus said: "The Kingdom of the Father is like a man who wished to kill a powerful man. He drew a sword in his house and stuck it into the wall, in order to know whether his hand would carry through: then he slew the powerful man."

Someone who builds a tower must calculate the cost first, and the king who goes out to war must review his resources beforehand (Luke 14:28-33). Both analogies are peculiar to Luke. Towers were well known from the building projects of Herod. Josephus describes them in detail and especially alludes to their strength and their facilities, such as water supplies. He begins his description by saying that for "magnitude, beauty, and strength" they were without their equal in the world. It would be very probable that Jesus' audience would think of these towers when he used his analogy, for they were constructed within living memory. Herod's buildings proved to be a crushing financial burden to his subjects.

A famous public figure who was not able to pay his debts was Agrippa. If Luke has him in mind, it would, of course, be redaction on Luke's part: Agrippa I was tetrarch of Batanea and Galilee from 37 to 41 C.E. and king of Judea from 41 to 44 C.E.

The parable of the king preparing for battle has two probable backgrounds. Herod was defeated by the Nabateans in 32 B.C.E. (*Ant.* 15:108-20). But a more pertinent allusion might be found for those Jews (revolutionaries) who believed in divine providence. Does Jesus offer this example in the light of their overconfidence in the providence of God vis-à-vis the power of Rome? We note also Jesus' analogy of the king who had not enough resources; he should make peace with the enemy while that enemy is still a great way off (Luke 14:32). C. F. Evans compares the whole of Luke 14:15-35 with Deuteronomy 20.[16] If he is correct, then Jesus' words may be influenced by Deuteronomy 20:10-11, which advises the Israelites to offer peace to a city as they draw near to fight against it and also when they besiege a city "for a long time."

I suggest, therefore, that Jesus' analogies here are not offered purely for moral and spiritual counsel, but rather in the light of the political situation before and after the great war. If this is correct, it brings out an interesting feature of Jesus' political stance vis-à-vis the Roman war: he recommended nonresistance, to make peace with the enemy, the superior power, while it is far off. Did Jesus warn his people to make peace with Rome before it would be too late?[17]

The Parable of the Widow and the Judge (Luke 18:1-8)

This parable is placed after Jesus' teaching about the coming of the kingdom (Luke 17:20-37). It makes two points: persistence in prayer, and assurance that God will come to vindicate (avenge) the faithful. A parable about vindication seems to have been changed into one concerning prayer.

Delling suggests that the parable is directed toward Jews who were waiting for the Son of Man to come to vindicate them.[18] But he says that there is no evidence of such a group. However, we know that the revolutionaries had this hope. Even when the destruction of Jerusalem was imminent, they expected God to intervene on their behalf.

The faithful may have to wait a time for their vindication, but they should not think that their prayer goes unanswered. They should accept the fact that there may be a delay in the parousia. However, God will certainly vindicate them. This, perhaps, is the greatest contrast between the unjust judge and God. It is possible that Jesus told this parable in view of the revolutionaries, who were not prepared to wait but planned a holy war of retribution.

Thus, when seen in its historical context, instead of being a parable that teaches perseverance in prayer, it admonishes Jesus' audience not to take vengeance themselves but to leave that to God. This would be an important message for those who lived in the spirit of the Maccabees, for religious fanatics who followed the example of Phinehas, and for those who accepted the idea of holy war and vengeance.

Summary

In this chapter we see a number of "quietist" features in the Lukan Jesus. He will not retaliate with wrath when he hears that some of his compatriots have been slaughtered by Pilate, who has added sacrilege to violence by killing them as they offer sacrifice to God. He does not think that those who suffer from unforeseen accidents are worse sinners than other persons. He tells the parable of the fig tree as an illustration of God's mercy and love in allowing further time for repentance before the fall of Jerusalem. He counsels humility rather than ambitious craving after prestigious positions and rank. Luke has omitted the violent features from the parable of the great banquet and turned the theology of holy war into a theology of meeting the requirements of the gospel.

Jesus' demands of his disciples are as radical as those demanded of persons in military service. He will not exclude the handicapped. He teaches his followers not to take vengeance but to await God's vindication of their cause, and to pray unceasingly.

Chapter 8

THE PASSION AND DEATH
OF JESUS

The passion and death of Jesus are his final and decisive examples of non-violence. This is true of the passion account in all four Gospels. But in Luke and John, Jesus' nonresistance and heroic courage are painted with unusual poignancy. We also see the climax of Jesus' kindness to his enemies. My intention is to demonstrate the peculiar features of Luke's passion that reveal Jesus both as ideal martyr and as the Savior who terminates his life, as he began it, among those unloved and ostracized, to whom various kinds of hostility were shown. Jesus, as the evangelist shows, is completely innocent of revolutionary and violent tendencies, even for self-defense.

Luke may have possessed a special source for his passion, but even if he used Mark, he has radically redacted his material to bring out the unique characteristics of his theology.

In order to understand the special nonresistance features of Luke's passion it is necessary to contrast his account with those of Mark and Matthew. This will be presented at the beginning of each section that follows.

The Triumphal Entry (Luke 19:28–40; Mark 11:1–10; Matt. 21:1–9)

Luke's account of the triumphal entry into Jerusalem is quite close to that of Mark and Matthew.[1] Mark portrays Jesus as a triumphal figure, hailed by enthusiastic crowds who greet him, and he makes an explicit reference to the kingdom of David. Matthew is similar, although he adds a quotation from Zechariah 9:9, which, although alluding to a humble king, comes from a bellicose context. Zechariah 9:13b–14 reads:

I will brandish your sons, O Zion,
over your sons, O Greece,
and wield you like a warrior's sword.

108

Then the Lord will appear over them,
and his arrow go forth like lightning;
the Lord God will sound the trumpet [of battle],
and march forth in the whirlwinds of the south.

Although Matthew quotes only Zechariah 9:9, his readers would immediately recall the context. Matthew refers to the Son of David. Both Mark and Matthew mention branches spread before Jesus by the crowd.

Luke's account does reveal some significant differences from Mark and Matthew. First, Luke deliberately links the approach to Jerusalem with the expectation of the disciples expressed in Luke 19:11, "they supposed that the kingdom of God was to appear immediately." To correct this misapprehension Jesus told the parable of the pounds to emphasize that there would be a delay in the coming of the kingdom. The approach to Jerusalem is introduced with the words, "And when he had said this, he went on ahead, going up to Jerusalem." The parable was intended by Luke to mitigate enthusiastic expectations and avoid a political interpretation of what was to come.

Secondly, for Luke, Jesus is a king (v. 38) but with qualifications. Although the evangelist retains the description of the garments being spread before Jesus as he rides, it is not the crowds who do this but *only the disciples* in contrast to Mark and Matthew. Spreading garments symbolizes the right of a king to trample on his own property.

By excluding the crowd, Luke deemphasizes a general acclamation of Jesus as king. He is king only for his disciples.

Thirdly, Luke omits mention of the branches (Mark 11:8; Matt. 21:8). The reason for this becomes clear when one looks at John's Gospel. John says they were palm branches (John 12:13). Farmer points out that the Maccabean coins bore the image of a palm tree and were inscribed with the words "for the redemption of Israel."[2] Similar coins are found only between 66 and 70 C.E. and between 132 and 135 C.E., the revolutionary years. Palms were used in the triumphal procession when Judas rededicated the temple (2 Macc. 10:1–9). They were also employed by Simon Maccabee when he cleansed the citadel (1 Macc. 13:52). The rare word *baion* (palm) is found in 1 Maccabees 4:52–59 and in John's account of Jesus' entry into Jerusalem.[3] For John, Jesus may be following in the footsteps of the Maccabees. Luke omits the branches: they could be too closely associated with the warlike Maccabees.

Fourthly, Luke also avoids any reference to the "Son of David" (Matt. 21:9) or the "kingdom of our father David" (Mark 11:10). Recall how Luke reduces the importance of David in his genealogy of Jesus. For Luke, Jesus is not the Davidic king with the inevitable political connotations. Conzelmann observes that the entry into Jerusalem has lost all political significance because the "concept of the Davidic Lordship is replaced by the simple title of King, the nonpolitical sense of which is preserved (19:38)."[4] I should say "nonmilitary" rather than "nonpolitical." The regal acclamation of the disciples in Luke is simpler. Yet Luke does definitely designate Jesus as "the

King ("he" in Mark and Matthew) who comes in the name of the Lord."

Further, the acclamation in Luke's account echoes the phrase from the infancy narratives, "Peace in heaven and glory in the highest." Yet significantly, and in contrast to the shepherd pericope, this peace is in heaven, not on earth. Perhaps this is intentional: Luke knows the disastrous outcome of the 66–74 C.E. war, and that earthly peace was not gained.

Finally, Luke alone records that the Pharisees asked Jesus to rebuke his disciples and he alone records Jesus' reply. Jesus says that the very stones will cry out. Job 31:38 speaks of the land crying and its furrows weeping together. In Hebrew thought the land is personified and is affected by the good and evil doings of its inhabitants. It is especially affected by the conduct of or toward the king. It might be that the stones mentioned by Jesus would cry out against those who reject a peaceful king. Even inanimate nature is affected by the rejection or acceptance of the kingship of Jesus.

The Fate of Jerusalem (Luke 19:41–48)

Eduard Lohse remarks that according to Matthew 21:10–11 Jesus' arrival in Jerusalem caused great enthusiasm among the people and he was hailed as the prophet from Nazareth.[5] In Jerusalem he performed a number of physical healings and received homage and praise from children (Matt. 21:14–17). None of this appears in Luke. His Jesus is not proclaimed publicly. In place of an ebullient healing ministry, the Lukan Jesus gives a solemn warning of imminent judgment on Jerusalem and teaches quietly in the Temple.

An arresting nonviolent feature in Luke is seen in his omission of the cursing of the fig tree.[6] In the ancient world a curse was a dynamic, destructive act; it was greatly to be feared.

Instead of the cursing, Luke describes Jesus weeping or rather wailing over Jerusalem (Luke 19:41–48). In other words he is not the agent of destruction but one who shows deep sympathy. Nevertheless, the reader learns a similar message: Jerusalem (Israel) will be destroyed, not by divine curse, but by earthly enemies. The material may be pre-Lukan. It is partially dependent upon Jeremiah 6:6–20, which relates how Jerusalem's trees will be cut down; a siege will be laid; the city will be punished because there is oppression in it; there will be violence and destruction within it; it is warned that it may become a desolation, "an uninhabited land." All this happens because the Jews treat the Lord's word with scorn. Jesus, like Jeremiah (8:18ff. and 15:5), laments over Jerusalem; Jeremiah (cf. Jesus) preaches against resistance to the enemy. Jesus' lament is also influenced by Isaiah 29:1–4, which warns the people of Jerusalem that the city will be besieged. Thus Jesus' lament is well within the prophetic tradition. Jeremiah, especially, was a prophet of nonresistance.

In Luke 19:41–44 the words "peace" (v. 42) and "visitation" (v. 44) echo the infancy narratives (Luke 1:68, 78; 2:14, 19). But the concepts have undergone a radical change in the main part of the Gospel. "Peace" is acceptance of Jesus' message. "Visitation" by God brings *political disaster,* not political victory, for Israel.

Although Luke's description of the siege, the throwing up of a palisade, and the building of a stone siege dyke could be a general description of sieges in the ancient world, it is also akin to Josephus's account of the siege of Jerusalem in 70 C.E. (*B.J.* 5:264ff.). Trees were felled; the timber was used for the earthworks.[7] The Romans brought "quick-firers" (scorpions) and stone projectors and the "rocks which they hurled weighed a talent and had a range of two furlongs or more." Then battering rams were set round the city. Eventually, after protracted fighting on both sides, Titus determined to build a wall around Jerusalem (*B.J.* 5:499–510).

Luke further elaborates Jesus' prediction of the fall of Jerusalem in his redaction of the synoptic apocalypse (Luke 21:20–24; Mark 13:14–20; Matt. 24:15–22). It seems to me that in both descriptions Luke, in contrast to Matthew and Mark, speaks clearly about the destruction of Jerusalem by the Romans (vv. 20 and 24). What is interesting, however, is how Luke, and Luke alone, speaks of this catastrophe: "for these are days of vengeance (*ekdikēseōs*), to fulfil all that is written (v. 22)." In other words, the prediction is directly contrary to the nationalistic expectations of the infancy narratives (cf. the Magnificat). Vengeance or retribution does not come upon Israel's enemies but upon itself.

Luke 19:41–44 is the second lamentation over Jerusalem (cf. Luke 13:34–35). The third occurs as Jesus carries his cross (Luke 23:28–31).

Thus the triumphal entry according to Luke ends on a note of solemn and mournful warning rather than triumph. This is contrary to Matthew. Luke's message is not new; prophets (cf. First Isaiah and Jeremiah) counseled nonresistance to the enemy and predicted disaster if it were not implemented.

In summary, Luke has removed the triumphal aspect to the entry in the following ways. (1) The parable of the pounds begins to play down the political tone, and to deny that an earthly kingdom is to be established. (2) Luke softens enthusiasm by omitting that the crowds accompanied Jesus; only the disciples accompany him. (3) Jesus is king for the disciples, not for the crowds. (4) Luke omits the branches associated with royalty and with military victory. (5) He eschews the title "Son of David," which would denote a warrior king. (6) He records Jesus' reply to the Pharisees that the earth would protest if the disciples did not proclaim his (irenic) kingship. (7) Luke records Jesus' wailing over Jerusalem rather than cursing it.

The Cleansing of the Temple
(Luke 19:45–46; Mark 11:15–19; Matt. 21:12–13)

The cleansing of the Temple, especially as portrayed by John (2:13–17), has been the cause of controversy. It appears to be an act of violence. Indeed, in Mark and Matthew, Jesus drove out the merchants and the buyers and turned over the tables of those who exchanged foreign coins for Jewish currency. He also upset the seats of those who sold pigeons. In John, Jesus drove out the oxen and sheep with a whip and poured out the coins. The scene is one of complete pandemonium, the bullocks, sheep, and goats running wild, probably in full cry, birds flapping their wings and twittering and humans crying out, many in rage. Jesus acts like a zealot (John 2:17).

It is remarkable that Luke drastically abbreviates the whole episode. He merely reports that Jesus drove out only the merchants, not even the animals. There is no reference to buyers or to the overturning of tables or seats. There is no mention of Jesus' prohibiting anything from being carried through the Temple (Mark 11:16). Considering Luke's frequent affinity to John, his abbreviation of this episode is arresting. Unlike Mark (11:17), Luke does not mention that the Temple will be a house of prayer for all nations. Most probably he knew this would not be realized: the Temple must have fallen by the time he wrote his Gospel.

Thus Luke's account is very restrained. Jesus' action seems to be simply a prelude to his using the Temple as a place for teaching. The chief priests, scribes, and leading citizens sought to destroy him, implicitly because of his teaching (v. 47), not because of the cleansing of the Temple (cf. John's account). The reason for Luke's short account is clear and is consonant with the rest of his Gospel: his Jesus must not appear to be like a destructive zealot.

Jesus' Teaching in the Temple and the Role of the Pharisees (Luke 19:47-48 and 20:1-21:4)

Here the first two verses are an introduction to Jesus' teaching. I shall not give detailed examination to passages that are common to all the Gospels, but rather concentrate on what is peculiar to Luke and germane to the main subject of this book, nonviolence.

There is an important difference in Luke's Gospel. The Pharisees take no part in the passion. The last time they are mentioned is in Luke 20:1. Luke may be loath to implicate them because of Christian Pharisees in the Lukan church, or because of the Pharisaic academy at Jamnia whose leader, Johanan ben Zaccai, was an advocate of nonresistance.

Rhoads observes that many Pharisees were upset over Roman insensitivity to the observance of Jewish law, and they may have joined the revolt.[8] On the other hand, the Pharisaic house of Hillel "continued to urge the ways of peace and to warn the nation about the consequences of its revolutionary activity." However, as the war progressed, less heed was given to these exhortations for caution. Yet, in assessing the role of different sects during the actual time of the war, Rhoads argues that, on the whole, the Pharisees appear to have been moderates.[9] He notes that Pharisees were called, together with the chief priests and leading citizens, to dissuade the people from revolution (*B.J.* 2:411). Further, Josephus was in hiding during the civil war in Jerusalem, but he "ventured out of the Temple and once more consorted with the chief priests and the leading Pharisees'' (*Life* 21). Obviously, he was less afraid of terrorism from them. Moreover, there is the example of Simon ben Gamaliel, a Pharisee of the house of Hillel, who was a moderate and worked for peace (*Life* 192ff.).

Rhoads observes that "Yohanan ben Zakkai was typical of many later Pharisees who condemned the war as a consequence of 'baseless hatred.' ''[10] It was the Pharisaism of Yohanan ben Zakkai that survived the war and "became instrumental in shaping subsequent Judaism." Perhaps Luke thought he would be preaching to the converted if he directed his nonviolence polemic toward the Pharisees. However, he does criticize certain Pharisees, possibly those of the house of Shammai, who were of a stricter and more severe school (Luke 11:37–44).

The Last Supper and the Dispute about Greatness (Luke 22:24–30)

Luke has completely omitted from his Gospel the narrative of James and John's seeking places of honor near Jesus in his kingdom (Mark 10:35–45; Matt. 20:20–28). Yet some of that teaching is reflected in his account of the last supper.

The sons of Zebedee were attracted by political preeminence, to which many Jewish revolutionary pretenders and their followers aspired. It would seem that the family, or perhaps dynasty, descended from Hezekiah, the archbrigand, aspired to kingship for nearly a century (*B.J.* 1:204; *Ant.* 14:159–60). The best known aspirant of this family is Menahem, whose messianic claims were repudiated by other revolutionaries during the War (*B.J.* 2:442–48). He played the tyrant, was clad in royal robes, and was followed by a suite of armed fanatics (*B.J.* 2:442–48). Perhaps James and John wished for a similar leader in Jesus. The memory of Menahem would be ripe in the minds of the members of the Lukan church.

Although Luke would be reluctant to mention the incident concerning James and John, he wished to record Jesus' teaching on leadership as service. Therefore, he reports the dispute about greatness at the last supper. He has placed this and Jesus' response in a passover setting, which commemorated the Hebrew slaves' freedom from Egyptian oppression. Subsequently, the Hebrews received God's covenant on Sinai and accepted Yahweh as their only King and Lord. In the last meal in the preresurrection life of Jesus, Luke shows that a new covenant is made with the disciples and Jesus promises that they will share the eschatological banquet. Preparation for this is a life of humility and service, not of political and military leadership and rivalry.

The Two Swords (Luke 22:35–38)

This pericope is peculiar to Luke. Jesus advises his disciples to equip themselves with the requisites for a journey (contrast Luke 9:1–6 and 10:1–7). He also appears to advise them to purchase a sword. This passage deserves a fairly detailed examination.

Manson observes:

> This short dialogue throws a brilliant light on the tragedy of the minis-
> try. It goes with the Q lamentation over Jerusalem (Luke 13:34f.; Matt.
> 23:37–39); and, like that elegy, it is full of bitter disillusionment. The
> grim irony of verse 36 is the utterance of a broken heart.[11]

Whereas in the earthly ministry Jesus and his disciples could be dependent on the good will of the people, now they can be so no longer. For Conzelmann the Satan-free period is over. He proposes that in Luke Satan is presented as leaving Jesus after his temptation, "he departed until an opportune time" (Luke 4:13). He does not return until the time of the passion, when he enters into Judas Iscariot (Luke 22:3).

The disciples miss the irony; they think that Jesus means to defend himself against the growing hostility and, armed, they will join him and defend him. Manson believes that the saying in verse 36 is a "vivid pictorial way of describing the complete change which has come about in the temper and attitude of the Jewish people since the days of the disciples' mission."

Bartsch sees the counsel to buy a sword as absurd in the mouth of either Jesus or the evangelists.[12] He discusses Conzelmann's interpretation of the sword. It symbolizes the daily Christian fight against attacks, especially per-secution. It signifies a new way of life; the disciples are no longer under the protection of Jesus. The time of the church is contrasted with that of Jesus.

Bartsch discusses the literary origin of the pericope. He thinks it unlikely that the early Christian community placed this saying on the lips of Jesus, for in other respects it endeavored to keep Jesus dissassociated from the revolu-tionary movement. Rather the supposition that it was a genuine saying of Jesus is more likely. It would have been suppressed in the rest of the synoptic tradition to keep Jesus far away from any connection with the revolution-aries.[13] Bartsch deems it improbable that the whole pericope is from Luke. It is an apocalyptic saying in connection with the messianic eschatological war. Luke may have directed the statement toward Jewish-Christians at the time of the Jewish war. Some fled to Pella but some must have remained to partici-pate in the fighting. Jesus' words applied to the 66–74 C.E. war. He would expect Christians not to use violent means to resist the Romans.

Hahn adopts a metaphorical meaning.[14] He points out that several men would use one cloak to cover themselves at night and thus Jesus' suggestion of selling a cloak for a sword is symbolic of dire need, a threat to life itself. He does not see revolutionary traits in Jesus.

Minear seems to offer the most persuasive interpretation of the text under discussion.[15] He observes that Conzelmann refers to this text seventeen times. It is a pivotal text. He himself thinks that the "but now" (v. 36, *alla nun*) is very important. It does, indeed, point to a new period, just beginning. The disciples are now vulnerable to temptation. As is the case for so much important teaching in Luke, the logion is found in the context of a meal; in this instance the last supper. It contains the most important table talk within the Lukan meal settings. Minear draws attention to the fact that following the narrative about the last supper there are eighteen verses, which comprise four units:

(1) verses 21–23, the prophecy about the betrayal of Jesus by Judas, which occurs before the supper in Mark and Matthew, but afterward in Luke;

(2) verses 24–30, the dispute about greatness among the twelve;

(3) verses 31–34, the prediction that Satan will sift Peter;

(4) verses 35–38, the two-swords passage.

By rearranging his materials, placing them all at the last supper, and adding some of his own, Luke has amalgamated all four units.

When we read all these four, not stopping where Mark and Matthew do, a climax is reached in the prophetic disclosures of the last unit of material, the verses about the sword. Minear sees a threefold betrayal: by Judas, by the apostles, and by the soldiers. The disciples and Jesus' captors bear weapons; Jesus does not. Therefore, there is an implicit rebuke with regard to violence in Jesus' behavior and an explicit one in his words when he is captured (vv. 51–52). Minear proposes that the twofold use of the sword—by the disciples and by the captors—makes for a dual sword witness, which he sees as the power of darkness (v. 36).

The disciples' possession of the two swords is an act of disobedience. Minear would translate verse 38: "This is quite enough to fulfil the prophecy"—that is, that Jesus will be reckoned with transgressors (v. 37). For Minear transgressors are those who bear swords (weapons). The two swords reveal the disciples' treachery, of which they, including Peter, were ignorant. For this very reason the apostles are counted with transgressors.

For Minear the *alla nun* ("but now") of verse 36 does not point to the time of the church (Conzelmann) but to the garden scene.

Interpreting the pericope in this way, Minear sees certain common features in the meal pericopes (Luke 5:29f.; 7:36f.; 10:38f.; 11:37f.; 14:1f.; 22:1f.). In all these cases Luke has used a common tradition, but he has expanded it with largely didactic material. In all these pericopes, with the possible exception of 5:29f., Luke has rearranged the setting and adapted the teaching to the circumstances. In all the meals, the table is the scene of a controversy, and the table talk throws light on the means of salvation taught by Jesus; his teachings "collide with prevailing norms." Each occasion is used for training the disciples and should have prepared them for the passion. Implicitly these teachings pronounce "authoritative woes" upon those who are scandalized by his dining with sinners.

Minear's study seems to cast the most light on the difficult two-swords pericope and it has the advantage of drawing together climactic points in the Gospel. He has put together Jesus' first great banquet with toll collectors and others, his acceptance of a prostitute, his approval of a woman disciple, his critique of self-satisfied Pharisaism, his teaching on table etiquette and, particularly, his counsel to invite to a meal the handicapped, who were outcasts in society (Luke 14:12–14). All these passages reach their highest peak in the last supper with its covenant character. Jesus' teaching on this occasion has the maximum significance—namely, that *the members of violent resistance movements are to be numbered with transgressors.* For him these are the real transgressors, not tax collectors, "others," harlots, women disciples, and the handicapped. This is a sobering thought. It is a readjustment of values.

The purpose of this pericope is the conversion of violent revolutionaries. According to the Lukan theological pattern—word and then deed—this word of Jesus will be complemented by his conduct in the garden, his healing of the severed ear, his forgiveness of the criminal on the cross, and his acceptance of him into paradise "today" (cf. Luke 4:18–21).

Thus the two-swords passage is central to Luke's theology of the passion and to the understanding of Jesus' teaching on nonviolence and nonresistance. Jesus' teaching is dramatically implemented in the garden where the disciples finally learn that the eschatological war will not commence. There is no need for swords on the part of Jesus' friends or foes. Jesus' teaching at the last supper forms a climax to all his teachings that accompanied meals during his earthly life. It means that sword bearers are classified with transgressors. Jesus will implement his own teaching about nonresistance in the next scene, in the garden.

The two-swords passage prepares the reader for the trial of Jesus according to Luke. Here the evangelist is clearly concerned to demonstrate that Jesus is not a violent revolutionary.

Gethsemane (Luke 22:39–46; Matt. 26:30–46; Mark 14:26–42)

In Mark and Matthew Jesus and the eleven disciples sing a hymn, probably the Hallel (Ps. 113–118), and proceed to the Mount of Olives. Jesus predicts that the shepherd will be struck and the flock scattered; he warns the disciples that they will "all fall away." Peter declares that he will support him even unto death, but Jesus warns him that he will deny him three times. Peter repudiates this, and the other disciples give similar assurance.

Mark and Matthew report that they came to a place called Gethsemane. Jesus took aside with him Peter, James, and John. He was sorrowful and troubled and quoted scripture to that effect (Ps. 42:5–6). Three times he went apart from the disciples and three times prayed that the hour (cup) might pass from him. Returning to the disciples he rebukes them for sleeping. When he goes back to the disciples the last time, he announces that the hour has come and the Son of Man will be betrayed into the hands of sinners.

In Luke the account of Jesus' going to the garden is briefer and significantly altered. There is no quotation from Zechariah 13:7 about the shepherd being struck and the flock scattered. Jesus does not predict that the disciples will fall away, and the prediction of Peter's denial has been placed during the last supper. These changes may arise from Luke's desire to portray Jesus as poised and courageous; he is nonresistant but not stricken. He is the ideal martyr. Luke will show Peter and the disciples to be less vulnerable than in Mark and Matthew. At the last supper Jesus said that they had continued with him in his temptations (Luke 22:28, past perfect tense). This is demonstrated by the fact that they are more faithful than in Mark and Matthew.

In the garden Luke does not report that Jesus took Peter, James, and John aside with him. Jesus moves only "a stone's throw" from the eleven so that he is within sight and hearing of his companions, thus maintaining a propinquity not suggested by Mark and Matthew.

Jesus kneels rather than throws himself to the ground. More importantly, Luke does not record the quotation from Psalm 41:6 indicating Jesus' soul to be "very sorrowful even to death."

In Luke, Jesus prays only once, not three times. His prayer is more resigned to the divine will (v. 42). In Mark and Matthew Jesus makes a direct (not conditional) request to the Father to remove the cup (Mark 14:36, 39; cf. 41; Matt. 26:39; but cf. 42 and 44).

In Mark and Matthew Jesus' last words before his captors arrive are "the Son of man is betrayed into the hands of sinners . . . my betrayer is at hand." In Luke, Jesus' final words are more fitting for a pacifist. They are less condemnatory: "pray that you might not enter into temptation," perhaps the temptation to use weapons. These selfsame words are found at the beginning of Luke's garden scene (v. 40). They are still on Jesus' lips "when his passion breaks over him full tide in the approach of the crowd led by Judas to the arrest . . . (v. 47)."[16] Thus in the garden scene Luke portrays Jesus a poised figure in complete control of the situation. There is, however, one slight complication.

The Sweat of Blood

In many manuscripts verses 43–44 of Luke 22, about Jesus' agony, are omitted.[17] This "strongly suggests that they are not part of the original text of Luke."[18] Yet the fact that they are found in many texts and in early Christian writings is proof that the tradition is ancient. They seem to have been added by an early source, either oral or written. The editorial committee of the Greek New Testament prepared by the United Bible Society decided to retain them in the text.

Thus we are presented with what appears to be a contradictory portrayal of Jesus; he is poised yet he is in an agony. However, scholars cited by Feuillet have offered a solution.[19]

In verse 44 *agonia* ("agony") is peculiar to Luke.[20] This word is used very frequently in Greek literature with reference to athletes. "Agony" is an interior concentration that characterizes athletes about to begin their performance; they turn pale, tremble throughout their bodies, and perspire profusely. Thus, in these verses Jesus is perhaps depicted as a perfect athlete.

His prayer has some relevance to the needs experienced by athletes. The angel who comes to strengthen him plays a role analogous to that of the trainer of an athlete. Paul, the traveling companion of Luke, used imagery from the athletic world.

Feuillet says that these proposals seem attractive at first, but turn out to be rather exaggerated. However, I think that they may have been meaningful to Greek readers who would admire athletes. This explanation contributes substantially to the picture of Jesus as a heroic figure.

For Holleran this *agonia* is "the supreme concentration of powers in the face of imminent decisions or disaster."[21] The word "agony" embodies Jesus' "concern for victory in the face of the approaching decisive battle on which the fate of the world depends" (cf. Luke 12:49–50).

The phenomenon of sweating blood is found in the writings of Aristotle; the cause is violent and profound emotion.[22] It might be associated with the baptism of blood mentioned in Luke 12:49–50, or with the last supper (Luke 22:20), or with the blood from the side of Christ (John 19:34). The theological importance, however, is that for Luke the blood that redeems humankind begins to flow in the garden.[23] Holleran says that it is part of the theme of the portrayal of Jesus as ideal martyr.[24] Just as the blood in the eucharistic cup is a prelude to the blood shed on the cross in all the synoptics, so, in Luke, the sweat of blood is an anticipation of it.

Thus Luke's account of the agony (1) shows a more poised Jesus than in Mark and Matthew; (2) he undergoes emotions similar to those experienced by an athlete; (3) his redemptive blood begins to flow in the garden.

Jesus as Ideal Martyr

It has been observed that mainline Judaism commemorated the Maccabean and revolutionary martyrdoms rather than their military exploits. Luke speaks of Jesus in a similar vein. It is especially in Luke's Gospel that Jesus is portrayed as the ideal martyr. Feuillet compares Jesus in Luke's passion with Jewish martyrs in the following points:

(1) It is Satan who fights against the martyrs (*Mart. Isa.* 3:11 and Luke 22:53).

(2) Every martyr must expect a struggle; the Lukan account begins with the agony in the garden.

(3) There is the hope of help from heaven (2 Macc. 7:6; 3 Macc. 5:7–9; cf. Luke 22:43, although Luke omits Matthew's reference to twelve legions of angels).

(4) The apparition of a heavenly being usually gives succor (3 Macc. 6:18; Dan. 3:49; Luke 22:43).

(5) Political motifs play a role—for example, in apocryphal literature the Maccabees and Isaiah do not submit to the king's orders. Luke, more than Mark or Matthew, emphasizes the political motifs in the accusations against Jesus.

(6) The martyr announces the destiny of other persons (2 Macc. 7:14, 16, 18–19, 31–38; 4 Macc. 9:26–32). In Luke 23:28–31 are found the prophetic words of Jesus to the weeping women and on the cross his prediction of the salvation of the repentant "thief."

(7) The innocence of the martyrs is recognized and even their enemies admire them (2 Macc. 7:12; 4 Macc. 6:6; 17:16–17). Luke stresses the innocence of Jesus more emphatically than do Mark and Matthew (cf. Luke 23:4, 14, 15, 22).

Holleran also finds an affinity between the accounts of the Jewish and Christian martyrs and Jesus' struggle in the garden. The cup is common in martyrologies; so is the strengthening angel and the struggle in prayer.[25] He cites Aschermann who finds a parallel for sweat and blood in the martyrdom of the Maccabean Eleazar in 4 Maccabees (6:6, 11; 7:8). Aschermann claims that the use of these themes, together with the strengthening angel, reveals the intention of the author of these verses to depict the prayer-struggle of Jesus in the passion as possessing this martyrological character.[26]

Barbour makes an important point when he says the agony "is almost the only point at which the passion narrative has not altogether yielded to the overriding sense of predestination and fulfillment of the scripture; or, rather, in which that predestination is carried through by means of a recognizably human, responsible act against odds."[27]

Holleran observes: "At the very moment when he [Jesus] is humanly most anxious for deliverance, Jesus makes his appeal and his surrender to God's foreordaining purpose, negating in self-sacrifice [and] struggle any will of his own independent of that purpose."[28]

It would seem that the agony was complete by the time of the crucifixion. According to Barbour, in the garden rather than on the cross "we are witnessing the necessary unrolling of a heroic and tragic course of events which we well know will be canceled on Easter morning."[29] We can readily understand the acceptance of the Maccabees and the members of Qumran to die for the atonement of their land, but it "was another thing for Jesus, charged with that ultimate eschatological message, . . . to confront apparently total failure."

Most significantly, Luke has espoused the philosophy of the peaceloving Hillelites and the ideology of the rabbis in general in lauding and exulting the martyr over the warrior.

Above all, he has given all Christians the moral and spiritual example that they are to imitate when they embrace the philosophy of nonviolence and nonresistance. The next scene in Luke will show this philosophy put into practice.

Thus Luke's portrayal of Jesus in the garden is a pivotal scene. If verses 43–44 are to be retained, we see a unique struggle between the divine and human wills; the last great battle against Satan; a vivid representation of the ideal martyr, who overshadows the Maccabean martyrs as well as the revolutionaries following in the spirit of martyrdom. The garden is a prelude to the sacrifice on the cross, which will bring to a climax the picture of the ideal martyr.

Jesus' Arrest (Luke 22:47-53; Matt. 26:47-56; Mark 14:43-52)

Mark and Matthew begin the scene of the arrest by describing Judas with a crowd of persons armed with swords and clubs. They report Judas's instructions to capture the person whom he identifies with a kiss and (Mark) to "lead him away under guard." After the identification they lay hands on Jesus and seize him. One of the disciples retaliates and cuts off the ear of the servant of the high priest. Jesus reproaches the crowd for coming out to make an armed arrest of a revolutionary (robber). At this point all the disciples flee.

Once again Luke has either redacted his sources or used a special one. At the beginning of the scene he mentions only Jesus, not the armed crowd; he omits Judas's instructions and the violent seizure of Jesus: we hear that he is seized only in the next pericope (v. 54). By these changes Luke radically reduces the violence of the scene. We learn that the crowd has weapons only in verse 52. Luke does not state specifically that it was an armed arrest, only implicitly in the words of Jesus himself (v. 52). Taylor says that there is nothing in the passage to suggest "an armed band hostile to Jesus."[30]

These alterations seem to suggest that Luke wished to minimize, but not completely overlook, the idea of the crowd explicitly regarding Jesus as an armed revolutionary.

Luke does not elaborate on Judas's kiss; indeed, it is not clear whether he actually gave one or not. Taylor quotes Rehkopf who maintains that:

> . . . in Luke the kiss, the treachery, and the character of Judas himself appear in another light. In Mark Judas is the crafty, cold-blooded traitor who chooses the sign of affectionate greeting to effect the arrest; in Luke one thinks rather of a Judas who perhaps from a sudden anxiety and a still existent sense of awe is driven to the strange action of greeting Jesus with a kiss. The words of Jesus are not a warning or a reproach, but an expression of grief.[31]

Taylor adds, "His words . . . breathe the sadness of a deeply wounded love."[32] This is the second time that Luke has avoided explicitly condemning Judas (cf. Matt. 26:45-46; Mark 14:41-42). This is an important aspect of Luke's theology of the enemy (philo-echthrology).

Another important aspect of the Lukan account is that the disciples are the aggressive party. They ask Jesus whether they should strike with the sword and, without waiting for a reply, one of them cuts off the right ear of the priest's servant. In Mark, Jesus does not rebuke the disciple. In Matthew he says: "Put your sword back into its place; for all those who take with the sword will perish by the sword. Do you think that I cannot appeal to the Father, and he will at once send me more than twelve legions of angels?" (vv. 52-53). Luke has: "But Jesus said, 'No more of this!' " Jesus does not indicate that the Father has armed forces at his Son's disposal. A legion comprises about six thousand infantry and about the same number of auxiliary and cavalry troops plus technicians. Perhaps Luke does not wish this thought even to have entered Jesus' mind.

Of most importance is the fact that Luke, and Luke alone, reports that Jesus healed the ear of the servant of the high priest. This is significant because an insult to a servant was an affront to his or her master (see 2 Sam. 10:4f.; Mark 12:1ff.). In Luke it is the chief priests and their assistants who condemn Jesus. Thus this healing is a dramatic implementation of Jesus' precept to love one's enemies and to do good to those who hate one (Luke 6:27–28, 32–36). It is the climax of Jesus' nonviolent deportment in the garden. Indeed, both Jesus' words and actions show an active endeavor to avoid violent resistance and show love of the enemy.

As in the other synoptics Jesus rebukes the crowd for coming to capture him as if he were a revolutionary or armed bandit (lestēs, the word that Josephus uses so frequently for political rebels). Wilson remarks that Jesus' words have every mark of a genuine logion. He adds that in Luke the saying is recorded without any reference to scripture:

This very apt and pointed remark by Jesus at the crucial moment of his arrest would probably have been well remembered by his disciples. It was, in fact, probably the last words they heard from his lips before he was raised onto the cross. The fact that it is found in all three synoptic gospels, and in similar form in John, adds to our assurance. There can be little doubt that Jesus objected to his seizure as a teacher of violence and rebellion.[33]

Luke ends this pericope with Jesus' words: "But this is your hour and the power of darkness" (v. 53). These words are peculiar to Luke and imply that armed resistance belongs to the realm of supernatural evil (cf. Satan entering Judas at the beginning of the passion, Luke 22:3).

The Lukan account of the arrest, therefore, in contrast to Matthew and Mark, is noteworthy for the following points: (1) it is briefer and simplified; (2) the disciples are shown to be more volatile in that they retaliate before Jesus is seized; (3) Jesus, in word and action, is seen not only as nonviolent but as a healer of his enemy; (4) the narrative ends with words that strongly suggest that violent hostility is supernaturally inspired.

These points seem to decrease any emphasis on armed conflict and lessen the risk that readers might mistake Jesus for a revolutionary. The account would also imply that bearing arms is demonic.

Peter's Denial
(Luke 22:54–62; Mark 14:53–54, 66–72; Matt. 26:57–58, 69–75)

Although Peter is mentioned in Mark and Matthew as following Jesus at a distance after his arrest, Peter's denial of Jesus comes after the trial before the Sanhedrin. Luke has a different position for the denial: before Jesus' interrogation by the Jews. The change is important because in this way Peter's denial follows immediately upon Jesus' rebuke to his captors that they have come out to capture him as if he were a revolutionary. Thus, in Luke, the essence of Peter's denial is the repudiation that he himself was a revolutionary and, therefore, could be threatened with the punishment of crucifixion like his teacher.

According to Dietrich the Lukan narrative is more forensic; two men witness against Peter, and thus their testimony as males could be valid.[34]

If the maid and the two men thought that Peter was a revolutionary, the "also" (*kai*) spoken by the maid (v. 56) and by the first man (v. 57), and the words "Truly, you also . . ." uttered by the second man (v. 59), reach a climax and seem to suggest quite clearly that Peter's questioners thought Jesus and his followers were all revolutionaries.

Thus the Lukan account of Peter's denial fulfils Jesus' words at the last supper; the disciples, symbolized by Peter, continue with Jesus in his temptations. Jesus' prayer for Peter's protection against Satan is answered and he appears in a much better light than in the other Gospels. He does not warm himself by the fire; he does not curse and swear in his denial, and he does not leave the court and go to the gateway (Mark 14:68; Matt. 26:71). Jesus and Peter are both in the house of the high priest.

The scene comes to a climax in Luke when Jesus looks at Peter. This is recorded only by Luke and would have been impossible without unity of place. The differences in Luke's account of Peter's denial may be accounted for in that Luke wished to portray Peter in a better light because Jesus' prayer for his protection against Satan must not be ineffectual (Luke 22:31–34).

Luke has shown the weakness of a disciple, when he is accused of being a revolutionary, in contrast to the heroic behavior of the Teacher under the same accusation.

The Mockery of Jesus (Luke 22:63–65; Mark 15:16–20; Matt. 27:27–31)

The mockery of Jesus as recorded by Luke is markedly different from that in Mark and Matthew. Mark and Matthew report a simple mockery of Jesus by the Jews after his trial before the Sanhedrin (Mark 14:65; Matt. 26:67). It comprises spitting on him, striking him, and bidding him to prophesy. In Mark he is blindfolded. However, the chief mockery in Mark and Matthew occurs after the sentence of death delivered by Pilate. It is a repugnant game played by the Roman soldiers, performed before the whole battalion. Jesus is dramatically ridiculed as a regal messianic pretender. This is seen by the investiture with a purple (Matthew, scarlet), royal cloak; the crown; the acclamation, "Hail, King of the Jews"; and the kneeling in homage. In Matthew a scepter (reed) is placed in Jesus' right hand. Before the Romans, according to Mark and Matthew, Jesus is accused of treason and is seen as a political messianic pretender.

Luke omits any vestige of this. In his view the Romans have no evidence that Jesus is a political criminal. However, Luke describes the mockery of Jesus by those who arrested him before the informal trial by the Jews. The mockery is not perpetrated by those who condemn Jesus but is preliminary to the trial.

The key to our passage is the blindfolding of Jesus and his being tested as a prophet. Taylor thinks that the blindfolding may be an addition to the Markan text, in which case Luke is the only one to retain this important detail.[35] Catchpole asserts that a similar test was applied to Bar Kochba (Bar Koziba), who led the second revolt against Rome (132-135 C.E.) and claimed to be Messiah.[36] According to the Mishnah (*Sanh.* 93b), a messianic candidate was required to show his ability to work without the aid of sight or hearing and so to fulfil Isaiah 11:3. The text reads:

The Messiah—as it is written, *And the spirit of the Lord shall rest upon him . . . And shall make him of quick understanding . . . in the fear of the Lord.* R. Alexandri said: This teaches that he loaded him with good deeds and suffering as a mill [is laden]. Raba said: He smells [a man] and judges (to tell whether he is guilty or innocent), as it is written, and *he shall not judge after the sight of his eyes, neither reprove after the hearing of his ears, yet with righteousness shall he judge the poor* (since he does not use his eyes or ears he must judge through the sense of smell). (Bar Koziba reigned two and a half years, and then said to the Rabbis, "I am the Messiah." They answered, "Of Messiah it is written that he smells and judges: let us see whether he [Bar Koziba] can do so." When they saw that he was unable to judge by the scent, they slew him.) [italics added]

Thus Luke's mockery scene does not imply that Jesus is accused of a political crime. Jesus is accused of a religious offense. This is confirmed by Luke's words in verse 65, that many blasphemed against him; one does not blaspheme against a king. Thus Luke has removed the political element from the mockery and secured Jesus against the charge of being a royal messianic pretender. But he does indicate that the Jews thought of him as a false prophet.

Jesus before the Sanhedrin and Pilate
(Luke 22:66–23:5; Matt. 26:57–27:26; Mark 14:53–15:20)

Blinzler observes that the most arresting change in Luke's passion narrative is the transfer of Jesus' trial to daytime.[37] On this point many scholars give preference to Luke. A trial by night would not be consonant with the Jewish law.

However, Luke's account does not give the impression of a formal trial. He gives no special part to the high priest, as do Mark and Matthew; rather

Jesus' interrogators are "they"—the elders of the people, the chief priests, and the scribes. The lack of emphasis on the high priest would seem to suggest that this was a preliminary examination before Jesus was sent to Pilate. This is confirmed by that fact that Luke mentions no witnesses, true or false (Mark 14:56, Matt. 26:60), and he does not state that a verdict was given. Luke omits the accusation about destroying the temple and rebuilding it (Mark 14:57–60; Matt. 26:61–62).

There is a further change of some consequence in Luke. According to Mark (v. 61) and Matthew (v. 63) the high priest asks Jesus whether he is the Christ (the Messiah), the Son of God (Mark, "the Son of the Blessed"). To this question Jesus replies in the affirmative and then speaks about the eschatological advent of the Son of Man.

Instead of the one question that we find in Mark and Matthew, Luke has two. They are clearly distinct: (1) Is he the Messiah? (2) Is he the Son of God? Walaskay proposes that in dividing the question into two distinct parts Luke has clarified the religious and political aspects of the accusations against Jesus.[38] "Messiah" is a political accusation. "Messiah" does not usually imply supernatural claims. "Son of God" is clearly a religious accusation. It was blasphemous to claim equality with God.

Jesus gives two distinct replies. As Walaskay states, "To the question about the messiahship, Jesus gives a most obscure answer, certainly nothing like a confession."[39] To the question about the divine sonship, Jesus replies in the affirmative: "You say that I am." That this was a positive answer is shown by the reaction of the Jews: "And they said: 'What further testimony do we need? We have heard it ourselves from his own lips' " (v. 71).

Walaskay deduces from this clear distinction of the charges that Luke wanted his readers to know that the Jews brought only a religious charge against Jesus.[40] Indeed, Luke tends to destroy any "semblance of legitimacy" in the Jewish trial. Walaskay observes: "By comparison with the Roman trial which follows, the hearing before the Sanhedrin is a mockery; it is not a trial by any standards. Though Luke has followed his source's outline of the trial scene, his additions and omissions bring into sharp relief the difference between the Jewish and Roman justice."[41] Walaskay notes that almost immediately after Luke's account of the Sanhedrin's examination and religious charge against Jesus, the council presents a completely contradictory charge to Pilate, a political one (Luke 23:5). "Luke has made clear to his readers that the Sanhedrin knew the *politico-religious* distinction but chose, in its accusation to Pilate, to place the emphasis solely on the *political* side."[42]

The contradiction is all the more vivid because Luke has no intervening verses: Mark and Matthew have the Jewish mockery and the denial by Peter. In Luke the condemnation of Jesus on a *religious* charge by the Jews is "eyeball to eyeball" with their *political* charges before Pilate. These charges are threefold: (1) perverting the nation; (2) forbidding that tribute be given to Caesar; (3) claiming to be king (Luke 23:2).

These charges are thrown into greater relief when compared with the one accusation found in Mark and Matthew, that Jesus claims to be king of the Jews. However, they attribute the accusation to Pilate, not to the Jews.

Of the three Lukan accusations brought before Pilate, two have already been repudiated in the gospel material prior to the passion. All three Gospels show that Jesus did not explicitly deny that tribute should be paid to Caesar (Luke 20:20–26; Mark 12:13–17; Matt. 22:15–22). Luke's account of the entry into Jerusalem clearly depicts only the disciples', not the crowds', recognition of Jesus as king. In the light of the gospel material, then, these accusations are false. The whole tenor of Luke's Gospel disclaims the third accusation.

A fourth accusation is brought against Jesus by the Jews when Pilate had declared him innocent, the accusation of stirring up the people and teaching throughout Judea "from Galilee even to this place" (Luke 23:5).

All these accusations are political and may well be anachronisms, historically related to the turbulence from about 40 to 74 C.E.

Blinzler observes that the Romans did not trouble themselves about Jewish laws (cf. Acts 18:15; 23:29; 25:18–20). Therefore the Jews could hope to convict Jesus only if they showed the Roman governor that their prisoner had committed a crime against Roman law.

At the time of a religious festival it would have been relatively easy to gain access to the Roman governor, because he usually took up residence in Jerusalem at such times in order to deal with riots.

Bringing treason charges against a person would not have been difficult in Palestine at the time of Jesus and, more especially, at the time of Luke. Walaskay draws attention to the fact that accusations similar to those made against Jesus were becoming increasingly frequent in the civil court of Jerusalem before the destruction of the city (70 C.E.).[43] Josephus, referring to the state of affairs before the outbreak of the war, says:

Nero's death, moreover, brought universal confusion; many were induced by this opportunity to aspire to the sovereignty, and a change which might make their fortune was after the heart of the soldiery [B.J. 1:4–6].

Josephus speaks also of "numbers of persons who aspired to the sovereignty"—for example, Judas the Galilean; Simon, a royal slave in Perea who "assumed the diadem"; a shepherd called Athrongaeus who, "like a king, handled matters of graver moment," and also assumed the diadem (B.J. 2:55–65); and an Egyptian prophet who planned to capture Jerusalem and become a tyrant (B.J. 2:261–63).

Most importantly, Menahem, son of Judas the Galilean, secured Masada and then returned "like a veritable king to Jerusalem." He was such an "insufferable tyrant" that another revolutionary, Eleazar, and his followers attacked him, and he withdrew to Masada.

In the light of these disorders, so close to the time of writing his Gospel,

Luke must have felt it incumbent on him to demonstrate very clearly that Jesus was not a revolutionary and not an aspirant after the diadem like the leaders named above. This would have been more important in Luke's time than in Jesus' time: the rebellions had gathered momentum and broken into a full-scale war. Even after the fall of Jerusalem and Masada, the country cannot have been completely under control, especially in rural areas, which were honeycombed with convenient caves.

It is interesting that two of the accusations against Jesus are those brought against the Jews before the war. Agrippa II, who tried to dissuade the Jews from war with Rome, blames them for not paying their tribute to Caesar, being guilty of insurrection, and cutting down the porticoes communicating with the Fort Antonia (Pilate's headquarters) (*B.J.* 2:402–5).

As Walaskay observes, it is extremely surprising that Pilate judged Jesus to be innocent.[44] It would be natural for him to be suspicious of any charges of sedition, especially when these charges were brought by accusers who appeared to be pro-Roman.

Sherwin-White remarks that Jesus' case was not without parallel.[45] The Roman courts were so accustomed to the absentee accuser that Emperor Claudius passed a number of decrees to protect defendants in this situation. Sherwin-White suggests the affinity of Jesus' trial and those of the martyrs some seventy years later. Those who did not defend themselves were given three chances to change their minds before being sentenced. He compares Acts 25:16 where Festus does not want to condemn Paul until his accuser is present. In Mark and Matthew, Jesus is interrogated twice, but in Luke he is asked once and the prosecution is asked three times (Mark 15:2–4; Matt. 27:11–15; Luke 23:3, 13–22). Sherwin-White adds that, although Mark and Matthew seem to have more accurate knowledge on certain points, Luke is remarkable in that "his additional materials, the full formulation of the charges before Pilate, the reference to Herod, and the proposed acquittal with an admonition, are all technically correct."[46]

To recapitulate, Luke's account of the trial before Pilate is important from a political point of view. (1) Unlike Matthew and Mark, Luke has Jesus accused of three specific charges of treason against the Roman government. (2) Having clarified these charges, Luke can then demonstrate that Pilate declares his prisoner to be innocent. (3) Luke's account of the trial appears more correct from the point of view of Roman legal proceedings. (4) The result of Luke's version of the trial by Pilate is that Jesus is acquitted of all political charges.

Thus Jesus stands in a situation entirely different from the false prophets and messianic pretenders of the first century C.E.

This is very important for the Lukan church, for it would wish its founder to be as far removed as possible from those many Jews and, perhaps, Christians who might have been involved in seditious resistance against Rome. In the aftermath of the 66–74 C.E. war, the Romans must have been extremely vigilant with regard to further revolts. Some of the Jews who escaped from

Palestine began to cause disturbances against Rome in the Diaspora—for instance, the *sicarii* both in Egypt (*B.J.* 7:407-19) and in Cyrene, together with Jonathan the Weaver, who won the ear of the indigent and performed signs and wonders (*B.J.* 7:436).

Jesus before Herod (Luke 23:6–16)

The mention of Galilee in the Jews' fourth accusation gives Pilate the opportunity to send Jesus to Herod Antipas. He may have been in Jerusalem for the feast (*Ant.* 18:122). Pilate could have been anxious to placate Herod, whom he might have offended over the Galilean massacre (Luke 13:1) or over the introduction of the votive shields into Jerusalem (Philo, *Leg.* 299-304). This occurred in approximately 32-33 C.E.

Sherwin-White observes that "Herod the Great, according to Josephus, had the abnormal privilege of extraditing offenders who had fled from his kingdom to other parts of the Roman empire. Possibly a remnant of this privilege underlay the sending of Christ to the second Herod; most of the activities of Christ had taken place in Galilee."[47] In Josephus's words: "Herod's formidable influence extended, moreover, beyond his realm to his friends abroad; for no other sovereign had been empowered by Caesar, as he had, to reclaim a fugitive subject even from a state outside his jurisdiction" (*B.J.* 1:474). Thus Pilate could realistically hope that Herod would acquit Jesus. Herod had desired to see Jesus. Luke has foreshadowed this in 9:9 and 13:31. It would appear that Herod wanted Jesus to prove himself a prophet with signs and wonders. His mockery focuses on this. It is different from the Roman mockery (Matthew and Mark) in that all the regal features are omitted.

Herod arrayed Jesus in a bright robe that might have been understood as a mock *toga candida* (white robe) of a candidate for office.[48] I suggest that Luke may have had a revolutionary candidate in mind. We recall that Simon bar Giora, perhaps the most noteworthy of all the Jewish revolutionary leaders, made his surrender clothed in white tunics and emerging from the subterranean tunnels on Mount Zion from the very place where the temple had stood (*B.J.* 7:25-36). If Luke intended this allusion, then he is taking "poetic license" because it is an anachronism. Yet the theological meaning is clear. Luke wanted to show that Herod could not condemn Jesus as if he were a man like Simon bar Giora: an eminent military leader, severe disciplinarian, radical social revolutionary, and vehemently opposed to the rich.

However, the climax to this scene is Jesus' return to Pilate and the third declaration of innocence. Pilate says, "not even Herod" found Jesus guilty of a capital offense (Luke 23:15). Thus Herod and Pilate provide a dual witness to Jesus' innocence—the dual witness required by Jewish law.

Encouraged by Herod's acquittal of Jesus, Pilate makes another attempt to release Jesus. When Pilate mentions that Herod found no fault in Jesus, he adds that he will chastise him and release him.

The Lukan text has two important differences from that of Mark and Matthew: the chastisement takes place *before* the sentence of death; Mark and Matthew refer to a severe beating that was part of the punishment of crucifixion.[49] They use the word *phragellō*; Luke uses *paideuō*. This is a lighter whipping with *fustes* ("rods"), not thongs with embedded bone or metal pieces, and its purpose was a warning before the prisoner was released.

Luke records two efforts on the part of Pilate to placate the Jews by scourging Jesus (Luke 23:16 and 22). There is also a second denial by Pilate that Jesus was causing sedition (Luke 23:14). Thus Luke is exceptionally careful to exonerate Jesus from any political charge of being a revolutionary and shows Pilate taking extreme efforts to release him.

The Death Sentence (Luke 23:17-25; Mark 15:6-15; Matt. 27:15-26)

Luke's account of Pilate's sentence differs considerably from that of Mark and Matthew. He makes no reference to the custom of releasing a prisoner at passover time.

Matthew does not even report that Barabbas was a revolutionary, although Mark indicates that he was guilty of murder in an insurrection.

Luke clearly states that Barabbas was a political prisoner, "a man who had been thrown into prison for an insurrection started in the city, and for murder" (v. 19).[50] He is not content to mention this only once but repeats almost the selfsame words in verse 24: this is only five verses later. It is very obvious that Luke wishes Barabbas ("Son of a Father"), a revolutionary, to be the complete antithesis to Jesus, the Son of God, a champion of nonresistance.

The Jews demand crucifixion. According to the Temple Scroll found at Qumran, it could have been a Jewish punishment for blasphemy (the accusation before the Sanhedrin), sorcery, or betraying one's country to the enemy (see "Temple Scroll" in *EJ*). It is in this pericope that the word "crucify" is first used; it occurs three times (v. 21 [twice] and v. 23). The total picture in Luke is that of a nonviolent, innocent man condemned to a revolutionary's death and the release of a man whom all recognized to be guilty of sedition and murder.

The Way to Golgotha (Luke 23:26-31; Matt. 27:32; Mark 15:21)

Matthew and Mark devote only one verse to the way to Golgotha. Luke has six. Luke makes an important change with reference to Simon of Cyrene. In Mark 15:21 and Matthew 27:32 he is pressed into service (*aggareuō*, the technical term for forcing duties on a subject people) but Luke uses "catch," "take hold of" (*epilambanomai*). Thus Luke avoids the provocative reference to a forced pressing into service, and Simon appears as a concrete example of a disciple taking up his cross and following Jesus. The technical word "follow" pertaining to discipleship (*akoloutheō*) is attributed to the great crowd that accompanies Jesus in the next verse (v. 27). Thus in Luke the masses are not only relieved of the guilt of condemning Jesus, but they accompany him to the cross as disciples. The wailing women are especially pointed out. They take the place of the mockers in Mark and Matthew.

Luke gives special emphasis to these women who accompanied Jesus and lamented over him. Manson[51] refers to Dalman who quotes a pertinent rabbinic passage:

> When a man goes out to be crucified, his father weeps for him; his mother weeps for him and beats [her breast] for him; and one says "Woe is me"; and the other says, "Woe is me." But the real woe is to him who goes out to be crucified [*Sifre Dt.* 308].[52]

This scene brings to a climax Luke's theology of the people. In contrast to the chief priests and leaders, the masses do not condemn Jesus but rather remain faithful to him in his final trial. Manson says that they raise "the death-wail over him in anticipation. He in his turn raises, as it were, the death-wail over Jerusalem in anticipation."[53]

When Jesus speaks to the women he warns them that, if they knew what was to happen to Jerusalem, they would wail for themselves rather than for him. Jesus uses the formula of the prophetic oracles in the Old Testament.

Conzelmann wishes to see the women as participating in the "going down" (*katabasis*) and "going up" (*anabasis*) of Jesus,[54] but they seem to be from Jerusalem, not Galilee. Women mourners were not uncommon. They provided opiates for the condemned:

> When one is led out to execution, he is given a goblet of wine containing a grain of frankincense, in order to benumb his senses, for it is written, *Give strong drink unto him that is ready to perish and wine unto the bitter in soul.* And it has also been taught: the noble women in Jerusalem used to donate and bring it. If these did not donate it, who provided it? As for that, it is certainly logical that it should be provided out of public [funds] [*Sanh.* 43a; italics added].

It is very interesting that Luke, who wishes to portray the ideal martyr, does not mention the analgesic (cf. Matt. 27:34; Mark 15:23). We must consider, however, that the Jews must have been accustomed to offer this analgesic to those whom their leaders did not consider guilty but who were condemned by the Romans. It would hardly be logical for Luke to show the Jewish authorities condemning Jesus and then following this custom. Therefore the women of nobility and the public funds do not furnish this for Jesus. The middle-class or poor women who accompanied Jesus might not have been able to afford it.

P.W. Käser observes that the blessing of the childless must not be isolated from its historical context.[55] It is parallel to the woe in 21:23a over those who are pregnant or nursing babies during the destruction of Jerusalem. There is, in fact, an affinity in vocabulary.

Fertility was highly prized in the ancient world in all cultures, and Jesus speaks of sterility as a blessing because of the dire necessities of the time. This does not seem to be an invention of Luke. In a nonbiblical Jewish text (Mid. *Tehillim* 137:5) we are informed that after the Temple was destroyed "ascetics increased in Israel. . . ."

Baba Bathra (60b) discusses this idea more fully and speaks about abstinence from meat, wine, marital intercourse, and begetting children as a mark of sorrow for national catastrophe. One might ask whether this asceticism, unusual for Jews, influenced Luke.

Jesus' saying about the green wood and the dry wood means that green wood, which is unseasoned, does not burn quickly, but dry wood burns readily. We may also compare R. Jose ben Joezer, who was mocked by his nephew as he was on his way to be crucified. His response was, "If this [crucifixion] happens to those who offend him [God], what of those who do his will. . . . If this happens to those who do his will, what of those who offend him?"

In summary, Luke's account of the way of the cross has introduced the theme of discipleship as exemplified in Simon, the crowd accompanying Jesus, and the wailing women. In such ways, the mockers in Matthew and Mark are replaced by disciples who sympathize with Jesus. Jesus' reply to the women mourners is important because it brings a further insight into the heartfelt sorrow and sympathy of Jesus for the very ones who brought about his death, and who themselves will suffer so much at the hands of the Romans. It is the most appropriate response on the part of one who espouses nonviolence, and this deportment will reach a climax in the crucifixion.

Already the nonviolent Jesus has attracted followers prepared to suffer the same fate as he.

The Crucifixion (Luke 23:32–43; Mark 15:22–32; Matt. 27:33–44)

Mark (v. 27) and Matthew (v. 38) report that Jesus was crucified between two revolutionaries (*lestai,* rebels or armed robbers), one on his right side and one on his left (cf. Mark 10:37–40; Matt. 20:21–23). Luke (23:33) has a different wording. He calls the criminals "evildoers" (*kakourgoi*), not revolutionaries. Luke has carefully proved at the Roman trial that Jesus was not a revolutionary. Now he does not want to depict him between two revolutionaries or armed social bandits.

Yet there may be a deeper meaning in Luke's choice of words. Not only does Luke avoid the word for revolutionaries or bandits, but "evil-doers" could comprise the classes of "sinful" persons with whom Jesus had identified himself from the very beginning of his ministry: tax collectors, toll collectors, traders, merchants, usurers, gamblers, adulterers, and the like. The word *kakourgos*, both in classical Greek and New Testament Greek, is used also of those "who commit gross misdeeds and serious crimes."

Thus Jesus died in the company of those to whom he had a special ministry. There is a direct link between the calling of the ostracized and the crucifixion. This relationship between the Lukan Jesus, exonerated from the charge of being a revolutionary, and his ministry to so many who were prone to violence and suffered violence in various forms is a weighty matter for Luke. It reaches a climax in two passages, peculiar to Luke, that concern forgiveness.

Forgiveness of others, especially those involved in violence, is an essential part of pacifism. Luke brilliantly illustrates this side of Jesus' character. Jesus' intimacy with such persons was one important reason for his crucifixion.

Jesus Forgives His Enemies (Luke 23:34)

Luke's portrayal of Jesus may be contrasted with that of the Jewish zealot (violent) freedom fighters. In verse 34 Luke records that Jesus, as he was being fastened to the cross, asked the Father to forgive his enemies. Once again he implemented his own teaching in the sermon on the mount and the sermon on the plain. Even though some early and important manuscripts and versions omit this verse (v. 34), Metzger believes that the omission cannot be explained as a deliberate deletion from the original text by those who thought that the fall of Jerusalem showed that Jesus' prayer for forgiveness of his foes had not been answered.[56] He concludes that, although the logion probably was not part of the original Gospel, it "bears self-evident tokens of its dominical origin."

This prayer of Jesus makes him different from the Maccabean and many other Jewish martyrs. For example, in 2 Maccabees 7, we see an obvious contrast. The second Maccabean boy-martyr says to his persecutor, "You accursed wretch, you dismiss us from this present life, but the King of the universe will raise us up to an everlasting renewal of life." The fourth son retorts to his torturer, "But for you there will be no resurrection to life!" The fifth son says to the king, "Keep on, and see how his [God's] mighty power will torture you and your descendants!" The sixth son exclaims, "But do not think that you will go unpunished for having tried to fight against God." The last (seventh) son declares, "But you, who have contrived all sorts of evil against the Hebrews, will certainly not escape the hands of God . . . you unholy wretch, you most defiled of all men, do not be elated in vain and puffed up by uncertain hopes. . . . You have not yet escaped the judgment of the almighty, all-seeing God . . . you, by the judgment of God, will receive just punishment for your arrogance."

In contrast to these Jewish martyrs, Jesus dies forgiving his enemies with not a word of reproach. He is shown as not only nonviolent but nonresistant and forgiving.

We must ask whether his prayer is on behalf of the Jews or the Romans. Daube has given the best interpretation of this verse, which is so characteristic of the Gospel of Luke and of Acts.[57] He notes that Harnack thought that the prayer was offered on behalf of the Romans but that later it was misinterpreted as a prayer for the Jews. A similar prayer is attributed to James, the brother of the Lord, by Hegesippus (Eusebius, *H.E.* 2, 23, 16).[58]

An obvious parallel to the first part of Jesus' prayer is the first part of Stephen's oration in Acts 7:60, but the second part of Jesus' prayer finds no echo in Stephen. Nevertheless, it is very Lukan. The evangelist states a relationship between sin and ignorance. The theme occurs five times in Acts (3:17; 13:27; 14:16; 17:30; 26:9).

The rest of verse 34, which reports the sharing of Jesus' garments by the soldiers, supports the view that the prayer is for the Romans. Yet the people (*laos*) mentioned in the next verse must surely mean the Jewish people. Daube argues that the prayer for forgiveness could, indeed, also be offered for the Jews.[59] In verses 28ff. Jesus points to the "fearful consequences which even those among the crowd who weep cannot foresee, and where the verb 'do' [as in v. 34] is used of the conduct of his [Jesus'] adversaries: 'for if they do these things in a green tree. . . .' " Further, ignorance or unwitting sin of the Jews is emphasized in Acts.[60]

In both Jewish and gentile sources there are precedents for the forgiveness of unwitting sin.[61] Unwitting sin is contrasted with "sin committed with a high hand" in the Old Testament (Num. 15:9; Deut. 17:12; cf. *P. Sheb.* 33a; *b. Yoma* 36b). In Leviticus 16:21 there is a discussion of three types of sin: sin through presumption; sin through rebellion; and sin through ignorance. *Baba Bathra* 60b, quoted above, says: "It is better that the Israelites should transgress in ignorance than willfully." *Makkoth* 2:5 and 10b speak of the difference between murder and homicide. The sinner who does not know the Torah is less culpable.[62] *Baba Metzia* 33b states: "a student's unwitting sin counts as intentional, an ignoramus's intentional sin counts as unwitting: the latter is not informed."

The theology of unwitting sin is understood clearly from the day of atonement. On this day Numbers 15:26 is read: "And it shall be forgiven all the congregation of the children of Israel and the foreigner who sojourns among them, *seeing that all the people were in ignorance*" (italics added). In fact, this sentence was taken out of its context and placed at the beginning of the 24-hour service on the day of atonement.[63] It seems to have been inserted into the liturgy in the Middle Ages, but it can be traced back to Eleazar the Great (first century), who thought that this sentence also covered presumptuous sin. There are several references to ignorance in Numbers 15:24-26.[64]

Yoma 36b (the tractate on the day of atonement) also refers to forgiving iniquity with reference to Exodus 34:7, God's compassion after Israel's sin over the golden calf. Daube observes: "It is noteworthy that the topic of this baraitha is the high priest's confession of sins on behalf of Israel on the day of atonement."[65] We may compare also the high priest in the Epistle to the Hebrews who has compassion on the weak and ignorant (Heb. 5:2). Daube states:

> Considering a doctrine like that of Eleazar the Great and an intercession like that of Moses for his backsliding people . . . it would be unreasonable to deny the possibility of Luke 23:34 being a prayer for the Jews and having a thoroughly Jewish background.

Yoma 36b distinguishes between "wrongs" as "deliberate misdeeds," "transgressions" as "rebellious deeds," and "sins" as "inadvertent omissions." Thus the high priest on the day of atonement prays, "I have sinned, I have done wrong, I have transgressed before Thee, I and my house." In this way he covers all sin, witting and unwitting.

Daube also adds that from a baraitha we are virtually certain that Jonah was used as an afternoon reading on the day of atonement.[66] This is appropriate for the book ends thus: "And should I not spare Nineveh that great city wherein are more than sixscore thousand persons that do not know between their right hand and their left hand, and also much cattle?" The Ninevites were gentiles who had not heard of Yahweh. Thus Daube shows that Luke 23:24, Acts 3:17 and 13:27, and James's prayer in Hegesippus are consonant with a Jewish environment. Jesus' prayer as he was fastened to the cross is like that of the high priest on the day of atonement.

I should like to add one point to Daube's thesis. If scholars who argue that Jesus' homily at Nazareth (Luke 4) inaugurated a jubilee year are correct, then that jubilee year, eschatological or not, would commence on the day of atonement. Jesus' ministry is one of atonement for religious and social outcasts. It is, therefore, fitting that Luke should portray Jesus on the cross as the new high priest on a new day of atonement, who at his own most traumatic hour intercedes for all sinners: those who sinned wittingly and those who sinned unwittingly; Jews and gentiles. In fact, the prayer of forgiveness complements Luke 4 and reinforces the bold assertion of Jesus in his opening sermon that the anointed prophet comes to announce "a year of favor" but omits the day of vengeance, which is so closely related to the figure of Melchizedek, the priest of the Most High God. This day of vengeance was emphasized by the Qumran community and the revolutionaries, especially the religious fanatics. Luke ends his Gospel (24:51) with Jesus, a priest comparable to Simon in Sirach 51, who gives a blessing to his people before his ascension, a blessing that they did not receive from Zechariah because he was struck dumb by the appearance of the war angel Gabriel.

Most significantly, the theme of the day of atonement is prominent for Luke at the very commencement of Jesus' ministry (Luke 4) and at the very end (Luke 23).

Jesus Forgives the Criminal (Luke 23:39-43)

The climax of the crucifixion is the part played by the two criminals and by Jesus in relationship to them. Only Luke records the words of the repentant criminal and Jesus' response. From the beginning of the crucifixion scene Luke has emphasized the presence of the criminals. Their dialogue with Jesus is given considerable space. Luke alone recounts the words of the criminal who defended Jesus against the taunt of the other one, his appeal to Jesus to remember him when he comes into his kingdom, and Jesus' reply that "today" he will be with him in paradise. Obviously Luke believes in the efficacy of a martyr's intercession. This pericope is the climax of Jesus' ministry with "tax collectors and others," the climax of his ministry of forgiveness.

Ellis sees the passage about the forgiveness of the criminal as the focal point in Luke's crucifixion narrative:

> He [the good criminal] is offered more than he asks for. If his thoughts are fixed on the entry to the kingdom of God at the end of the world, Jesus promises him salvation here and now, the certainty of being in paradise with him that very day. Jesus' kingly power is to be operative for salvation forthwith.[67]

The whole incident shows the difference between condemnation and salvation. Even when he is dying a slave's and criminal's death, Jesus turns to the outcasts. With the word "today" Jesus indicates that the new time of salvation, which was predicted on the occasion of his birth (2:11) and proclaimed at the commencement of his ministry (4:21; cf. 5:26; 19:9), has been fully implemented.

The Final Declaration of Jesus' Innocence (Luke 23:47)

Matthew 27:46 and Mark 15:34 record the last words of Jesus' earthly life as, "My God, my God, why hast thou forsaken me?" Instead, the last pre-resurrection words of Jesus in Luke are: "Father, into your hand I commend my spirit." They are uttered with the same "loud voice" mentioned by Matthew and Mark with respect to the cry of despair.

Luke's Jesus has a cry of triumph.

Lastly, Luke records the words of the centurion. They are different from those remarked by Mark (15:39) and Matthew (27:54): "Truly this was a son of God." Luke's centurion says, "Truly this person was innocent (*dikaios*)."

There has been not a little debate about the meaning of *dikaios*. Kilpatrick has argued convincingly that *dikaios* can be translated "innocent."[68] For example, Matthew 27:4 speaks of "innocent blood" (*haima dikaion*). Kilpatrick observes that Pilate is emphatic about Jesus' innocence in Luke 23:4, 14, and 22. The innocence of Jesus is also attested to by Herod (23:15) and the thief (23:41).

In Luke the centurion's words are the climax to these assertions that Jesus was innocent. Luke has proclaimed Jesus innocent six times; by Pilate (three times), by Herod, by the criminal, and by the centurion—innocent of being a violent, revolutionary person. It was important to point out that Christians were not to be revolutionaries who resisted Rome. This was all the more necessary as Christianity moved into more educated and wealthier circles in the Greco-Roman world. Theophilus, to whom Luke's Gospel and Acts are dedicated (Luke 1:3), may have belonged to these classes.[69]

Thus Luke's account of the crucifixion and death of Jesus brings to a climax his portrayal of Jesus as one who taught and lived an ethic that was completely dissimilar to the militant ideology of the Maccabees, the Hasmoneans, and the revolutionary groups of the first century C.E. He died between two "sinners" just as he has associated with "sinners," or religious and social outcasts, during his entire ministry. He died forgiving those who fastened him to the cross as well as the repentant criminal hanging beside him whom he admitted to eternal life with him. These actions dramatically demonstrate that he can fully implement his own teaching and offer it as lifestyle differing from that of such sectarians as the members of the Qumran community, who were taught to have everlasting hatred and no mercy toward sinners. Moreover, his forgiveness, as Daube has shown, extends beyond the Roman soldiers. Like a Jewish high priest on the day of atonement he prays for forgiveness for his Jewish brothers and sisters. For Luke Jesus' life does not end on a note of grim despair but triumphal joy (cf. Heb. 12:2).

Last, but not least, the Roman centurion declares Jesus innocent. He and Pilate represent for Luke the unmitigated judgment of the Roman Empire, which exonerated Jesus and, with him, the nascent Christian movement, from treason, violence, and revolution vis-à-vis Rome.

Chapter 9

SUMMARY AND CONCLUSION

The whole of Palestine was in turmoil shortly before Luke wrote his Gospel. During the decade of his writing it was suffering the aftermath of the war that Josephus calls "the greatest not only of the wars of our own time, but . . . well nigh of all that ever broke out between cities or nations" (*B.J.* 1:1). At the end of his account of the war Josephus reports that the defeat of the Jews had repercussions in the Diaspora and that some of the revolutionaries had escaped and were causing further unrest. One of the purposes of the Gospel of Luke was to respond to these postwar conditions and to show to Palestinian and Diaspora Christians that the peace that Christ came to bring was not won through weapons but through love, forgiveness, and acceptance of enemies into covenant community.

Luke was an artist, as well as a historian and theologian. He planned his Gospel with consummate skill. He set his first scene in the period of Israel and dramatically portrayed the families of John the Baptist and of Jesus as righteous Jews who anticipated a prophet and a king who would conduct a holy war, win international power for Israel, and render retribution to their enemies. John the Baptist expected a warrior king who would baptize with wind and fire.

In his fourth chapter Luke introduces this awaited leader. He is wholly transformed.

He is the Anointed of God who will announce a year of favor for both the Jews *and* their opponents. His message is received with such astonishment and hostility that his fellow citizens try to assassinate him. Yet the year of favor that Jesus proclaims is the Jubilee era, which, if properly implemented, would solve many of the social, economic, and religious problems within Palestine.[1] The program could also be accommodated to the Christian communities in the Diaspora.

After his provocative homily in Nazareth (Luke 4:21–27), which inaugurates and epitomizes his ministry, the Lukan Jesus begins to implement it by showing the churches that there must be a change of attitude toward those

136

who had caused such resentment and disgust in society at large—namely, tax collectors and "sinners." Luke then addresses the continuing problem of the hostility between the Jews and the Samaritans, which had intensified for a whole year during the governorship of Cumanus. Having dealt with two of the major causes of the great war with Rome (66–74 C.E.)—taxation and Samaria—the Lukan Jesus addresses other social and political issues, very often by teaching in parables that have a political aspect to them. Jesus deals especially with the problem of the *lex talionis* (law of retaliation), wealth and poverty, and discipleship.

It is, however, in Luke's treatment of the passion of Jesus that his teaching on love of enemies reaches its zenith. By his teaching and his conduct the Lukan Jesus is exonerated from any suspicion of being a political malcontent. He heals the servant of those who will condemn him. He is presented as the martyr par excellence who, unlike many of the Jewish martyrs, intercedes for those who persecute him. Moreover, he admits to eternal felicity—salvation—a condemned criminal.

It is surely Luke's intention that all Christians should follow in Jesus' footsteps.

It is not my contention that all the evangelists teach what we now call "pacifism" but, rather, that this is one of the special features of Luke (and John). In the contemporary world, where terrorism, violence, crime, war, and poverty are the most important issues of the day, this aspect of Luke's Gospel is acutely pertinent.

In reflecting on Luke's work one should realize that his message is not confined to first-century Christians and their position vis-à-vis Rome. It is addressed also to twentieth-century Christians.

The challenge with which Luke's Gospel confronts us includes the following. Can we—contemporary wealthy Western society—implement the jubilee principles, especially with regard to the Third World? Do we accept Jesus as the new high priest, like Melchizedek in the Epistle to the Hebrews, who empathizes with human frailty in its multitudinous forms in modern society? He taught good news, not reproach, to the poor and weak and was their co-sufferer in pain and temptation, with "loud weeping" (Heb. 4: 14–5:10). Do we proclaim a year of good favor to the oppressed in body and mind, and those in substandard social situations? What is our attitude to the contemporary "tax collector"? Would we dine with members of the mafia, with adulterers, prostitutes (male and female), robbers, or drug addicts?

What does the Lukan attitude to the Samaritans teach us? Does it not have relevance to the situations in Ireland, Israel, Lebanon, Iran, Iraq, and all other war-torn countries?

Above all, would the Jesus who rebuked James and John for desiring fire from heaven to incinerate the Samaritans condone proliferation of nuclear weaponry or another holocaust like Hiroshima?

The answer to all these questions is found in the words of the Holy Spirit who inspired the Lukan account of the passion and death of Jesus of Nazareth. What greater love can we have but to take up our cross daily and lay down our life for both friend and enemy—or admit them to covenant intimacy?

NOTES

Preface

1. For chapters 2–8 the reader will find it helpful to use *Gospel Parallels*, by B. H. Throckmorton (Nashville, 4th ed., 1979). It presents the text of the first three Gospels in parallel columns so that similarities and differences are readily observed.

2. David M. Rhoads, *Israel in Revolution 6-74 C.E.* (Philadelphia, 1976), pp. 154–56.

3. N. N. Glatzer, *Hillel the Elder* (New York, 1956), pp. 63–73.

4. Ibid., p. 65.

5. Ibid.

6. Ibid., pp. 68–69.

7. Rhoads, *Israel*, pp. 63–64.

8. Ibid., p. 83.

9. Ibid., p. 175.

Chapter 1

1. M. I. Rostovtzeff, *The Social and Economic History of the Roman Empire* (Oxford, 1926), p. 146.

2. R. H. Horsley, "Ancient Jewish Banditry and the Revolt against Rome," CBQ, 43 (1981) 410–11.

3. Ibid., p. 411.

4. E. J. Hobsbawm, *Primitive Rebels* (New York, 1965), pp. 15f.

5. C. Roth, *The Dead Sea Scrolls* (New York, 1965), p. 177.

6. P. W. Barnett, "The Jewish Sign Prophets—A.D. 40–70—Their Intention and Origin," NTS, 27 (1981) 679–97.

Chapter 2

1. M. Hengel, *Die Zeloten* (Leiden, 1970), pp. 243–46.

2. Ibid.

3. See *Sōtēr* in TDNT.

4. R. E. Brown, *The Birth of the Messiah* (New York, 1977), p. 311; italics added.

5. J. A. Fitzmyer, "The Contribution of Qumran Aramaic to the Study of the New Testament," NTS, 20 (1973–74) 394.

6. Ibid., p. 393.

7. Ibid., p. 392.

8. Ibid., p. 393.

9. P. Skehan, "The Hand of Judith," CBQ, 25 (1963) 108.

10. Ibid., note 11.

11. Brown, *Birth*, p. 348.

12. For the use of *kurios* in Luke's Gospel, see P. Winter, "Some Observations on the Language in the Birth and Infancy Stories of the Third Gospel," NTS, 1 (1954) 111-21. Only in Luke 1:43 does *kurios* refer to Jesus; elsewhere in the infancy narratives it refers to God.

13. F. W. Danker, *Jesus and the New Age* (St. Louis, 1972), p. 14.

14. Brown, *Birth*, p. 349.

15. Douglas Jones, "The Background and Character of the Lukan Psalms," JTS, ns 19 (1968) 22.

16. F. M. Cross, "The Divine Warrior," in *Biblical Motifs*, A. Altmann, ed. (Cambridge, Mass., 1966), pp. 11-30. See also P. D. Millar, *The Divine Warrior in Early Israel* (Cambridge, Mass., 1975).

17. The use of the aorist in vv. 51-55 has been much discussed. It probably represents the Hebrew iterative perfect to show what God customarily does for the people.

18. I. H. Marshall, *Commentary on Luke* (Grand Rapids, 1978), p. 84.

19. Jones, "Background," pp. 25-26.

20. H. Schürmann, *Das Evangelium Lukas* (Berlin, 1976), pp. 63-66.

21. W. R. Farmer, "Judas, Simon and Athronges," NTS, 4 (2, 1958) 148-49.

22. *A Complete Concordance of Flavius Josephus,* K. H. Rengstorf, ed. (Leiden, 1968), suppl. 1.

23. For tandem relationship, see R. E. Brown, *The Gospel of John* (New York, 1970), vol. 2, pp. 1137-39.

24. With respect to Maccabean names, according to Mark and Matthew there are several among Jesus' "brothers": James, John, Judas, and Simon; they are mentioned in Mark 1:3 and Matt. 4:55, but significantly omitted in Luke 4:22.

25. Jones, "Background," p. 28.

26. *1 Enoch* 83-91.

27. D. Rhoads, *Israel in Revolution 6-74 C.E.* (Philadelphia, 1976), pp. 85-86, 99-100, 107, 113, 169-70 (God using the Roman army to purify the Temple, according to Josephus).

28. Jones, "Background," p. 37.

29. See P. Minear, "Luke's Use of the Birth Stories," SLA, pp. 111-30.

30. See Danker, *New Age.*

31. H. Braunert, "Der römische Provinzialzensus und der Schätzungsbericht des Lukas-Evangeliums," *Historia*, 6 (1957) 192-214.

32. See E. Schürer, *The Jewish People in the Time of Jesus Christ* (Edinburgh, 1885), p. 103, note 12.

33. Cited by Marshall, *Commentary*, p. 107; see also H. Sahlin, *Der Messias und das Gottesvolk* (Uppsala, 1945), p. 207; cf. *J. Ber.* 2:4, cited in S-B, 1, p. 83.

34. P. Neirynck, "That Mary Preserved All These Things in Her Heart," *Coll. Brug.*, Jan. 5, 1959, pp. 455ff., translated for me by Dr. Martin Schoenberg.

35. See G. Voss, *Die Christologie der Lukanischen Schriften in Grundzügen* (Paris, 1965), pp. 45-55.

36. Brown, *Birth*, p. 415.

37. Cited by Neirynck, "Mary Preserved," pp. 441-42.

38. Cited by Neirynck, ibid., pp. 441-43.

39. P. Winter, "Some Observations," p. 117, note 1.

40. So R. A. Aytoun, "The Ten Lucan Hymns of the Nativity in their Original Language," JTS, 18 (1917) 286.

41. Brown, *Birth*, pp. 404-5.

42. See Marshall, *Commentary*, p. 112.

43. C. H. Hunzinger, "Neues Licht auf Lc 2, 14 *anthrōpoi eudokias*," ZNW, 44 (1952) 85-90. See J. A. Fitzmyer, *The Semitic Background of the New Testament* (Missoula, Montana, 1974), pp. 101-4. Cf. Sir. 15:15 and 39:18.

44. Jones, "Background," p. 41.

45. J. F. Stenning, *Targum of Isaiah* (Oxford, 1949).

Chapter 3

1. H. Conzelmann, *The Theology of St. Luke* (New York, 1960), pp. 12-21 and 92-94.

2. For further details concerning Herod Antipas, see Harold W. Hoehner, *Herod Antipas* (Cambridge, 1972).

3. See E. M. Smallwood, "High Priests and Politics in Roman Palestine," JTS, 13 (1962) 14-34.

4. This role is also predicated of the Qumran community. I *QS* 8:12–16 reads:

And when these things come to pass for the Community in Israel at these appointed times, they shall be separated from the midst of the habitation of perverse men into the desert to prepare the way of Him: as it is written, *In the wilderness prepare the way of . . . Make straight in the desert a highway for our God.* This [way] is the study of the Law which He has promulgated by the hand of Moses, that they may act according to all that is revealed, season by season, and according to that which the Prophets have revealed by his Holy Spirit.

5. Isa. 40–55 contains several references to the new creation and redemption that God will achieve.

6. W. Wink, *John the Baptist in the Gospel Tradition* (Cambridge, 1968), p. 42.

7. Ibid., p. 42.

8. Ibid., p. 43.

9. Ibid., p. 47.

10. Conzelmann, *Theology*, pp. 18–22.

11. Wink, *John the Baptist*, p. 58.

12. D. M. Rhoads, *Israel in Revolution 6–74 C.E.* (Philadelphia, 1976), *passim* but esp. pp. 72–76.

13. Richard A. Horsley, "Ancient Jewish Banditry and the Revolt against Rome," CBQ, 43 (1981) 409–32.

14. Ibid., p. 412.

15. Ibid., p. 413.

16. Ibid., p. 427.

17. H. Braunert, "Der römische Provinzialzensus und der Schätzungsbericht des Lukas-Evangeliums," *Historia*, 6 (1957) 213ff.

18. C. C. Caragounis, "*Opsōnion*: A Reconsideration of Its Meaning," *Nov. Test.*, 16 (1974) 35–37.

19. Ibid., p. 50.

20. M. Hengel, *Die Zeloten* (Leiden, 1970), p. 326.

21. Charles H. H. Scobie, *John the Baptist* (Philadelphia, 1964), p. 64.

22. Ibid., p. 65.

23. G. Vermès, *Scripture and Tradition* (Leiden, 1961), pp. 56–66.

24. Josephus remarks that more women than men were converted to Judaism. He states that nearly all the women in Damascus were converts.

25. Marshall, *Commentary*, p. 160.

26. M. D. Johnson, *The Purpose of the Biblical Genealogies* (Cambridge, 1969), p. 231.

27. Ibid., pp. 77–82.

28. A. Lefèvre, RSR, 37 (1950) 291f., cited by Johnson, ibid., p. 82.

29. Ibid., p. 82.

30. J. Jeremias, *Jerusalem in the Time of Jesus* (London, 1969), pp. 330–31.

31. Johnson, *Genealogies*, pp. 237–38.

32. Ibid., pp. 242–4. Other nonbiblical texts include the *Letter of Aristeas*, and Eusebius, *Quaestiones Evangelicae ad Stephanum* 3:2. See also the *Apocalypse of Zerubbal*, according to which Menahem ben Ammiel was born in the time of David but was hidden until his revelation. He was the son of Hephzibah and Nathan the prophet.

33. Aptowitzer, *Parteipolitik*, pp. 113–16 and notes, cited by Johnson, *Genealogies*, p. 246.

34. Johnson, *Genealogies*, p. 251.

35. Sahlin, *Der Messias*, p. 89.

36. E. L. Abel, "The Genealogy of Jesus *HO CHRISTOS*," NTS, 20 (1974) 206.

37. J. Jeremias, *Jerusalem*, p. 276.

38. Ibid., p. 277. He also mentions the burning of genealogies by Herod the Great (pp. 281–82). Josephus is silent about this.

39. For the political implications of Herod Antipas's marriage to Aretas's daughter, see Hoehner, *Herod Antipas*, pp. 129–30.

40. Ibid., p. 142.

41. Ibid., pp. 142–45; see esp. note 7, p. 143.

42. See C. H. Kraeling, *John the Baptist*, 1951, pp. 90–91. John's rebuke of Herod was politically provocative.

43. Scobie, *John the Baptist*, pp. 19ff.

44. Ibid., p. 20.

45. Ibid.

Chapter 4

1. See D. Tiede, *The Charismatic Figure as Miracle Worker* (Missoula, Montana, 1972); T. Weeden, *Traditions in Conflict* (Philadelphia, 1971); Morton Smith, *Jesus, The Magician* (New York, 1978).

2. See S. Freyne, *Galilee, From Alexander the Great to Hadrian, 323 B.C.E. to 135 C.E.* (Notre Dame, Indiana, 1980), pp. 122–28.

3. Ibid., pp. 245–47.

4. For a literary analysis of Luke 4:16–30, see H. Schürmann, "Zur Traditionsgeschichte der Nazareth-Perikope Lk. 4, 16–30," in A. Descamps et al., *Mélanges bibliques* (Gembloux, 1970), pp. 187–205.

5. R. North, "Maccabean Sabbatical Years," *Biblica*, 34 (1953) 501–15.

6. C. H. Gordon, "Sabbatical Cycle or Seasonal Pattern?" *Orientalia*, 22 (1953) 79-81.

7. A. Strobel, "Die Ausrufung des Yobeljahres in der Nazareth-predigt Jesus: zur apokalyptischen Tradition, Lc. 4, 16-30," in W. Eltester, ed., *Jesus in Nazareth* (Berlin, 1972), pp. 38-50. The positions taken by Strobel and North cannot be reconciled.

8. Strobel, "Die Ausrufung," p. 44.

9. M. P. Miller, "Isa. 61:1-2 in Melchizedek," JBL, 88 (1969) 467.

10. Miller, "Isa. 61:1-2," p. 468.

11. Quoted from A. Dupont-Sommer, *The Dead Sea Scrolls: A Preliminary Survey* (Oxford, 1952), pp. 95-96.

12. Ibid., p. 96, note 4.

13. Contrast the good Samaritan in Luke.

14. J. A. Sanders, "From Isaiah 61 to Luke 4," in J. Neusner, *Christianity, Judaism and Other Greco-Roman Cults* (Leiden, 1975), part 1, p. 90 (cited not quoted).

15. J. A. Fitzmyer, "Further Light on Melchizedek from Qumran Cave 11," JBL, 86 (1967) 29. See also A. S. Van der Woude, "Melchisedech als himmlische Erlösergestalt in den neugefundenen eschatologischen Midraschim aus Qumran Hohle X," *Oudtestamentische Studien*, 14 (1965) 354-73; he dates the fragment to the first century C.E. (p. 357).

16. Fitzmyer, "Further Light," p. 31.

17. Ibid., p. 32.

18. Ibid., p. 34.

19. Ibid., p. 36.

20. F. L. Horton, *The Melchizedek Tradition* (Cambridge, 1976).

21. Ibid., p. 73.

22. J. A. Sanders, "Dissenting Deities and Phil. 2:1-11," JBL, 88 (1969) 290.

23. Horton, *Melchizedek*, p. 80.

24. But Horton is working from only one column; see *Melkizedek*, p. 66, and J. T. Milik, "Milki-Sedeq et Milki-Resa dans les anciens écrits juifs et chrétiens (1)," JJS, 23 (1972) 95-144. For Horton's discussion of Melchizedek in Philo, see *Melkizedek*, pp. 54-60; for Melchizedek in Josephus, pp. 82-83. For his discussion of Gnostic texts, see pp. 131-51.

25. M. De Jonge and A. S. Van der Woude, "11 Q Melchizedek and the New Testament," NTS, 12 (1965-66) 306.

26. Ibid., p. 309.

27. Ibid.

28. Ibid., pp. 309-10.

29. Ibid., p. 310.

30. Ibid., p. 311.

31. Ibid., p. 312.

32. Ibid., p. 305.

33. It could be a dative of advantage, as in Acts 13:22; 14:3; 15:8; 22:5; Gal. 4:15; Col. 4:13. Note the frequency of this meaning in Luke.

34. B. Violet, "Zum rechten Verständnis der Nazarethpericope, Lc. 4:16-30," ZNW, 73 (1939) 251-71.

35. Ibid., p. 256.

36. Ibid., p. 258-63.

37. J. Jeremias, *Jesus' Promise to the Nations* (London, 1969).

38. L. C. Crockett, "Luke 4:25–27 and Jewish-Gentile Relations," JBL, 88 (1969) 177–83.

39. Crockett, "Luke 4:25–27," p. 178.

40. Ibid., p. 179.

41. Ibid., p. 181.

42. M. Miyoshi, *Der Anfang des Reiseberichts Lk. 9:51–10:24* (Rome, 1974), p. 18.

43. See A. Hastings, *Prophet and Witness in Jerusalem* (Baltimore, 1958), *passim*.

44. J. W. Elias, "The Beginning of Jesus' Ministry in the Gospel of Luke, a Redaction—Critical Study of Luke 4:14–30" (Toronto School of Theology, 1978).

Chapter 5

1. See E. Schürer, *The Jewish People in the Time of Jesus Christ* (Edinburgh, 1885), p. 372. O. Michel (TDNT, 7, p. 97) states that it was not paid into the *aerarium populi Romani* but into the imperial treasury (*fiscus*).

2. See Schürer, *The Jewish People*, p. 373.

3. See H. Loewe, *Render to Caesar* (Cambridge, 1940), p. 81.

4. Ibid., p. 83.

5. Ibid., p. 84.

6. J. S. Kennard, "Judas of Galilee and his Clan," JQR, 36 (1945) 281–86.

7. M. Black, "Judas of Galilee and Josephus' Fourth Philosophy," *Josephus Studien*, O. Betz, K. Haacker, and M. Hengel, eds. (Göttingen, 1974), pp. 45–47.

8. G. H. Dalman, *Sacred Sites and Ways* (London, 1935), p. 119, cited by Black, "Judas of Galilee," pp. 46–47.

9. W. Farmer, "Judas, Silas and Athronges," NTS, 1958, p. 151.

10. S. W. Applebaum, "The Zealots: The Case for Reevaluation," JRS, 61 (1971) 165.

11. J. Jeremias, "Zöllner und Sünder," ZNW, 30 (1931) 293–300; John R. Donahue, "Tax Collectors and Sinners," CBQ, 33 (1971) 39–61.

12. Michel, TDNT, under *Telōnes*, p. 102.

13. Ibid., p. 98.

14. J. Jeremias, *Jerusalem in the Time of Jesus* (London, 1969), p. 307.

15. Ibid., p. 303.

16. Ibid., p. 305.

17. Ibid., p. 306.

18. Ibid.

19. Ibid., p. 308.

20. Ibid., p. 309.

21. Ibid., p. 312.

22. Donahue, "Tax Collectors," p. 57.

23. See N. Perrin, *Rediscovering the Teaching of the New Testament* (London, 1967), pp. 93–102.

24. E. E. Ellis, *The Gospel of Luke* (London, 1974), p. 107.

25. D. Daube, "Responsibilities of Master and Disciples in the Gospels," NTS, 19 (1972) 5. The quotation comes from Seneca's *Troades*, 290.

26. W. Grundmann, *Das Evangelium nach Lukas* (Berlin, 1966), p. 132.

27. See I. H. Marshall, *Commentary on Luke* (Grand Rapids, 1978), p. 678.

28. J. Jeremias, *The Parables of Jesus* (London, 1963), p. 140.

29. Ibid., p. 142.

30. "Zöllner," p. 295.

31. J. Jeremias, *Parables*, p. 144.

32. Marshall, *Commentary*, p. 694.

33. W. P. Loewe, "Towards an Interpretation of Lk. 19:1-10," CBQ, 36 (1974) 321-31.

Chapter 6

1. For the history and theology of the Samaritans, see J. A. Montgomery, *The Samaritans* (Philadelphia, 1907); M. Gaster, *The Samaritans* (London, 1925); John Macdonald, *The Theology of the Samaritans* (London, 1964).

2. For further details, see H. Kreissig, *Die sozialen Zusammenhänge des jüdischen Krieges* (Kriens, 1970), pp. 17-20.

3. The Loeb translation of *Antiquities* (18:30, note d) cites J. Carcopino, "Encore le réscrit impérial sur les violations de sépulture," *Rev. Hist.*, 166 (1931) 90.

4. D. Rhoads, *Israel in Revolution 6-74 C.E.* (Philadelphia, 1976), pp. 71-73.

5. Tacitus (*Ann.* 12:54) says Cumanus was governor of Galilee and Felix of Samaria.

6. *Ant.* 20:118 calls it Giraea.

7. Josephus (*B.J.* 3:48) says, "The province of Samaria lies between Galilee and Judea, beginning at the village of Ginaea situated in the Great Plain."

8. Not mentioned in *Ant.* 20.

9. Rhoads, *Revolution*, pp. 71-73.

10. For discussion on the central section of Luke's Gospel, see C. C. McCown, "The Geography of Luke's Central Section," JBL, 57 (1938) 51-66; J. Blinzler, "Die literarische Eigenart des sogenannten Reiseberichtes im Lukas-Evangelium," in J. Schmid and A. Vogtle, eds., *Synoptische Studien* (Munich, 1953), pp. 20-52; J. Schneider, "Zur Analyse des Lukanischen Reiseberichtes," ibid., pp. 207-29; H. Conzelmann, *The Theology of St. Luke* (New York, 1960), pp. 53-66; B. Reicke, "Instruction and Discussion in the Travel Gospel," TU, 73 (1959) 206-16; W. Grundmann, "Fragen der Komposition des Lukanischen 'Reiseberichtes,' " ZNW, 50 (1959) 252-70; J. H. Davies, "The Purpose of the Central Section of St. Luke's Gospel," TU, 87 (1963) 164-69; G. Ogg, "The Central Section of the Gospel according to St. Luke," NTS, 18 (1971-72) 39-53.

11. C. F. Evans, "The Central Section of St. Luke's Gospel," in D. E. Nineham, ed., *Studies in the Gospels* (Oxford, 1957), pp. 37-53.

12. See R. H. Charles, *Pseudepigrapha* (Oxford, 1913), p. 407.

13. Evans, "Central Section," p. 40.

14. Ibid., pp. 42-50.

15. R. H. Charles, *Apocrypha and Pseudepigrapha of the Old Testament* (Oxford, reprint, 1964), vol. 2, p. 407.

16. Ibid.

17. Ibid.

18. W. Wink, *John the Baptist in the Gospel Tradition* (Cambridge, 1968), p. 45.

19. H. Flender, *St. Luke Theologian of Redemptive History* (London, 1967), p. 34. He adds: "In an earlier stage of this tradition it may have referred to Elijah *redivivus* (cf. Mark 6.15/Luke 9.8). At any rate the desire expressed by the sons of Zebedee for fire to descend from heaven points in this direction."

20. Ibid.

21. A. R. C. Leaney, *The Gospel according to St. Luke* (London, 1958), pp. 70–72.

22. M. Enslin, "Luke and the Samaritans," HTR, 36 (1943) 277–97.

23. Ibid., p. 281.

24. I. H. Marshall, *Commentary on Luke* (Grand Rapids, 1978), p. 465; cf. J. Jeremias, *The Parables of Jesus* (London, 1963), p. 205.

25. S-B, vol. 4, pp. 537, 543f.

26. G. Sellin, "Lukas als Gleichniserzähler: Die Erzählung vom barmherzigen Samariter (Luke 10:25-37)," ZNW, 65 (1974) 166–68 and 66 (1975) 19–60.

27. Cited by Sellin, ibid., pp. 27–28.

28. C. G. Montefiore, *The Synoptic Gospels* (New York, 1968), vol. 2, p. 467.

29. E. Linnemann, *Parables of Jesus* (London, 1966), p. 51–58.

30. Sellin, "Lukas," p. 40.

31. Ibid., p. 41.

32. Evans, "Central Section," p. 43.

33. Derrett, *Law in the New Testament* (London, 1970), p. 220.

34. Y. Yadin, "Temple Scroll," BA, 30 (1967) 135–39. See also Johann Maier, *Die Tempelrolle vom Toten Meer* (Basel, 1978), pp. 32–34 and 86–87.

35. Sellin, "Lukas," p. 29.

36. G. V. Jones, *The Art and Truth of Parables* (London, 1964), p. 115.

37. D. Crossan, "Parable and Example in the Teaching of Jesus," NTS, 18–19 (1972) 292.

38. F. D. Bruner, *A Theology of the Holy Spirit* (Grand Rapids, 1970), p. 176.

Chapter 7

1. M. Hengel, *Die Zeloten* (Leiden, 1970), p. 300.

2. S. G. F. Brandon, *Jesus and the Zealots* (Manchester, 1967), p. 159.

3. See J. Jeremias, *The Eucharistic Words of Jesus* (London, 1966), p. 207, note 4.

4. J. Blinzler, "Die Niedermetzelung von Galiläer durch Pilatus," *Nov. Test.*, 2 (1958) 32–37.

5. C. B. Caird, *St. Luke* (Harmondsworth, 1963), pp. 169–70.

6. J. Jeremias, *The Parables of Jesus* (London, 1963), pp. 170f.

7. Jerome Murphy-O'Connor, "The Rule of the Community," RB, 76 (1969) 528–49.

8. See Mary Douglas, *Purity and Danger, An Analysis of the Concepts of Pollution and Taboo* (New York, reprint, 1980).

9. See Jeremias, *Parables*, pp. 178–79.

10. Ibid.

11. Caird, *St. Luke*, p. 177.

12. A. Edersheim, *The Life and Times of Jesus the Messiah* (Grand Rapids, 1947), pp. 440–41.

13. Brandon, *Jesus*, p. 57.

14. See M. Hengel, *Crucifixion* (Philadelphia, 1977).

15. Jeremias, *Parables*, pp. 196–97.

16. C. F. Evans, "The Central Section of St. Luke's Gospel," in *Studies in the Gospels*, D. E. Nineham, ed. (Oxford, 1955), p. 48.

17. C. H. Dodd finds another parable that can be understood in the context of the revolutionary movement—the parable of the wicked tenants (*The Parables of the*

Kingdom [London, 1961], pp. 124ff.). It reflects the revolutionary attitude of the Galilean peasants to the foreign absentee landlords aroused by the zealots (revolutionaries) whose headquarters were in Galilee. Much of the hill country of Galilee and the north and northwest shores of the Sea of Galilee comprised latifundia (large agricultural estates). If the owner of the vineyard is abroad this explains why the tenants could not only illtreat the messengers but kill the son and hope to take over the property. If the land were not claimed within a certain time, it could be taken possession of by others.

18. G. Delling, "Das Gleichnis vom gottlosen Richter," ZNW, 53 (1962) pp. 1–25.

Chapter 8

1. H. Conzelmann (*The Theology of St. Luke* [New York, 1960], pp. 74–76) argues that Luke connects the entry with the Temple, not the city. According to Conzelmann, Luke gives the impression of a fairly long period of activity. Jesus cleanses the Temple and "occupies it as a place belonging to him."

2. W. R. Farmer, "The Palm Branches in John 12:13," JTS, ns 3 (1952) 62–66.

3. For the affinity between John and Luke, see J. A. Bailey, *The Traditions Common to the Gospels of Luke and John* (Leiden, 1963).

4. Caird, *St. Luke*, p. 139.

5. Edward Lohse, *History of the Suffering and Death of Jesus Christ* (Philadelphia, 1967), pp. 27–28.

6. The other destructive miracle is the killing of the Gadarene swine.

7. Biblical law prohibits the cutting down of fruitbearing trees.

8. D. M. Rhoads, *Israel in Revolution 6-74 C.E.* (Philadelphia, 1976), p. 155.

9. Ibid., pp. 155–56.

10. Ibid.

11. T. W. Manson, *The Sayings of Jesus* (London, 1949), p. 341.

12. H. -W. Bartsch, "Jesu Schwertwort, Lukas 22:35–38," NTS, 20 (1974) 190–93.

13. Ibid., p. 193.

14. F. Hahn, *The Titles of Jesus in Christology* (London, 1969), pp. 153–55.

15. P. Minear, "A Note on Luke 22:36," *Nov. Test.,* 7 (1964) 129–34.

16. V. Taylor, *Jesus and His Sacrifice* (London, 1937), p. 194.

17. B. M. Metzger, *A Textual Commentary on the New Testament* (London, 1971), p. 177.

18. Ibid.

19. A. Feuillet (*L'Agonie de Gethsemani* [Paris, 1977], p. 147) cites G. Gamba, "Agonia di Gesù," *RB,* 16 (1968) 159, and M. Galizzi, *Gesù nel Gethsemane* (Zurich, 1972), pp. 20–22 and 202–3. K. G. Kuhn ("Jesus in Gethsemane," EvT, 12 [1952–53] 268–69) thinks that the agony has a hellenistic background.

20. Feuillet, *L'Agonie*, p. 147.

21. J. W. Holleran, *The Synoptic Gethsemane* (Rome, 1973), p. 99.

22. Feuillet, *L'Agonie*, p. 148.

23. Ibid., pp. 149–50.

24. Holleran, *Gethsemane*, p. 101.

25. Ibid., p.97.

26. Ibid.

27. R. S. Barbour, "Gethsemane in the Passion Tradition," NTS, 16 (1970) 247. He suggests one to five different sources for the narrative of the agony.

28. Holleran, *Gethsemane*, pp. 88–89.

29. Barbour, "Gethsemane," p. 240.

30. V. Taylor, *The Passion Narrative of St. Luke* (Cambridge, 1972), p. 73.

31. Ibid., p. 74.

32. V. Taylor, *Behind the Third Gospel* (London, 1926), p. 47.

33. W. R. Wilson, *The Execution of Jesus* (New York, 1970), p. 111.

34. W. Dietrich, *Das Petrusbild der Lukanischen Schriften* (Stuttgart, 1972), pp. 139–57. He makes an analogy with Luke 5:8, where Peter is also a sinful man.

35. Taylor, *Passion*, p. 79.

36. D. R. Catchpole, *The Trial of Jesus* (Leiden, 1971), p. 175.

37. J. Blinzler, *The Trial of Jesus* (Westminster, Md., 1959), p. 115.

38. P. W. Walaskay, "The Trial and Death of Jesus in the Gospel of Luke," JBL, 94 (1975) 82.

39. Ibid.

40. Ibid., p. 83.

41. Ibid.

42. Ibid., p. 82.

43. Ibid., p. 84, note 9.

44. Ibid., p. 85.

45. A. N. Sherwin-White, *Roman Society and Roman Law in the New Testament* (Oxford, 1963), p. 25.

46. Ibid., p. 32.

47. Ibid., p. 118.

48. See H. Hoehner, *Herod Antipas* (Cambridge, 1972), p. 243, note 1.

49. "The Temple Scroll . . . may indicate that crucifixion was sometimes used as a punishment by the Jews" (*Encyclopaedia Judaica*, under "Temple Scroll").

50. Blinzler (*Trial*, p. 210) observes that some scholars connect Barabbas with Luke 13:1 and *Ant.* 18:6–12, the rebellion under Judas the Galilean, but he finds this mere conjecture.

51. Manson, *Sayings*, p. 343.

52. G. Dalman, *The Words of Jesus* (Edinburgh, 1909), p. 193.

53. Manson, *Sayings*, p. 343.

54. Conzelmann, *St. Luke*, p. 47.

55. P. W. Käser, "Exegetische und theologische Erwägungen zur Seligpreisung der Kinderlosen, Lc. 23:29b," ZNW, (1963) 240–54.

56. Metzger, *Commentary*, p. 180.

57. D. Daube, "For They Know Not What They Do, Lk. 23:24," TU (*Studia Patristica*), 79 (1961) 58–70.

58. Ibid., p. 58.

59. Ibid., p. 59.

60. Ibid., p. 60.

61. Ibid., p. 61.

62. Ibid., p. 62.

63. Ibid., p. 65.

64. Ibid., p. 66.

65. Ibid., p. 67.

66. Ibid., pp. 67–68.

67. E. E. Ellis, *The Gospel of Luke* (London, 1974), pp. 268–69.

68. G. D. Kilpatrick, "A Theme of the Lucan Passion Story and Luke 23:47," JTS, 43 (1942) 34–36.

69. R. P. C. Hanson, "Does *Dikaios* in Luke xxiii 47 explode the Proto-Luke Hypothesis?" *Hermathena*, 55 (1942) 74–78. Hanson disagrees with Kilpatrick.

Chapter 9

1. There is a good discussion of the jubilee principles in A. Trocmé, *Jesus and the Non-violent Revolution* (Scottdale, Pa., 1973), pp. 27–76.

DISCUSSION QUESTIONS

Ask the participants to bring with them their Bibles and, if they possess a copy, their Gospel Parallels.

The questions below are intended as a point of departure for group discussion. They may also be appropriate for individual persons in their own reflections on the themes of this book. They are by no means exhaustive but they do represent an example of the possible application of Luke's principles to pastoral concerns and contemporary problems.

It would be best if only one chapter were discussed individually and if time were taken at the beginning to recall its salient points. Members of the group should be invited to share what points they considered most interesting or important—or even, most perplexing. This has the beneficial effect of putting the chapter firmly in mind, so that it can be discussed all the more concretely. It also helps to prevent the frustration of an irrelevant, rambling discussion. The printed questions could then be posed, allowing sufficient time for individual viewpoints and subsidiary questions to emerge. Further application should be encouraged.

The important thing is that group members be enabled and stimulated to interact vitally with the text. They should not try to be biblical exegetes or to give definitive answers to issues. A short interval for silence and prayer might be offered before or after the questions.

Chapter One

(1) The chapter describes first-century Palestine as a "seething cauldron." Is this description appropriate for the Middle East in our own times? Why or why not?

(2) The contemporaries of Jesus were obliged to endure Roman military occupation, burdensome taxation, and at least occasional instances of official misconduct. Have people in the world today or you yourself had any experience of these? Under what circumstances? How do you think your experience differs from (or concurs with) that of the people in first-century Palestine?

(3) In Palestine in Jesus' day there were internal as well as external tensions. What groups today remind you of the competing factions and revolutionary parties described in the chapter? Why?

(4) What do you think is the proper role of the Church in addressing these internal and external conflicts? Should Christians become involved in political or social disputes? Or should they seek to be neutral and to reduce animosities on both sides? Is it possible to do both? How? Give examples.

(5) Are you horrified by the number of crucifixions alluded to in this chapter? In the light of these do you understand more clearly (a) the courage of Jesus and (b) the fear of the disciples, especially when they deserted him in the garden of Gethsemane. Who runs the risk of torture today?

(6) What effect did the occupying troops have on Palestine? How do occupying armies make conditions more difficult for people today? What can be done about this?

(7) What were the class conflicts in first-century Palestine? Are similar tensions found in our world? Are they found in your town or country?

(8) Is there any phenomenon similar to "social banditry" today? If so, how can we alleviate this?

(9) Do you know of anyone in the contemporary world who believes in God as warrior and in holy war? Is this consistent with the teaching of Jesus?

(10) Are there any prophets and prophetesses living today?

Chapter Two

(1) Perhaps most people are accustomed to think of a single, composite Christmas story, without realizing the differences between the versions found in the Gospels of Matthew and Luke. What points distinguish the two (you will find the use of Gospel Parallels helpful here)? Do you prefer one or the other? Is one more "political" than the other? How would you characterize Luke's narrative and his point of view?

(2) How do most people view and "practice" Christmas today?

(3) How do you suppose the advent of Jesus appeared to the figures mentioned in Luke's narrative? What had each been told, and what did each expect? What do you make of Luke's emphasis on Mary's family connections? Do you think, generally speaking, that Luke writes from Mary's point of view, or do you think that she would have written a somewhat different account? Is it fair or accurate for Luke's contrast of Jesus to the bellicose expectations of his contemporaries to be described as a feminine perspective?

(4) According to Luke, Jesus emphasized love of enemies at a time when others looked for vengeance and retribution. Granted that his teaching is beautiful and inspiring, do you think that it is also practical? Can it be implemented without having already attained moral perfection? Is retribution a necessity in the "real world"? If forgiveness is no less real or practical, why? Give examples.

(5) Have you gained a new insight into Mary's character by reading this chapter? If so, how does it alter your relationship with her? Does she become a more real and more courageous person in your eyes?

(6) Has this chapter altered your view of angels?

(7) What do "names" mean to you? Do you fulfill the expectation of your baptismal name given by your parents and your confirmation name chosen by yourself? What names would you choose for yourself now? Why?

(8) Select some Christmas hymns which are appropriate for a more realistic view of the birth of Christ (they need not come from the Christmas season).

(9) Write a prayer of thanksgiving for Mary after the birth of her child and one for the shepherds when they visit the Messiah.

Chapter Three

(1) Scholars have disagreed whether the ministry of John the Baptist was more closely related to the Old Testament (as the last of the prophets) or the New Testament (as precursor of Jesus). What do you suppose Luke thought? On the basis of his message, what do you think?

(2) How should Christians see John? Was he basically "one of us"? Was he a saint or martyr in the sense of those who were later followers of Jesus? Is he a "good example" for us? If so, in what way? Or should he be played down as a somewhat crude and bellicose figure, who in any case was far eclipsed by Jesus?

(3) What is the importance of Luke's genealogy of Jesus? Is it inconsistent that he should trace the line of Adam to Joseph, only to maintain that Jesus had no natural, earthly father? If Luke is trying to make a different sort of point, what might it be? What is our own attitude to ancestry and genealogy, and how does it differ from the attitude presupposed in the Bible?

(4) Luke is shown in this chapter to tone down the political significance of John, especially as pertains to his treatment of Jesus. Do you consider that Luke was revealing a unique aspect of John and Jesus or simply changing the facts to suit his own purposes and point of view? Does Luke, in downplaying violence and revolution, make John (and later Jesus) more politically indifferent than they probably were in actuality?

(5) John gave ethical teaching to soldiers, tax collectors, and the poor. What ethical principles should contemporary people in these groups follow (substitute police for soldiers, if you prefer)?

(6) Jesus spoke about the simplicity and courage of John's status as a prophet. What characteristics do you think he would ask of prophets and prophetesses today?

(7) Marshall lists several purposes of genealogies. Which purpose is most appropriate (a) to Matthew and (b) to Luke? How does the view of a genealogy as a "work of art" rather than a subject for literal interpretation help us to understand scripture in both the Old Testament and the New Testament?

(8) Write a "job" description for a prophet or prophetess or religious leader in general. Would your description be consonant with charismatic

work in (a) your parish and (b) on conservative, Christian television broadcasts?

(9) The authoress of this book has called John a "transitional figure," not as belligerent, as were some of his contemporaries, but not as pacific as Jesus. Is there some role for transitional personages today?

(10) John sent his disciples to ask for Jesus' credentials as "He Who Was To Come." What are the credentials which are necessary for Christians today?

Chapter Four

(1) Luke's account of Jesus' first "homily" shows him preaching relief for the poor and oppressed, but without the violence and vengeance which people had come to expect of the new "Melchizedek." For this reason the congregation turned against him. Why should the preaching of peace have made the people angry? Can you think of anyone whose preaching of the peaceful pursuit of justice has promoted resentment and ill treatment in our own time? What limits should be placed on how peace is preached from the pulpit?

(2) According to one Jewish expectation, a warrior messiah would be able to restore the rights and interests of the people. Do you think this was realistic? Was the violent overthrow of foreign oppressors justifiable? Was it likely to succeed? Many modern nations, including the United States, are the products of revolution. Are we in a position to condemn all violent revolutionaries? Some? Why do some revolutions result only in more revolutions?

(3) Jesus announces that the prophecy of Isaiah has been fulfilled and proclaims a new age of clemency and justice. Since we are still waiting for such a time to be inaugurated, was Jesus wrong? In what sense has Isaiah's prophecy been fulfilled? Is it enough to say that Jesus has brought peace only for his followers? Does church history bear this out? Can justice with peace and clemency ever really be attainable?

(4) The Roman Catholic church celebrates a jubilee year every twenty-five years, but this is not really socially orientated. Would it be possible to practice the principles of the jubilee year as found in the Bible? If it is not possible to implement all the features, could certain ones be used, e.g., the redistribution of wealth?

(5) The Qumran community appears to have taught a doctrine of "holy hatred." Do some religious people practice this today? If so, is it consonant with the gospel and modern ethical standards?

(6) Is it possible for Moslems and Christians to come to some agreement about the principles of "holy war"?

(7) Jesus confronted the congregation and they attempted to assassinate him. What responsibility and consequences do we accept when we choose to confront anyone or any group?

(8) Jesus appears to have omitted part of a verse from scripture. How does this become germane to the issue of the inspiration or inerrancy of scripture?

(9) Some people still believe in a Day of Vengeance. What would be a fruitful way of discussing this with them?

(10) The early church faced much conflict over the question of "table fellowship," Jews dining with gentiles. Are there any comparable issues in modern times?

Chapter Five

(1) What did people in Jesus' time think of tax collectors? Why? What do you think of tax collectors yourself? Why? How would you explain our resentment of taxes and frequent inclination to cheat on our 1040s if only a little? How does Luke's account of Jesus' attitude to tax collectors apply to us? Is it enough to respect the collector but resent the tax? Should taxes be withheld when they are being used for apparently immoral purposes?

(2) There were many other occupations which Jews in the time of Jesus rejected as dishonest or impure. Are there occupations we reject today on grounds of snobbery or disrespect of common work? Are there occupations we reject with good reason? Give examples.

(3) How should we follow Jesus' example of association with "sinners"? Can fellowship with "sinners" and approval of sin be kept entirely separate? What do you think is the proper relationship of a Christian today to a robber, swindler, or male or female prostitute? Is it really possible, as some have suggested, to simultaneously love the sinner but hate the sin?

(4) Who are the social outcasts in your area? What is the outreach of your parish or community to them? Do you think of their welfare as part of your responsibility as a Christian? Should one distinguish between supplying their spiritual and physical needs? Would you be glad to see persons of another race, nationality, or social class taking a more active and visible role in your parish or community? In the neighborhood where you live?

(5) Do you feel any sympathy with the principles of the revolt of Judas the Galilean? With any resistance movement today?

(6) Although there has been a history of resistance to taxes, they do provide necessary service for a country, e.g., in Palestine the fine Roman roads. What benefits can taxes serve today?

(7) The Jews saw themselves as tenants on God's land. How do we regard our possession or lack of possession of land and property?

(8) Tax collectors were akin to members and leaders of the mafia. What would have been Jesus' reaction to the films *Godfather I* and *Godfather II?*

(9) If you gave a meal for Jesus, who would you invite and what menu would you serve?

(10) Rewrite the parable of the tax collector and the Pharisee in modern terms so that it is appropriate for a modern, general situation.

Chapter Six

(1) The conflict between the Jews and the Samaritans was partly ethnic, partly religious, and partly simply the result of animosities accumulated over time. Can you think of a contemporary example of such rivalry. What are the parallels? Who are "the Samaritans" in the world today? In our own country? Why are ethnic and religious bigotry so difficult to overcome?

(2) In Luke's Gospel Jesus shows considerable acceptance of this despised religious and ethnic group, in spite of a longstanding tradition. How does this example apply to our own prejudice? What can you do to overcome bigotry in your own family, neighborhood, parish, city, or community? How does the Christian deal with the past injustices which may have been committed by the other side?

(3) With this discussion in mind, retell the parable of the Good Samaritan in modern terms, substituting contemporary social groups for those represented by the biblical characters. Does the parable seem different to you? How do you think members of your parish would react to the reading of your modernized version on Sunday morning?

(4) How do you explain the fact that Matthew appears to have a different approach to the Samaritans than Luke? Is it possible for Christians to differ so radically today?

(5) Jesus was not expected to drink from the same vessel as the Samaritan woman. Give examples of practices of ritual purity (in different religions) which appear to ostracize certain people or conditions.

(6) A rival temple was offensive to the Jews. Are we offended by rival temples or churches? If so, why?

(7) Herod made his wedding an interlude to the siege of Jerusalem, thereby adding to the pain of the Jews. In which areas have we been insensitive to others?

(8) Cumanus did not fulfill his responsibilities toward the country "under his care." How is the United States fulfilling its responsibility toward less privileged neighbor states?

(9) Jesus accepted the inhospitality of the Samaritans with equanimity. How do we react when we are rejected?

(10) The Jews saw the death of their spiritual leaders as "assumptions." How do we look on the deaths of those who are respected and loved?

Chapter Seven

(1) In Luke's Gospel Jesus identifies with the poor, the handicapped, and the underprivileged; he rejects the assumption that their lot in life is a punishment for sin. Are there people today who believe that the poor deserve their fate or that they have brought their condition upon themselves?

(2) Luke reports much of Jesus' teaching about fellowship in the form of

stories about meals. Do you think that sharing meals helps to create a sense of unity? How important do you think it is, in these days of busy schedules, for families to dine in common rather than "on the run"?

(3) Jesus dined with tax collectors and sinners. In the parable of the Great Supper, it is those on the fringe of life who join the feast. How does this cordiality apply to the epitome of table fellowship—of community with God and community in the Church—which we know in the Eucharist?

(4) Write the parable of the Rich Fool in terms of nuclear warfare.

(5) Jesus girded himself with a towel and washed the feet of his disciples. What personal form of service is most appropriate for the Christian today?

(6) Jesus reacted with poise and magnanimity to the news of the tower killing a number of people and to the death of his Galilean countrymen. What light does this shed on the contemporary practice of taking people to court for accidents?

(7) What would Jesus think about our present "table etiquette"? Can you imagine Jesus in a MacDonalds? Would he communicate with his fellow diners?

(8) Two thousand persons were crucified near Jesus' home when he was a teenager. What psychological effect would this have on him and his mother and on his attitude to nonviolence? How can we apply this to situations today?

(9) Some peoples still believe in holy war. What is your answer to them as a Christian?

(10) Many Christians are convinced that a Day of Vengeance is coming. Is this, or is it not, consonant with the teaching of Jesus in Luke's Gospel?

Chapter Eight

(1) Luke emphasizes that Jesus went to his death quietly, courageously, and with forgiveness for those who betrayed him. Is it humanly possible to set aside our self-interest for the sake of loving our enemies, even at the risk of death? What would be the consequences in international relations of forgiving those who wish us harm and submitting to their abuse?

(2) Is violence in self-defense a necessary evil?

(3) Recent years have seen a stream of best-selling books whose theme has been that we should pursue our own personal fulfilment. In the light of the cross, is this a credible philosophy of life for the Christian? Give examples of what the humility of a Christian might require (or would not require!) in the vicissitudes of daily life.

(4) Jesus came to his resurrection only through suffering and shame. How does this example compare with the assumptions about power and glory which we find reflected in film and television?

(5) Power has potential for both great good and great harm. Nuclear energy can be used to generate electricity or cause utter destruction. What is the lesson of Luke's depiction of Jesus about real power and its use?

(6) Jesus cleansed the temple of "filthy lucre." How can we be careful not to make religion the source of gain? What can we do if we find that we have made a financial profit from it?

(7) How can the discipline of athletes teach us about the necessity of self-control and discipline in our religious life?

(8) Jesus, apparently, was wrongfully accused of political misdemeanor. Can we think of similar cases in our own day?

(9) Jesus' crucifixion was unbelievably cruel and obscene. What forms of death and punishment do we permit which are inhumane and degrading? What form of death would you yourself choose?

SELECT BIBLIOGRAPHY

Books

H. von Baer. *Der Heilige Geist in den Lukanschriften*. Stuttgart, 1926.

J. A. Bailey. *The Traditions Common to the Gospels of Luke and John*. Leiden, 1963.

E. Bammel, ed. *The Trial of Jesus*. London, 1970.

G. R. Beasley-Murray. *Jesus and the Future*. London, 1954.

P. Benoit. *Exégèse et théologie*. Paris, vol. 1, 1961; vol. 2, 1961; vol. 3, 1968.

―――. *The Passion and Resurrection of Jesus Christ*. London, 1969.

O. Betz et al. *Abraham unser Vater*. Leiden, 1963.

O. Betz, K. Haacker, and M. Hengel, eds. *Josephus Studien*. Göttingen, 1974.

―――. *What Do We Know about Jesus?* London, 1968.

M. Black. *An Aramaic Approach to the Gospels and Acts*. Oxford, 1967.

J. Blinzler. *The Trial of Jesus*. Westminster, Md., 1959.

J. Blinzler et al. *Neutestamentliche Aufsätze*. Regensburg, 1963.

G. Bornkamm. *Jesus of Nazareth*. London, 1960.

S. G. F. Brandon. *The Fall of Jerusalem and the Christian Church*. London, 1951.

―――. *Jesus and the Zealots*. Manchester, 1967.

―――. *The Trial of Jesus of Nazareth*. New York, 1968.

H. Braun. *Qumran und das Neue Testament*. Tübingen, 1966.

R. E. Brown, *The Birth of the Messiah*. New York, 1977.

―――. *The Gospel According to John*. London, 2 vols., 1971.

F. F. Bruce. *The Acts of the Apostles*. London, 1961.

J. Cadbury. *The Style and Literary Method of Luke*. Cambridge, Mass., 2 vols., 1920.

G. B. Caird. *St. Luke*. Harmondsworth, 1963.

R. Catchpole. *The Trial of Jesus*. Leiden, 1971.

R. H. Charles, ed. *The Apocrypha and Pseudepigrapha of the Old Testament in English*. Oxford, 1913.

H. Conzelmann. *Theology of Luke*. New York, 1960.

C. E. B. Cranfield. *St. Mark*. Cambridge, 1963.

J. M. Creed. *St. Luke*. London, 1930.

O. Cullmann. *The Christology of the New Testament*. London, 1959.

G. Dalman. *The Words of Jesus*. Edinburgh, 1909.

F. W. Danker. *Jesus and the New Age*. St. Louis, 1972.

D. Daube. *The New Testament and Rabbinic Judaism*. London, 1956.

W. D. Davies. *The Gospel and the Land*. Berkeley, 1974.

―――. *The Setting of the Sermon on the Mount*. Cambridge, 1964.

H. Degenhardt. *Lukas—Evangelist der Armen*. Stuttgart, 1966.

J. D. M. Derrett. *Law in the New Testament*. London, 1970.

A. Descamps et al., eds. *Mélanges bibliques*. Gembloux, 1970.

M. Dibelius. *Studies in the Acts of the Apostles*. London, 1956.

W. Dietrich. *Das Petrusbild der Lukanischen Schriften*. Stuttgart, 1972.

C. H. Dodd. *Historical Tradition in the Fourth Gospel*. Cambridge, 1963.

————. *The Parables of the Kingdom*. London, 1961.

A. J. G. Dreyer. *An Examination of the Possible Relation between Luke's Infancy Narratives and the Qumran Hodayot*. Amsterdam, 1962.

J. D. G. Dunn. *Baptism in the Holy Spirit*. London, 1970.

A. Dupont-Sommer. *The Essene Writings from Qumran*. New York, 1961.

B. S. Easton. *The Gospel According to St. Luke*. Edinburgh, 1926.

E. E. Ellis. *The Gospel of Luke*. London, 1974.

E. E. Ellis and E. Grasser, eds. *Jesus und Paulus*. Göttingen, 1975.

E. E. Ellis and M. Wilcox, eds. *Neotestamentica et Semitica*. Edinburgh, 1969.

W. Eltester, ed. *Judentum—Urchristentum—Kirche*. Berlin, 1964.

E. Fascher. *Prophētēs*. Giessen, 1927.

A. Feuillet. *l'Agonie de Gethsemani*. Paris, 1977.

J. Finegan. *Handbook of Biblical Chronology*. Princeton, 1964.

J. A. Fitzmyer. *The Gospel According to Luke 1-9*. New York, 1981.

H. Flender. *St. Luke Theologian of Redemptive History*. London, 1967.

J. Massyngbaerde Ford. *Revelation*. New York, 1974.

S. Freyne. *Galilee*. Notre Dame, Indiana, 1980.

R. H. Fuller. *Foundations of New Testament Christology*. London, 1965.

B. Gartner. *The Temple and the Community in Qumran and the New Testament*. Cambridge, 1965.

W. W. Gasque and R. P. Martin, eds. *Apostolic History and the Gospel*. Exeter, 1970.

M. Gaster. *The Samaritans*. London, 1925.

L. Gaston. *No Stone on Another*. Leiden, 1970.

R. Geldenhuys. *Commentary on the Gospel of Luke*. London, 1950.

B. Gerhardsson. *The Good Samaritan—The Good Shepherd?* Lund, 1958.

W. Grundmann. *Das Evangelium nach Lukas*. Berlin, 1966.

E. Haenchen. *The Acts of the Apostles*. Philadelphia, 1971.

F. Hahn. *The Titles of Jesus in Christology*. London, 1969.

D. R. A. Hare. *The Theme of Jewish Persecution of Christians in the Gospel according to St. Matthew*. Cambridge, 1967.

A. Hastings. *Prophet and Witness in Jerusalem*. London, 1958.

M. Hengel. *Crucifixion*. Philadelphia, 1977.

————. *Judaism and Hellenism*. Philadelphia, 2 vols., 1974.

————. *Nachfolge und Charisma*. Berlin, 1968.

————. *Die Zeloten*, Leiden, 1970.

H. Hoehner. *Herod Antipas*. Cambridge, 1972.

J. W. Holleran. *The Synoptic Gethsemane*. Rome, 1973.

Fred H. Horton. *The Melchizedek Tradition*. Cambridge, 1976.

W. Jens. *Der barmherzige Samariter*. Stuttgart, 1973.

J. Jeremias. *The Eucharistic Words of Jesus*. London, 1966.

————. *Jerusalem in the Time of Jesus*. London, 1969.

————. *Jesus' Promise to the Nations*. London, 1958.

————. *The Parables of Jesus*. London, 1963.

M. D. Johnson. *The Purpose of the Biblical Genealogies*. Cambridge, 1969.

E. Käsemann. *Essays on New Testament Themes.* London, 1964.

———. *New Testament Questions of Today.* London, 1969.

J. S. Kennard. *Render to God. A Study of the Tribute Passage.* New York, 1950.

R. Laurentin. *Structure et théologie de Luc 1-2.* Paris, 1957.

A. R. C. Leaney. *The Gospel according to St. Luke.* London, 1958.

E. Linnemann. *Parables of Jesus.* London, 1966.

———. *Studien zur Passionsgeschichte.* Göttingen, 1970.

H. Loewe. *Render unto Caesar.* Cambridge, 1940.

Edward Lohse. *History of the Suffering and Death of Jesus Christ.* Philadelphia, 1967.

John Macdonald. *The Theology of the Samaritans.* London, 1964.

J. G. Machen. *The Virgin Birth of Christ.* London, 1932.

T. W. Manson. *The Gospel of Luke.* London, 1930.

———. *The Sayings of Jesus.* London, 1949.

———. *The Teaching of Jesus,* Cambridge, 1935.

I. H. Marshall. *Commentary on Luke.* Grand Rapids, 1978.

———. *Luke: Historian and Theologian.* Grand Rapids, 1971.

B. M. Metzger. *A Textual Commentary on the Greek New Testament.* London, 1971.

R. Meyer. *Der Prophet aus Galiläa.* Leipzig, 1940.

J. T. Milik. *Ten Years Discovery on the Wilderness of Judea.* London, 1959.

D. G. Miller and D. Y. Hadidian. *Jesus and Man's Hope.* Pittsburgh, vol. 1, 1970; vol. 2, 1971.

M. Miyoshi. *Der Anfang des Reiseberichts Lk. 9:51-10:24.* Rome, 1974.

J. A. Montgomery. *Samaritans.* Philadelphia, 1907.

G. F. Moore. *Judaism.* Cambridge, Mass., 3 vols., 1927-30.

C. F. D. Moule. *An Idiom-Book of New Testament Greek.* Cambridge, 1953.

D. E. Nineham, ed. *Studies in the Gospels.* Oxford, 1955.

N. Perrin. *Rediscovering the Teaching of Jesus.* London, 1967.

A. Plummer. *St. Luke.* Edinburgh, 1922.

I. de la Potterie, ed. *De Jésus aux Evangiles.* Gembloux, 1967.

T. Rehkopf. *Die lukanische Sonderquelle.* Tübingen, 1959.

B. Reicke. *New Testament Era.* Philadelphia, 1974.

K. Rengstorf. *Das Evangelium nach Lukas.* Göttingen, 1937.

———. *Die Re-Investitur des verlorenen Sohnes in der Gleichniserzählung Jesu, Luk. 15, 11-32.* Cologne, 1967.

M. Rese. *Alttestamentliche Motive in der Christologie des Lukas.* Gütersloh, 1969.

D. M. Rhoads. *Israel in Revolution 6-74 C.E.* Philadelphia, 1976.

S. Safrai and M. Stern. *The Jewish People in the First Century,* vol. 2. Philadelphia, 1976.

H. Sahlin. *Der Messias und das Gottesvolk.* Uppsala, 1945.

———. *Studien zum dritten Kapitel des Lukasevangelium.* Uppsala, 1949.

A. Schlatter. *Das Evangelium des Lukas.* Stuttgart, 1960.

J. Schmid and A. Vogtle, eds. *Synoptische Studien.* Munich, 1953.

G. Schneider. *Verleugnung, Verspottung und Verhör Jesus nach Lukas 22, 54-71.* Munich, 1969.

T. Schramm. *Der Markus-Stoff bei Lukas.* Cambridge, 1971.

E. Schürer. *The History of the Jewish People in the Age of Jesus Christ,* vol. 1 (revised and edited by G. Vermès and F. Millar). Edinburgh, 1973.

H. Schürmann. *Das Lukasevangelium.* Freiburg, 1969.

F. Schutz. *Der leidende Christus*. Stuttgart, 1969.

H. Scobie. *John the Baptist*. London, 1964.

A. N. Sherwin-White. *Roman Society and Roman Law in the New Testament*. Oxford, 1963.

M. Smith. *Jesus the Magician*. New York, 1978.

E. Stauffer. *Christ and the Caesars*. Philadelphia, 1955.

————. *Jerusalem und Rom*. Bern, 1957.

————. *Jesus and His Story*. London, 1960.

B. H. Streeter. *The Four Gospels*. London, 1936.

C. H. Talbert. *Literary Patterns, Theological Themes and the Genre of Luke-Acts*. Missoula, Montana, 1974.

V. Taylor. *Behind the Third Gospel*. Oxford, 1926.

————. *The Gospel according to St. Mark*. London, 1953.

————. *Jesus and His Sacrifice*. London, 1937.

————. *The Passion Narrative of St. Luke*. Cambridge, 1972.

H. Thurman. *Jesus and the Disinherited*. Nashville, 1949.

D. Tiede. *The Charismatic Figure as Miracle Worker*. Missoula, Montana, 1972.

H. E. Tödt. *The Son of Man in the Synoptic Tradition*. London, 1965.

C. C. Torrey. *The Four Gospels*. London, n.d.

A. Trocmé. *Jesus and the Nonviolent Revolution*. Scottdale, Pa., 1973.

G. Vermès. *Jesus the Jew*. London, 1973.

————. *Scripture and Tradition in Judaism*. Leiden, 1961.

G. Voss. *Die Christologie der lukanischen Schriften in Grundzügen*. Paris, 1965.

M. Wilcox. *The Semitisms of Acts*. Oxford, 1965.

S. G. Wilson. *The Gentiles and the Gentile Mission in Luke-Acts*. Cambridge, 1973.

W. R. Wilson. *The Execution of Jesus*. New York, 1970.

W. Wink. *John the Baptist in the Gospel Tradition*. Cambridge, 1968.

P. Winter. *On the Trial of Jesus*. Berlin, 1974.

Y. Yadin. *The Art of Warfare in Biblical Lands in the Light of Archaeological Study*. New York, 1963.

————. *The War Scroll of the Sons of Light against the Sons of Darkness*. Oxford, 1962.

J. H. Yoder. *The Politics of Jesus*. Grand Rapids, 1973.

Articles

E. L. Abel. "The Genealogy of Jesus *HO CHRISTOS*." NTS, 20 (1973-74) 203-10.

Moses Aberbach. "The Conflicting Accounts of Josephus and Tacitus Concerning Cumanus' and Felix's Terms of Office." JQR, 40 (1949) 1-14.

H. Anderson. "Broadening Horizons: The Rejection at Nazareth Perikope of Lk. 4, 16-30 in Light of Recent Critical Trends."*Interpretation*, 18 (1964) 259-75.

S. A. Applebaum. "The Zealots: The Case for Reevaluation." JRS, 61 (1971) 165.

R. A. Aytoun. "The Ten Lucan Hymns of the Nativity in their Original Language." JTS, 18 (1917) 274-88.

J. Bajard. "La structure de la pericope de Nazareth en Lc. 4:16-30." EphT, 45 (1969) 165-71.

P. H. Ballard. "Reasons for Refusing the Great Supper." JTS, ns 23 (1972) 341-50.

E. Bammel. "The Baptist in Early Christian Tradition." NTS, 18 (1971-72) 95-128.

R. S. Barbour. "Gethsemane in the Passion Tradition." NTS, 16 (1969-70) 231-51.

P. W. Barnett. "The Jewish Sign Prophets—A.D. 40-70—Their Intention and Origin." NTS, 27 (1981) 679-97.

———. "Under Tiberius All Was Quiet," NTS, 21 (1975) 564-71.

C. K. Barrett. "The House of Prayer and the Den of Thieves." Ellis and Grasser, eds., *Jesus und Paulus*, pp. 13-20.

H. W. Bartsch. "Jesu Schwertwort, Lukas xxii, 35-38." NTS, 20 (1973-74) 190-203.

W. Bauer. "The 'Colt' of Palm Sunday." JBL, 72 (1953) 220-29.

Stephen Benko. "The Magnificat, A History of Controversy." JBL, 86 (1967) 263-75.

P. Benoit. "L'enfance de Jean-Baptiste selon Luc 1." NTS, 3 (1956-57) 169-94.

———. " 'Non erat eis locus in diversorio' (Lc. 2, 7)." Descamps et. al., eds., *Mélanges bibliques*, pp. 173-86.

———. " 'Et toi-même, un glaive te transpercera l'âme' (Luc 2, 35)." CBQ, 25 (1963) 251-61.

H. D. Betz. "The Cleansing of the Ten Lepers (Luke 17:11-19)." JBL, 90 (1971) 314-28.

O. Betz. "The Kerygma of Luke." *Interpretation*, 22 (1968) 131-46.

P. Billerbeck. "Ein Synagogengottesdienst in Jesu Tagen." ZNW, 55 (1965) 143-61.

J. N. Birdsall. "Luke XII, 16ff. and the Gospel of Thomas." JTS, ns 13 (1962) 332-36.

M. Black. "Judas of Galilee and Josephus' Fourth Philosophy." Betz et. al., eds., *Josephus Studien*, pp. 45-47.

J. Blinzler. "Die literarische Eigenart des sogenannten Reiseberichts im Lukas Evangelium." Schmid and Vogtle, eds., *Synoptische Studien*, pp. 20-52.

———. "Die Niedermetzelung von Galiläer durch Pilatus." *Nov. Test.*, 2 (1958) 24-49.

———. "Passionsgeschehen und Passionsbericht des Lukasevangeliums." *Bibel und Kirche*, 24 (1, 1969) 1-4.

Marc Borg. "The Currency of the Term 'Zealot.' " JTS, 22 (1971) 504-12.

Georg Braumann. "Die Lukanische Interpretation der Zerstörung Jerusalems." *Nov. Test.*, 6 (1963) 120-27.

H. Braunert. "Der Römische Provinzialzensus und der Schätzungsbericht des Lukas-Evangeliums," *Historia*, 6 (1957) 192-214.

R. E. Brown. "Luke's Method in the Annunciation Narratives." J. W. Flanagan and A. W. Robinson, eds., *No Famine in the Land*, Missoula, Montana, 1975, pp. 179-94.

W. H. Brownlee. "The Servant of the Lord in the Qumran Scrolls, 2." *Bulletin of the American School of Research*, 135 (1954) 36-38.

F. F. Bruce. "Render unto Caesar." C. F. D. Moule and E. Bammel, eds., *The Zealots and Jesus* (forthcoming).

L. Brun. "Engel und Blutschweiss Lc. 22, 43-44." ZNW, 32 (1933) 265-76.

F. C. Burkitt. "St. Luke XXII 15, 16: What is the General Meaning?" JTS, 569-72.

———. "Who Spoke the Magnificat?" JTS, 7 (1905-06) 220-27.

H. J. Cadbury. "A Proper Name for Dives." JBL, 81 (1962) 399-402.

C. C. Caragounis, "Opsōnion: A Reconsideration of its Meaning." *Nov. Test.*, 16 (1974) 35-57.

C. H. Cave. "Lazarus and the Lucan Deuteronomy." NTS, 15 (1968-69) 319-25.

T. Corbishley. "Quirinius and the Census." *Klio,* 29 (1936) 8–93.

J. M. Creed. "The Slavonic Version of Josephus' History of the Jewish War." HTR, 25 (1932) 279–314.

L. C. Crockett. "Luke iv 16–30 and the Jewish Lectionary Cycle: A Word of Caution." JJS, 17 (1966) 13–46.

H. S. Cronin. "Abilene, the Jewish Herods and St. Luke." JTS, 18 (1916–17) 147–51.

J. D. Crossan. "Parable and Example in the Teaching of Jesus." NTS, 18 (1972–73) 285–307.

N. A. Dahl. "The Story of Abraham in Luke-Acts." SLA, pp. 139–58.

D. Daube. " 'For they know not what they do' Luke 23, 34." TU, 79 (1961) 58–70.

———. "Inheritance in Two Lukan Pericopes." *Zeitschrift der Savigny-Stiftung für Rechtsgeschichte,* 72 (1955) 327ff.

———. "Responsibilities of Master and Disciples in the Gospels." NTS, 19 (1972–73) 1–15.

J. H. Davies. "The Purpose of the Central Section of St. Luke's Gospel." TU, 87 (1963) 164–69.

R. Deichgraber. "Lc 2:14 *Anthrōpoi eudokias.*" ZNW, 51 (1960) 132.

J. Delobel. "La rédaction de Lc. IV, 14–16a et le 'Bericht vom Anfang.' " P. Neirynihk, ed., *L'Evangile de Luc,* Gembloux, 1973, pp. 203–23.

J. D. M. Derrett. "Law in the New Testament: The Palm Sunday Colt." *Nov. Test.,* 13 (1971) 241–58.

———. "The Manger: Ritual Law and Soteriology." *Theology,* 74 (1971) 566–71.

———. "The Rich Fool, A Parable of Jesus Concerning Inheritance." HJ, 18 (1977) 131–51.

G. R. Driver. "Two Problems in the New Testament." JTS, ns 16 (1965) 327–37.

J. Dupont. "L'Ambassade de Jean Baptiste (Mt. 11:2–6 et 7:18–23)." NRT, 83 (1961) 805–21.

———. "Vin Vieux, Vin Nouveau (Luc 5:39)." CBQ, 25 (1963) 286–304.

R. A. Edwards. "The Redaction of Luke." *Journal of Religion,* 49 (1969) 392–405.

J. K. Elliott. "Does Luke 2,41–52 Anticipate the Resurrection?" ET, 83, (1971–72) 87–89.

E. E. Ellis. "Die Funktion der Eschatologie im Lukasevangelium." ZTK, 66 (1970) 387–402.

J. A. Emerton. "Melchizekek and the Gods: Fresh Evidence for the Jewish Background of John X. 34–36." JTS, ns 17 (1966) 399–401.

Morton S. Enslin. "Luke and the Samaritans." HTR, 36 (1943) 277–97.

V. Eppstein. "The Historicity of the Gospel Account of the Cleansing of the Temple." ZNW, 55 (1964) 42–58.

C. F. Evans. "The Central Section of St. Luke's Narrative." TU, 73 (1959) 206–16.

———. "Tertullian's References to Sentius Saturninus and the Lukan Census." JTS, ns 24 (1973) 24–39.

———. "Uncomfortable Words-V. (Lk. 16:31)." ET, 81 (1969–70) 228–37.

A. Feuillet. "La Coupe et le Baptême de la Passion." RB, 74 (1967) 356–91.

———. "Le récit lucanien de l'agonie de Gethsemani (Lc. xxii, 39–46)." NTS, 22 (1975–76) 399–417.

A. Finkel. "Jesus' Sermon at Nazareth (Luke 4, 16–30)." Betz et. al., eds., *Abraham unser Vater,* pp. 106–15.

J. A. Fitzmyer. "The Contribution of Qumran Aramaic to the Study of the New Testament." *NTS* (1973–74), pp. 382–407.

——. "Further Light on Melchizedek from Qumran Cave 11." JBL, 86 (1967) 25–41.

——. "Now this Melchizedek. . . Hebr. 7:1." CBQ, 25 (1963) 305–21.

——. "Peace Upon Earth Among Men of His Good Will (Lk 2:14)." TS, 19 (1958) 225–27.

F. Fluckiger. "Luk. 21, 20–24 und die Zerstörung Jerusalems." TZ, 28 (1972) 384–90.

D. Flusser. "Melchizedek and the Son of Man." Christian News from Israel, 17 (1966) 23–29.

——. "Sanctus und Gloria." Betz et. al., eds., Abraham unser Vater, pp. 129–52.

W. Foerster. "Lukas 22:31ff." ZNW, 46 (1955) 129–33.

G. Friedrich. "Lk. 9, 51 und die Entrückungschristologie des Lukas." P. Hoffmann et al., Orientierung an Jesus, Freiburg, 1973, pp. 48–77.

J. M. Furness. "Fresh Light on Luke 10:25–37." ET, 80 (1969) 182.

P. Gaechter. "Der Verkündigungsbericht Lk. 1:26–38." ZTK, 91 (1969) 567–86.

W. Gasse. "Zum Reisebericht des Lukas." ZNW, 34 (1935) 293–99.

A. George. "Israel dans l'Oeuvre de Luc." RB, 75 (1968) 481–525.

——. "Le parallele entre Jean-Baptiste et Jesus en Lc 1–2." Descamps, Mélanges bibliques, pp. 147–71.

——. "Tradition et rédaction chez Luc. La construction du troiseme Evangile." I. de la Potterie, ed., De Jesus aux Evangiles, pp. 100–129.

M. Gertner. "Midrashim in the New Testament." JSS, 7 (1962) 267–92.

C. H. Giblin. "The 'Things of God' in the Question concerning Tribute to Caesar (Lk. 20–25; Mk. 12:17; Mt. 22:21)." CBQ, 33 (1971) 510–27.

D. Gill. "Observations on the Lukan Travel Narrative." HTR, 63 (1970) 199–221.

O. Glombitza. "Die christologische Aussage des Lukas in seiner Gestaltung der drei Nachfolgewarte Lukas ix 57–62." Nov. Test., 13 (1971) 14–23.

——. "Der reiche Mann und der arme Lazarus." Nov Test., 12 (1970) 166–80.

J. Gnilka. "Der Hymnus des Zacharias." BZ, 6 (1962) 215–38.

C. H. Gordon. "Sabbatical Cycle or Seasonal Pattern?" Orientalia, 22 (1953) 79–81.

J. van Goudoever. "The Place of Israel in Luke's Gospel." Nov. Test., 8 (1966) 111–23.

M. D. Goulder. "Characteristics of the Parables in the Several Gospels." JTS, ns 19 (1968) 51–69.

——. "The Chiastic Structure of the Lucan Journey." TU, 87 (1963) 195–202.

M. D. Goulder and M. C. Sanderson. "St. Luke's Genesis." JTS, 8 (1957) 12–30.

E. Grasser. "Jesus in Nazareth (Mc 6:1–6a)." (Originally published in English in NTS, 16 [1969–70] 1–23.) W. Eltester, ed., Jesus in Nazareth, Berlin, 1972, pp. 1–37.

G. B. Gray. "The Nazirite." JTS, 1 (1900) 201–11.

W. Grimm. "Eschatologischer Saul wider eschatologischen David. Eine Deutung von Lc xiii 31ff." Nov. Test, 15 (1973) 114–33.

——. "Selige Augenzeugen, Luk. 10, 23f." TZ, 26 (1970) 172–83.

K. Grobel. ". . . Whose Name Was Neves." NTS, 10 (1963–64) 373–82.

T. Gruglewicz, "Die Herkunft der Hymnen des Kindheitsevangeliums des Lukas." NTS, 27 (1974–75) 265–73.

W. Grundmann. "Fragen der Komposition des Lukanischen 'Reiseberichtes.' " ZNW, 50 (1959) 252–70.

John Gunther. "The Fate of the Jerusalem Church." TZ, 29 (1973) 81–94.

O. Haggenmuller. "Der Lobgesang des Zacharias (Lk. 1:68–79)." *Bibel und Liturgie,* 4 (1968) 249–60.

R. S. Hanson. "Mary According to Luke." *Worship,* 43 (1969) 425–29.

R. P. C. Hanson. "Does *Dikaios* in Luke xxiii.47 Explode the Proto-Luke Hypothesis?" *Hermathena,* 55 (1942) 74–78.

C. H. A. Hickling. "A Tract on Jesus and the Pharisee? A Conjecture on the Redaction of Luke 5 and 16." HJ, 26 (1975) 253–65.

R. H. Hiers. "The Problem of the Delay of the Parousia in Luke-Acts." NTS, 20 (1973–74) 145–55.

D. Hill. "The Rejection of Jesus at Nazareth (Luke IV:16–30)." *Nov. Test.,* 13 (1971) 161–80.

———. "The Request of Zebedee's Sons and the Johannine *doxa* theme." NTS, 13 (1966–67) 281–85.

P. Hoffmann. *"Pantes Ergatai Adikias,* Redaktion und Tradition in Lk 13:22–30." ZNW, 58 (1967) 188–214.

R. A. Horsley. "Ancient Jewish Banditry and the Revolt against Rome." CBQ, 43 (1981) 409–32.

J. H. Hughes. "John the Baptist, the Forerunner of God Himself." *Nov. Test.,* 13–14 (1971) 191–218.

C. H. Hunzinger. "Neues Licht auf Lc 2, 14, *anthrōpoi eudokias"* ZNW, 44 (1952) 85–90.

J. Jeremias. "Perikopen-Umstellungen bei Lukas?" NTS, 4 (1958) 115–19.

———. "Zöllner und Sünder." ZNW, 30 (1931) 293–300.

B. M. F. van Jersel. "The Finding of Jesus in the Temple." *Nov. Test.,* 4 (1960) 161–73.

———. "La vocation de Levi (Mc. 2:13–17, Mt. 9:9–13, Lc. 5:27–32)." I. de la Potterie, ed., *De Jésus aux Evangiles,* pp. 212–32.

D. R. Jones. "The Background and Character of the Lukan Psalms." JTS, ns 19 (1968) 19–50.

M. de Jonge and A. S. Van der Woude, "11 Q Melchizedek and the New Testament." NTS, 12 (1965–66) 301–26.

J. G. Kahn. "La parable du Figuier Sterile et les Arbres Recalcitrants de La Genèse." *Nov. Test.,* 13 (1971) 38–45.

W. Käser, "Exegetische und theologische Erwägungen zur Seligpreisung der Kinderlosen, Lk 23:29b." ZNW, 54 (1963) 240–54.

A. Kee. "The Question about Fasting." *Nov. Test.,* 11 (1969) 161–73.

J. S. Kennard. "Judas of Galilee and his Clan." JQR, 36 (1945) 281–86.

G. D. Kilpatrick. *"Laos* at Lk. 2:31 and Acts 4:25, 27." JTS, ns 16 (1965) 127.

———. "A Theme of the Lucan Passion Story and Luke 23:47." JTS, 43 (1942) 34–36.

Paul Kingdon. "Who Were the Zealots and Their Leaders in A.D. 66?" NTS, 17 (1970) 72.

Gunter Klein. "Die Verleugnung des Petrus." ZTK, 58 (1961) 285–328.

H. G. Klemm. "Das Wort von der Selbstbestättung der Toten." NTS, 16 (1969–70) 60–75.

N. Krieger. "Ein Mensch in weichen Kleidern." *Nov. Test.,* 1 (1956) 228–30.

K. G. Kuhn. "Jesus in Gethsemane." EvT, 12 (1952–53) 260–85.

W. G. Kummel. "Current Theological Accusations Against Luke." *Andover Newton Quarterly,* 16 (1975) 131–45.

M. J. Lagrange. "Jean Baptiste et Jésus d'après le texte slave du livre de la guerre des Juifs de Josephe." RB, 39 (1930) 29–46.

A. R. C. Leaney. "The Birth Narratives in St. Luke and St. Matthew." NTS, 158 (1961–62) 158–66.

G. M. Lee. "Luke iii 23." ET, 79 (1968) 310.

L. Legrand. "L'Evangile aux Bergers. Essai sur le genre littéraire de Luc, II 8–20." RB, 75 (1968) 161–87.

J. Liver, "The Half-Shekel Offering in Biblical and Post-Biblical Literature." HTR, 56 (1963) 173–98.

W. P. Loewe. "Towards an Interpretation of Lk. 19:1–10." CBQ, 36 (1974) 321–31.

Edward Lohse. "Zu den Anfangen der Mission in Samarien." TZ, 10 (1954) 158.

S. Lyonnet. "Chaire kecharitōmerē" Biblica, 20 (1939) 131–41.

H. Z. Maccoby. "Jesus and Barabbas." NTS, 16 (1969) 55–60.

P. L. Maier. "The Episode of the Golden Roman Shields at Jerusalem." HTR, 62 (1969) 109–21.

H. Mann. "Jesus and the Sadducean Priests, Luke 10:25–37." JQR, ns 6 (1915) 415–22.

I. H. Marshall. "Recent Study of the Gospel According to St. Luke." ET, 80 (1968) 4–8.

A.T. Mattill. "The Jesus-Paul Parallels and the Purpose of Luke-Acts." Nov. Test., 17 (1975) 15–46.

C. C. McCown. "The Geography of Luke's Central Section." JBL, 57 (1938) 51–66.

V. E. McEachern. "Dual Witness and Sabbath Motif in Luke." Canadian Journal of Theology, 12 (1966) 267–80.

P. H. Menound. "Le sens du verbe biazetai dans Lc 16:16." Descamps, Mélanges bibliques, pp. 207–12.

B. F. Meyer. "But Mary Kept All These Things." CBQ, 26 (1964) 31–49.

J. T. Milik. "Milki-Sedeq et Milki-Resa dans les anciens écrits juifs et chrétiens (1)." JJS, 23 (1972) 95–144.

M. P. Miller. "Isa. 1:1–2 in Melchizedek." JBL, 88 (1969) 467–69.

P. S. Minear. "Jesus' Audiences according to Luke." Nov. Test., 16 (1974) 81–109.

———. "Luke's Use of the Birth Stories." SLA, pp. 111–30.

———. "A Note on Luke xxii.36." Nov. Test., 7 (1964) 128–34.

C. L. Mitton. "Uncomfortable Words, IX Stumbling Block Characteristics in Jesus." ET, 82 (1970–71) 168–72.

Hugh Montefiore. "Revolt in the Desert? Mk. 6:30." NTS, 8 (1961–62) 135–41.

J. Murphy-O'Connor. "The Rule of the Community." RB, 76 (1969) 528–49.

John Navonne. "The Lucan Banquet Community." Bible Today, 51 (1970) 155–61.

P. Neirynck. "That Mary Preserved All These Things in Her Heart." Col. Brug., 5 (1959) 455ff.

E. Nestle. "Die Hirten von Bethlehem." ZNW, 7 (1906) 257–59.

A. A. Neuman. "A Note on John the Baptist and Jesus in Josippon." Hebrew Union College Annual, 23 (1950) 137–49.

R. North. "Maccabean Sabbatical Years." Biblica, 34 (1953) 501–15.

G. Ogg. "The Central Section of the Gospel according to St. Luke." NTS, 18 (1971–72) 39–53.

———. "The Quirinius Question Today." ET, 79 (1967–68) 231–36.

H. H. Oliver. "The Lucan Birth Stories and the Purpose of Luke-Acts." NTS, 10 (1963–64) 202–26.

J. C. O'Neill. "The Six Amen Sayings in Luke." JTS, ns 10 (1959) 1–9.

J. J. O'Rourke. "Some Notes on Luke xv.11–32." NTS, 18 (1971–72) 431–33.

H. Patsch. "Der Einzug Jesu in Jerusalem. Ein historischer Versuch." ZTK, 68 (1971) 1–26.

E. Pax. "Denn sie fanden keinen Platz in der Herberge." *Bibel und Leben*, 6 (1965) 285–98.

C. Perrot. "Luc 4, 16–30 et la lecture biblique de l'ancienne synagogue." RSR, 47 (1973) 324–40.

R. Pesch. "Levi-Mattäus (Mc 2:14/Mt 9:9; 10:3)." ZNW, 59 (1958) 40–56.

I. de la Potterie. "Le titre Kurios appliqué à Jésus dans l'évangile de Luc." Descamps, *Mélanges bibliques*, pp. 117–46.

G. Rau. "Das Volk in der Lukanischen Passionsgeschichte. Eine Konjektur zu Lk. 23:13." ZNW, 56 (1965) 41–51.

B. Reicke. "Instruction and Discussion in the Travel Narrative." TU, 73 (1959) 206–16.

———. "Jesus in Nazareth—Lk. 4, 14–30." H. Balz and S. Schulz, *Das Wort und die Wörter*, Stuttgart, 1973, pp. 47–55.

J. L. Resseguie. "Interpretation of Luke's Central Section (Luke 9:51–19:44) since 1856." *Studia Biblica et Theologica*, 5 (1975) 3–36.

D. Rhoads. "The Assumption of Moses and Jewish History: 4 B.C.–A.D. 48," G.W.E. Nickelburg, *Studies in the Testament of Moses*, Cambridge, Mass., 4th ed., 1973, pp. 53–58.

E. Rivkin. "The Meaning of Messiah in Jewish Thought." USQR, 26 (1971) 383–406.

W. C. Robinson, Jr. "The Theological Context for Interpreting Luke's Travel Narrative (9:51ff.)." JBL, 79 (1960) 20–31.

J. M. Ross. "The Rejected Words in Luke 9, 54–56." ET, 84 (1972–73) 85–88.

C. Roth. "The Pharisees in the War of 66–73." *Journal of Semitic Studies,* 7 (1962) 67–68.

A. P. Salom. "Was Zacchaeus Really Reforming?" ET, 78 (1966) 87.

Borge Salomansen. "Some Remarks on the Zealots with Special Reference to the Term 'Qannaim' in Rabbinic Literature." NTS, 12 (1965–66) 167–68.

J. A. Sanders. "Dissenting Deities and Phil. 2:1–11." JBL, 88 (1969) 279–90.

———. "From Isaiah 61 to Luke 4." J. Neusner, ed., *Christianity, Judaism and other Greco-Roman Cults*, Leiden, 1975, Part 1, pp. 75–106.

———. "Outside the Camp." *Union Seminary Quarterly Review*, 24 (1969) 240.

J. T. Sanders. "Tradition and Redaction in Luke xv.11–32." NTS, 15 (1968–69) 433–38.

J.F.A. Sawyer. "Why is a Solar Eclipse Mentioned in the Passion Narrative (Luke xxiii, 44–5)?" JTS, ns 23 (1972) 124–28.

R. Schnackenburg. "Der eschatologische Abschnitt Lk. 17:20–37." Descamps *Mélanges bibliques*, pp. 213–43.

G. Schneider. "Die Verhaftung Jesu." ZNW, 62–3 (1971–2) 188–209.

J. Schneider. "Zur Analyse des Lukanischen Reiseberichtes." Schmid and Vogtle, *Synoptische Studien*, pp. 207–29.

H. Schürmann. "Der 'Bericht vom Anfang'. Ein Rekonstruktionsversuch auf Grund von Lk. 4,14–16." (Originally in TU, 87 [1964] 242–58. *Traditionsgeschichtliche Untersuchungen*, Düsseldorf, 1968, pp. 69–80.)

G. Schwarz. "Der Lobgesang der Engel (Lukas 2, 14)." BZ, 15 (1971) 260–64.

G. Sellin. "Lukas als Gleichniserzähler: Die Erzählung vom barmherzigen Samariter (Lk. 10, 25-37)." ZNW, 65 (1974) 166-89; 66 (1975) 19-60.

E. M. Smallwood. "High Priests and Politics in Roman Palestine." JTS, 13 (1962) 14-34.

M. Smith. "Mt. 5:3 'Hate Thine Enemy.' " HTR, 46 (1952) 71-73.

——. "Zealots and Sicarii, Their Origins and Relations." HTR, 64 (1971)1-19.

E. R. Smothers. "A Note on Luke 2:49." HTR, 45 (1952) 67-69.

S. Sowers. "The Circumstances and Recollection of the Pella Flight." TZ, 26 (1970) 305-20.

C. Spicq. "La parable de la Veuve Obstinée et du Juge Inerte, aux décisions impromptues (Lc. 18, 1-8)." RB, 68 (1961) 68-90

K. Stendahl. "Hate, Non-Retaliation and Love." HTR, 55 (1962) 343-55.

M. Stern. "Aspects of Jewish Society: The Priesthood and Other Classes." Safrai and Stern, *The Jewish People in the First Century*, pp. 561-630.

A. Stöger. "Eigenart und Botschaft der Lukanischen Passionsgeschichte." *Bibel und Kirche*, 24 (1969) 4-8.

A. Strobel. "Die Ausrufung des Yobeljahres in der Nazareth-predigt Jesus: zur apokalyptischen Tradition Lc 4, 16-30." W. Eltester, ed., *Jesus in Nazareth*, Berlin, 1972, pp. 38-50.

R.C. Tannehill. "The Magnificat as Poem." JBL, 93 (1974) 263-75.

——. "The Mission of Jesus according to Luke iv 16-30." W. Eltester, ed., *Jesus in Nazareth*, Berlin, 1972, pp. 51-75.

W. B. Tatum. "The Epoch of Israel: Luke 1-2 and the Theological Plan of Luke-Acts." NTS, 13 (1967) 184-95.

W. Trilling. "Le Christ, roi crucifié Lc 23:35-43." *Assemblées du Seigneur*, 65 (1973) 56-65.

E. Trocmé. "L'expulsion des marchands du temple." NTS, 15 (1968-69) 1-22.

G. W. Trompf. "La section médiane de l'évangile de Luc: 1 'organisation des documents." RHPR, 53 (1973) 141-54.

N. Turner. "The Relation of Luke 1 and 2 to Hebraic Sources and to the Rest of Luke-Acts." NTS, 2 (1955-56) 100-109.

Joseph B. Tyson. "The Lukan Version of the Trial of Jesus." *Nov. Test.*, 3 (1959) 249-53

W. C. van Unnik. "Die Motivierung der Feindesliebe in Lukas vi 32-35." *Nov. Test.*, 8 (1966) 284-300.

A.S. Van der Woude. "Melchizedek als himmlische Erlösergestalt in den neugefundenen eschatologischen Midraschim aus Qumran Hohle 11." *Oudtestamentische Studien*, 14 (1965) 354-73.

N. Vanhoye. "Structure du 'Benedictus.' " NTS, 12 (1965-66) 382-89.

A. W. Verrall. "Christ before Herod." JTS, 10 (1908-09) 321-53.

P. Vielhauer. "Das Benediktus des Zacharias (Lk. 2, 68-79)." ZTK, 49 (1952) 255-72.

B. Violet. "Zum rechten Verständnis der Nazarethperikope." ZNW, 37 (1938) 251-71.

P. W. Walaskay. "The Trial and Death of Jesus in the Gospel of Luke." JBL, 94 (1975) 81-93.

H. Wansbrough. "St. Luke and Christian Ideals in an Affluent Society." *New Blackfriars*, 49 (1968) 582-86.

N. W. Watson. "Was Zacchaeus Really Reforming?" ET, 77 (1966) 282–85.

R.M. Wilson. "Some Recent Studies in the Lucan Infancy Narratives." TU, 73 (1959) 235–53.

J. Winandy. "La prophétie de Syméon (Lc. ii, 34–35)." RB, 72 (1965) 321–51.

W. Wink. "Jesus and the Revolution." *Union Seminary Quarterly Review*, 25 (1969) 37–59.

P. Winter. "Luke XXII. 66b–71." ST, 9 (1956) 112–115.

———. "Lc 2, 49 and Targum Yerushalmi." ZNW, 45 (1954) 145–79.

———. "Lukanische Miszellen." ZNW, 49 (1958) 65–77.

———. "Magnificat and Benedictus—Maccabean Psalms?" *Bulletin of John Rylands Library,* 37 (1954) 328–47.

Y. Yadin. "A Note on Melchizedek and Qumran." *IEJ,* 15 (3, 1965) 152–54.

A. Zeron. "The Martyrdom of Phineas-Elijah." JBL, 98 (1979) 99–100.

GENERAL INDEX

171

INDEX OF SCRIPTURAL REFERENCES

OLD TESTAMENT

176